Grieving a Soulmate

The Love Story Behind "Till Death Do Us Part"

Grieving a Soulmate

The Love Story Behind "Till Death Do Us Part"

Robert Orfali

MILL CITY PRESS

MILL CITY PRESS

MINNEAPOLIS, MN
2011

Copyright © 2011 by Robert Orfali, LLC
www.GrievingaSoulmate.com

Mill City Press, Inc.

miLLCiTy PRESS

Minneapolis, MN 55401
Tel. 612-455-2294
www.millcitypublishing.com

Includes bibliographical references.

1. Loss—Bereavement   2. Grief—Psychological aspects 3. Soulmate —Final love 4. Death—End-of-life. I. Title

First Edition 2011

ISBN-13: 978-1-936400-66-9
LCCN: 2010941337

Cover design by Jayne Cloutier
Cover photos of Diamond Head and Jeri by Richie Rich & J. Cloutier
Typeset by Jay Garthwait

Printed in the United States of America

In Memory of My Soulmate
Jeri Edwards Orfali
September 5, 1952 - June 19, 2009

An extraordinary woman radiant in beauty and aloha.
She remains a constant source of inspiration and support.

Introduction

"I, Robert, take you, Jeri, to be my wedded wife, to have and to hold from this day forward, for better or for worse, for richer, for poorer, in sickness and in health, to love and to cherish, till death do us part."

—The Traditional Wedding Vow

This book is really a love story. Since the beginning of time, millions of love stories have appeared in every form of medium—stone tablets, papyrus, songs, poems, books, movies, and TV soaps. By now, everything should have been covered—first dates, courtship, marriage, honeymoon, lovemaking, parenting, dual careers, sex after menopause, and so on. What could have been left unsaid about love? Drumroll, the answer is: The "death do us part" thing. It never gets the proper coverage. No one likes to talk about what happens to love stories at the very end. The timeline just before and after the death of a soulmate remains the untold part of the story. There are some exceptions—for example, *Ghost*, which is a very tender and romantic movie.

Unfortunately, in the real-life version of *Ghost*, there is a high probability that one of the partners will eventually get sick and then die. The other partner first becomes a caregiver and then a griever. So the bad news is that sickness and death will eventually "do us part." The good news is that the love relationship only gets stronger with illness and death. It also survives death. Yes, one spouse dies, but the love continues to live forever in the surviving partner's heart. Of course, this assumes that the surviving partner does not perish during the grieving process.

So the big surprise is the incredible level of bonding, loving, and tenderness that takes place during sickness and the last days. It's the ultimate love affair. It's total and unconditional love. It's more romantic than courtship. It's more tender than mothering. And, it can be very sexy. You live in the moment. You savor every remaining microsecond that you can enjoy with your lover on this earth.

After death comes the grieving. At the beginning, you are assaulted with the red-hot pain bursts of young grief. It's like molten lava burning through your entire being. If you find some way to get rid of these grief bursts, you'll then withdraw into a period of sadness and meditation. This is a time when you can explore your relationship and give meaning to your lover's life and death. Incredibly, this meditation elevates you to another plateau of love. In your grieving, you rediscover what it was all about: You have loved and lost, but you also understand how lucky you were to have loved.

The "Final Love"

So, yes, this is a love story. It covers love at the end of life—the "final love." A few lucky lovers will leave this earth at the same time. For the rest of us, there will be grieving and, perhaps, a period of caregiving before death. Most lovers will experience this last part; it's almost universal. Deep inside, we all know it's going to happen—the marriage vows give us ample warning. Yet, none of us seem to know anything about the love experience in the final days. I certainly didn't. The subject is taboo. The tabloids never cover it. Hollywood gives us endless scenes of instant death. We don't ever see the entire process, even though it's pure love at its peak.

This book is about that process. It's about the death of a soulmate and the grieving that follows. It's the book I wish I had read before my soulmate, Jeri, died. I was so unprepared for both her death and the brutal period of grieving that followed. This book should help you get through both. It can be your guide through "death do us part" and its aftermath—the profound process of grieving a soulmate.

My Soulmate Jeri

Jeri died on June 19, 2009, at age 56. I met her in 1979. I was a happy bachelor then, but I knew I had found a gem. After our first encounter we became totally inseparable for the next 30 years. It's almost as if

Introduction

we were fused together—she was my lover, co-author, partner, and best friend. We were soulmates from the very first moment.

We were both in the computer industry in the early Silicon Valley days. Jeri joined some very exciting start-ups. She was a good techie who, at one time, managed hundreds of the best programmers in the Valley. She was able to turn out some great products, which she also knew how to market. In the early 1990s, Jeri was named *Silicon Valley Executive Woman of the Year*.

At one point, Jeri and I decided we would give back some of the knowledge we had acquired. We teamed up with Dan Harkey to write books that would help a new generation of programmers understand the technology of Client/Server and Java. We used simple terminology to explain some very difficult stuff—like the mission-critical software that runs the banks, stock markets, and telephone companies. Our books became bestsellers. We sold over a million copies.

In the last two years of our professional life, Jeri and I went together on two world tours to promote the technologies in our books. Although our books had been translated into 27 languages, we were surprised by how famous we were. We had a great time on the road with the "Jeri and Robert" show. Jeri was a very articulate and expressive speaker— the audiences loved her from Beijing to Stockholm.

At the end of our last world tour, we decided that Hawaii was the most beautiful place on this earth, so we made it our home. In July 1998, we packed and moved to Kailua, on the island of Oahu. We were in heaven. Unfortunately, Jeri was diagnosed with ovarian cancer just a short time later.

Jeri and I spent the next ten years fighting her cancer. She was on chemotherapy for most of those years. During her chemo years, Jeri learned how to surf. It became her passion. In record time, she became a very good surfer and was able to win fourth place in her age division. Most importantly, surfing helped Jeri fight her cancer and keep her alive. The ocean kept her radiant and fit until the very end. It was the best detox for her endless chemo. Jeri received one of the most moving surfer funerals ever. We scattered her ashes in the ocean at Waikiki where she had surfed.

I Was Caught Off Guard

During the ten years I helped Jeri fight her cancer, I was on top of the research. I knew everything about cancer treatments and her chemo choices. I also knew that her cancer would eventually kill her. We lived from one cancer count to the next, so I knew death was at the door all those years. But strangely, I was totally unprepared for both the death process and the grieving that followed. I was a death virgin and also a grief virgin. I had to learn about both the hard way—while they were happening. I kicked myself for not being better prepared and I ended up suffering too much during the grieving process. After years of helping Jeri, why was I not better prepared?

The answer comes in two parts. First, none of us spend very much time thinking about death and grieving. On an ordinary day, we tend to avoid both these topics like the plague. We try not to worry about them until they hit us. Some of us even delude ourselves with thoughts of immortality. Second, there is a lot of information out there, but it's spread out all over the place. It takes forever to find it and then digest it. During my grieving, I finally did the research—it became a matter of survival. I devoured everything that was written on the topic. It consumed hundreds upon hundreds of hours, about the same level of effort it takes to earn a master's degree in computer science.

Eventually, I completed my research. To my surprise, not all the pieces were there. There was nothing that could help stop these horrible grief bursts—the red-hot waves of pain. And there was nothing out there to help me grieve in a modern, secular way. If you don't subscribe to an organized religion with an after-death retirement plan, then you must become your own priest and philosopher. And because modern psychology doesn't do grieving well, you must also become your own psychologist. Finally, and most importantly, not all grieving is the same. The death of a soulmate is particularly harsh because the lovers are so intertwined and bonded. The pain you feel now is the flip side of the love you once had. The more you loved, the greater your grieving pain. Yes, grieving a soulmate can be pure hell.

So, Why Did I Write This Book?

I was left alone to face the death of my lover and grapple with the existential issues of life and death—from a secular perspective. Prodded by the red-hot pain, I had to develop, on the fly, an entirely new way to grieve my soulmate. I am grateful to the many people who gave me some guidance during this difficult period. I wrote this book to give back this knowledge I acquired the hard way. It's the book you will need to help you navigate through the final stage of your relationship. It's my gift to you and also my tribute to Jeri, my soulmate.

Of course, I am not going to profit from Jeri's death. All the proceeds from this book will go to charity (hopefully, St. Francis Hospice, where she died). I also want you to know that I did not write this book to help me grieve Jeri better. I was done with the painful part of my grieving before I began to write. My grief bursts are history. I now have happy memories of my life with Jeri. Instead of grief bursts, the memories bring smiles and good thoughts. It wasn't easy. It took me four months to get rid of the grief bursts completely. If I had this book, I could have done it in less than half that time. When you're suffering the pain of grief, every bit of help counts. Trust me, you want that horrible pain to stop. You want to get out of the pain zone as fast as you can. After you eliminate the pain, you can then enjoy the rest of your grieving. It becomes "good" grieving.

Who Is This Book For?

This book is for lovers of all ages. It prepares you for the end and it helps you grieve the death of your lover. In her book *The Year of Magical Thinking*, Joan Didion writes: "Life changes fast. You sit down to dinner and life as you know it ends." She was writing about the sudden death of her husband, writer John Dunne. Unfortunately, death is always a heartbeat away. It's an uninvited guest that shows up whenever and wherever it likes. All relationships end with death, our common destiny. So you will need to read this book at some point.

Jeri's "good death" and my ensuing grieving can be your guide. Ideally, you will be reading this book at least one year before the death of a lover. If you're brave, you can read it now. If not, just put it on a shelf and read it when you'll need it. Everyone prepares for marriage and birthing, but no one is prepared for the final passage of a relationship—the death of a lover. It pays to understand your options at the end and to prepare for the grieving that follows.

Grieving and End-of-Life

This book consists of three parts: living with a terminal illness, the end-of-life experience, and the grieving of a soulmate. Most of the book focuses on the grieving aspects. It's really a book on how to grieve your soulmate—a difficult topic that requires much understanding. Why do I cover dying in a book on grieving? Because understanding death helps us grieve better. Dying can be a long and messy affair. It's a lot like birthing, but in reverse. It takes time and effort for the engine to shut down.

As the surviving soulmate, the death you witnessed can leave you with deep feelings of guilt and remorse, which can haunt you throughout your grieving. Why? Because most of us have a sanitized view of death, which is really a messy, organic process. Because death is messy, you will blame yourself for not having done more for your dying lover. You go through endless "what ifs" and "if onlys" revisiting every aspect of the death. Again, the problem is that most of us are death virgins. So the better we understand death, the less pain we will experience during grieving.

How the Book Is Organized

The first three chapters are about living with a terminal illness and the end-of-life experience. The rest of the book is on the grieving process. Again, I cover both the theory and practice (in this case, mine) of grieving for a soulmate:

Introduction

- *Chapters 1 and 2* are about Jeri's epic battle with her cancer. For many of you, these two short chapters are optional reading. They do, however, contain a lot of invaluable information for people who are living with cancer. With almost ten years of continuous chemo, Jeri probably holds a world record. During that time, she was also a surfer and, probably, the most radiant person in all of Hawaii. She projected both inner and outer strength. I will share with you some of the things we did to achieve this state of body and mind. Maybe it can help you or a loved one, who is fighting cancer or some other chronic disease.

- *Chapter 3* is a lengthy chapter on death. I cover Jeri's death and the entire process of dying. It's the chapter I wish I had read before she died. It's a very concise guide that covers a lot of material on the process of dying—including hospice, palliative care, pain management, home nursing, caregiving, and what death itself looks like (the pre-active and active phases of dying). This chapter also provides a very intimate view of Jeri's death. In our society, the deathbed experience is private. What happens in the deathbed stays in the deathbed. After some hesitation, I decided that Jeri would not mind sharing her end-of-life experience with the rest of the world—especially if it could be of some benefit to others. She believed that knowledge is power to be shared. Her death is a textbook example of a good death, and there are definitely lessons to be learned here.

- *Chapter 4* is about mourning in the age of the Internet. I packed it with useful information. For example, I cover the importance of the memorial website we created for Jeri. It's the modern version of the tombstone. Jeri's memory now lives forever in the search engines of the Internet. As you can see, I do not subscribe to Freud's *Forget and Detach* view of grieving. The website helps me preserve the memories of my soulmate and feel her comforting presence. However, the website can also help separate the identities of the lovers, which is a key part of the recovery process. I also have a lot to say about cremation, viewing the dead body, writing the obituary, and the funeral itself. It's an insight into a more modern way of mourning—a little bit more high-tech than the traditional method of our parents.

- *Chapter 5* is about grief bursts, the red-hot pain of young grief. I explain why the loss of a soulmate is so traumatic and unique from a grieving perspective. I rely on e-mails I wrote during my red-hot grieving period to describe some typical grief bursts. The e-mails document my state of mind during this crucial period. The human mind tends to quickly forget painful experiences—it develops protective amnesia. I was lucky to have this trove of first-hand documentation.

- *Chapter 6* is about my search for the grief-burst cure. It's another lengthy chapter. I start with Freud's detachment theory and its most recent incarnations. I then go over Bowlby's very influential *Attachment Theory*. I spend some time reviewing the popular grief literature. These are the dozens of how-to guides by grief therapists that build on the Kübler-Ross five stages of grieving. Next, I visit what Kübler-Ross herself has to say about grieving and what the critics of her theory have to say. Finally, I cover the new frontier of grief theory including the *Dual Process Model*, Bonanno's new insights on *Resilience*, and the *Continuing Bonds* model. I conclude by presenting my own method for dealing with grief bursts. It's the cure I was looking for. I took the best everyone had to offer and then added the key missing pieces. It really worked for me.

- *Chapters 7 to 11* are about zapping my grief bursts into oblivion. I had to follow each grief burst to its source—the emotions, feelings, and events that were the triggers. Once I found the source, I could then zap the grief burst out of existence. It's an old trick from my computer software days—just trace the bugs. Once you find the root cause, you fix it and get rid of the bug. I had to classify and count the bugs. It's the same with grief bursts. Why five chapters? In my grieving, I had to deal with five types of grief bursts: *1) The last days* —I revisit the various "what ifs" and "if onlys" caused by Jeri's end-of-life process; *2) Survivor's guilt*—I'm alive but she isn't, she's not

here to enjoy what life has to offer, she died so young, and so on; *3)*
She's gone forever—I miss her physical presence on this earth, I
can't believe she's gone, she was just erased from every scene, and
so on; *4) Self-pity*—I have to face life without Jeri, she left a big hole
in my life, she left me with so many roles to fill, and so on; and *5)*
Deep existential issues—I must make meaning of Jeri's life and
death, I'm faced with a torrent of existential questions: Why did she
die? Where did she go? What was she thinking? Does anything still
make sense?... In each chapter, I go over my techniques for
eradicating a specific type of grief burst. These should serve as
templates for dealing with your own grief bursts. So you'll learn by
example.

Note: *Again, I borrowed some of these techniques from computer
software design. There, we use templates and patterns to capture the
better software practices and methods so that other programmers
can reuse them. Good software design is more art than science. The
same can be said about grieving techniques. Shameless plug: This is
so much better than anything else that is out there. It's a way of
applying some method to the grieving madness—even though death
shatters our lives in different ways.*

• ***Chapter 12*** is about the resolution of my grief. My definition of
healing consisted of two parts: 1) zero pain and 2) happy memories
of Jeri. I achieved both. This is also the final chapter where I try to
put it all together. I hope the lessons learned will get you to the other
side of your painful grief in record time.

Every grief has its own patterns. Mine can serve as a template to help
you deal with yours. You won't need a degree in grieving or computer
science. I put it all in one place for you. Remember that once you get
rid of the pain you can go back to living. Or, if you prefer, you can
continue to grieve. Without the grief bursts, it will be a much more
pleasant grieving experience. At the end, you will be left with happy
memories of your soulmate. You will be whole again. The memories

will help sustain you and give you inner strength as you continue to live. I now live for both of us.

Yes, There Is a Method to This Madness

This systemic treatment of grief may sound cold and analytic. Perhaps you may be thinking, "The grieving of a soulmate should be treated with poetry, not with conceptual thinking." Wrong! You must first deal with the pain; the poetry can come later. For me, dealing with the pain was a matter of survival. The pain attacks became all-consuming. I could not think of anything else, not even Jeri. So I had to use everything in my arsenal to get rid of the pain. From the grief literature, I borrowed anything that made sense to me; yet there were big holes. I had to improvise to fill in the missing parts. I used whatever conceptual training I had to complete the model. Jeri seemed to magically reappear after I got rid of the pain. This time she wasn't the Jeri of grief-burst nightmares. Instead, it was my loving Jeri—my soulmate. I rediscovered my Jeri. The love was back. My grieving could now turn poetic. You'll find that this book has more than its fair share of soul-searching and philosophical musings.

At the End, It's Still a Love Story

In conclusion, grieving your soulmate can be a beautiful poetic experience, but the red-hot pain is not. You must do whatever it takes to eradicate the pain, so that you can live again and rediscover your soulmate. Perhaps, now you can understand why I wrote this book. It's a survival guide for the final stages in a soulmate relationship. As the surviving soulmate, I tried to capture the powerful, final love experience and put it into words. There's more death and grieving in this book than you'll find anywhere else in print, but it's still a love story. I tried to convey, in intimate detail, that there is love during the dying and after the death. The love story will sustain us through the end-of-life and the grieving that follows. This is the all-important lesson in this book.

Table of Contents

Table of Contents

Chapter 1

You Have Ovarian Cancer

"Everyone who is born holds dual citizenship, in the kingdom of the well and in the kingdom of the sick. Although we all prefer to use only the good passport, sooner or later each of us is obliged, at least for a spell, to identify ourselves as citizens of that other place."

—*Susan Sontag*[1]

It all began on an autumn evening while we were walking on the promenade in Cannes. Earlier that day, we had landed in France—the start of a ten-city European lecture tour. The fresh Mediterranean air felt good after the long transatlantic flight. In the middle of our walk, Jeri suddenly said, "Stop, I'm feeling a sharp pain in the stomach." So we just sat down on a bench, waiting for the pain to go away. Jeri had just had a full gynecological exam before we left the U.S. and everything was fine. Consequently, we were not too worried. We assumed it was an upset stomach from the long plane ride. Sure enough, the pain just went away and we resumed our walk along the Riviera.

Over the next month, Jeri felt some intermittent pains as we flew from one country to the next. Again, we attributed it to airplanes and changing diets. By the time we returned home to Hawaii, the pain was gone.

One month later, however, the pain returned with a vengeance—this time, in the form of sharp pokes and a bloated stomach. We

---

[1] Susan Sontag, *Illness as Metaphor* (Picador Press, 1978).

1

immediately went to see Jeri's gynecologist, who then promptly ordered an ultrasound. The doctor called us the next morning with the results—something appeared to be very wrong. I remember my heart sinking when she said, "The ultrasound shows two large masses." My heart sank further when she referred us to Dr. Keith Terada, the top gynecological oncologist on the island. I asked her, "Does this mean Jeri has cancer?" She answered, "You'll need to talk to Dr. Terada." I could see from Jeri's face that she was devastated by the news. That night we did a lot of crying and hugging. The next morning we drove over the hill to meet Dr. Terada.

We Need to Operate

Our first encounter with Dr. Terada was scary. He was sitting at his desk looking at Jeri's ultrasound results with a frown on his face. "Not good," I thought. Finally, words came out of his mouth: "Umm...we'll need to operate to find out what's going on." He asked us if we had any questions. Jeri and I were both in a daze. I remember Jeri softly asking, "Do you think it's cancer?" The answer came back, "We'll know when we operate." All I could ask was, "What are the odds?" Dr. Terada paused, took a deep breath, and then answered, "I'd say 50/50." I did not like those odds at all.

Over the next ten years, we both grew to love Dr. Terada. He kept Jeri alive and well. We returned to that same office and sat facing him in the same two chairs over a hundred times. In every one of these visits, we dealt with matters of life and death. But, unlike that first uneasy encounter, Jeri could always make Dr. Terada smile (perhaps not at the very end). They both had a good sense of humor and got along very well. Most importantly, she completely trusted him with her life. These two developed a very deep relationship that only grew stronger with the years.

What Is Ovarian Cancer, Anyway?

As we left Dr. Terada's office, we both came up with one more question: "What type of cancer are we dealing with?" Phyllis, Dr.

Terada's nurse, looked surprised at our ignorance and answered, "It may be ovarian cancer, you know, the cancer of the ovaries." Of course, neither of us had heard of that cancer. Jeri had always been a model of good health. Like most women, the only two cancers she had been screened for every year were breast and cervical. So what was this ovarian cancer? It took less than 30 minutes of research on the Internet to get an answer: It's one nasty cancer.

Ovarian cancer is often called the "silent" killer because many times there are no symptoms until the disease has progressed to an advanced stage. This lack of symptoms means that about 75% of ovarian cancer cases will have spread to the abdomen by the time they are detected. Unfortunately, most patients die within five years. Ovarian cancer usually occurs in women over age 50, but it can also affect younger women. Its cause is unknown. About 21,550 women in the U.S. will learn they have ovarian cancer in 2010. About 14,600 will die from the disease.[2]

Tip: If you're a woman reading this you may be wondering: What can I do to protect myself against this horrible cancer? As Jeri would tell her friends, there are three things you must do: First, ask your doctor for a CA 125 test. Like the PSA for prostate cancer, this blood test is not always accurate. Consequently, it's not part of a woman's regular physical. Second, if your belly ever starts to bloat or ache, you should ask your doctor for a thorough examination—including a trans-vaginal ultrasound. Finally, if you have a family history of breast or ovarian cancer, you should have yourself tested for mutations in the BRCA1 and BRCA2 genes. It's another blood test. Typically, you get counseling from a geneticist before and after this test.

The Long Wait

Over the next few days, Jeri's pain and bloating became worse with each passing hour. She could only think of the pain, not the cancer.

---

[2] Source: The American Cancer Society.

Luckily, there was an opening in Dr. Terada's busy schedule and we were able to move up Jeri's operation date. She was on the operating table less than a week after the ultrasound. Because the events had moved so fast, we did not have the time to notify our friends and families. On the day of the operation, I found myself alone in the visitor's lounge, waiting for Dr. Terada to come out of the operating room.

Ten years later, I can still vividly remember the thoughts that were racing through my mind that fateful day. I remember pleading, "Please, don't let it be cancer." Then as the hours dragged on, all I could think was, "Please, let her come out of this operation alive." This was the first time I faced the possibility that Jeri could die on me. I was absolutely terrified. I could not conceive of life without Jeri. She was literally my other half. Then I had my first grief burst—a precursor of the horrible pain stabs I would feel after her death. I was in panic mode.

I must have looked terrible because I remember a kindly nurse asking me, "Sir, do you need help?" "Yes," I replied, "this operation has been going on forever. Could you please let me know if my wife, Jeri, is still alive?" She returned shortly after with very good news, "Jeri is alive. The operation will take a little while longer. Dr. Terada knows that you're waiting outside. He'll come and see you after the operation." I felt an incredible sense of relief. All that mattered was that Jeri would come out of this alive. Together, we could deal with any outcome—including cancer.

Thirty minutes later, Dr. Terada emerged from the operating room. He looked exhausted. I could see from his demeanor that the news was not good. He reported that both of Jeri's tumors were cancerous. The cancer was also in the lymph nodes, which meant it was not localized to the ovarian cavity—it was Stage 3. Dr. Terada felt he had done an excellent job removing the visible cancer. He had also performed a complete hysterectomy and removed the appendix and the omentum. So Jeri had been thoroughly "de-bulked." Finally, he mentioned something that made my hair stand up: "I had to cut out a piece of the colon around which the tumor had wrapped itself. We can reconnect the colon later. For now, she has a colostomy." The news put me in a state of shock. Thankfully, Jeri was still alive, but I now needed to take an inventory of the damage.

Tip: It's now become known that proper de-bulking greatly affects the survival outcomes in ovarian cancer. Jeri was extremely lucky that her gynecologist had referred her to Dr. Terada—a very skilled surgeon who is also a gynecological oncologist. If you're ever in this situation, just make sure that a very skilled surgeon performs the initial de-bulking operation.

Please, Google "Colostomy" for Me

As soon as Dr. Terada left, I got on the phone with friends and family to report on what had just happened. My first call was to a friend with a fast Internet connection: "Could you please do a search on "colostomy" for me?" The result came back: "It's a procedure which connects part of the colon to an opening in the abdominal wall to allow stools to drain. A colostomy may be permanent or temporary, depending on the reasons for its use."

The good news was that in Jeri's case the colostomy was reversible. The bad news was that she would have to live with colostomy bags in the interim. It was bad, but not terrible. The cancer, however, was a big problem. I dreaded having to tell Jeri the bad news.

How Do You Tell Your Wife She Has Cancer?

I went upstairs to the hospital room that would become our home for the next ten days. It was a private room with a spectacular view. The nurses fixed me a cot next to Jeri's bed. I looked at the ocean on the horizon, waiting for Jeri to be transported into the room. There was a beautiful Hawaiian sunset. An hour later, Jeri was finally wheeled in and then moved into her bed. She looked very pale, tired, and beautiful. She must have seen the tears in my eyes because her first words were, "Do I have cancer?"

Her question felt like a stab. I began to cry again and she knew the answer. Then I went over the status report I had received from Dr. Terada. I concluded by telling her, "And you also have this thing called a colostomy bag. But don't worry; it's only temporary." She nodded in a daze and gave herself a bolus of morphine. Her more immediate problem was how to recover from the long operation.

At 6:00 a.m. the next morning, we were both in deep sleep when Dr. Terada walked into the room. He went over the prognosis, this time with Jeri, who seemed to be a bit more lucid. At the end, she asked him one question, "Does this mean I'm going to die?" Dr. Terada was startled. If I remember correctly, his answer was, "No. Well, eventually we will all die. Well, there are statistics for your cancer."

This Is Our Cancer

The next few days were spent dealing with the various pains from the operation. Eventually, a nurse went over the colostomy procedures with us. Jeri's blood pressure jumped twenty points when she understood what it was all about. The next day a beautiful woman called Jackie showed up. She explained to Jeri how she went about life with her own colostomy bag. It seemed doable. Jeri felt much better.

One night, after the pain had subsided, Jeri invited me to sit next to her in the hospital bed. For a long time, we hugged and held each other. We also had a good cry. Then I turned over towards Jeri and said, "Look, we still have each other. This is our cancer; we'll fight it together. Somehow, we'll win." After that I felt much better. At this point, I had no idea how we would win. What I knew was that the team was still intact—Jeri was alive. Together, we could face almost anything life would throw at us—including being touched by cancer.

Chapter 2

The Longest Chemo

"My self-diagnosis is that I had a pre-existing case of fogginess that lifted during and immediately after my chemotherapy regimen: I suddenly experienced acute clarity.... I became a walking platitude, telling friends without a trace of irony to live every day as though it were their last. Because, man, I've been there. And if I weren't so repressed I'd give you a hug."

—Dan Barry[1]

Jeri's cancer was terminal. Though we're all terminal, she had received an official death sentence. *Anticipatory grief* is the normal mourning that occurs when expecting death. Typically, it includes grieving symptoms such as depression, extreme concern for the dying person, preparing for the death, and completing any unfinished business. The expectation of loss often makes the attachment to the dying person stronger.

However, this chapter is not about grieving. Instead, it's a brief account of Jeri's wins in her long fight with cancer. Even though the chemo was a constant for nearly ten years, those were very happy times for both of us. They say, "You're never really the same after being touched by cancer." Yet, cancer can also give your life new meaning. Yes, chemo would temporarily fog up Jeri's brain. But when the fog lifted, she became incredibly clear-headed and laser-sharp about what really mattered in life.

If cancer is not your thing, just skip over this chapter. If you are being touched by cancer, I hope you'll find something here that can be of

---

[1] Dan Barry, "My Brain on Chemo Alive and Alert," *New York Times*, August 31, 2009.

help. After years of dealing with chemo, we learned many valuable lessons—mostly the hard way. As a battle-scarred chemo warrior, Jeri always wanted to write a brief survival guide to help others in her situation. In this chapter, I will do my best to provide this missing piece. Of course, it would have been much better had Jeri written this chapter. As a caregiver, I can only explain how to deal with the external physical issues surrounding chemo. However, something awful seems to be happening deep inside the mind that only the person going through it could explain. It may be that this mind experience cannot be captured in words. Many times, I asked Jeri to explain what she experienced when she had that glazed, out-of-it look. She never gave me a complete answer. She would just say, "It's that horrible chemo fog."

The Invisible Caregiver

You may have noticed that I now called myself a "caregiver." Here's what happened. After the hospital stay, I decided to drop everything so that I could spend the maximum amount of quality time with Jeri. I now had more time to be her lover, companion, soulmate, and playmate. In addition, I became her caregiver, which really meant I would throw myself into the fight against her cancer. She would do all the heavy lifting and I would provide the support. So her cancer became our cancer.

Tip: It was important that Jeri not see herself as a cancer patient. She was a normal person who was fighting cancer. We would not let the cancer define her. If all you think of is the cancer, then you have lost half the battle—you become a victim. Although I was always there for Jeri, I was not just her caregiver. It's crucial that you do not create separating roles like patient and caregiver. Life after cancer must continue as normally as possible. The sad truth is that you will need the help of a caregiver to fight cancer effectively and on a sustained basis. The trick is to make this caregiving invisible.

Dealing with Easy Problems: Meet Rosie

Our most immediate problem was learning how to live with the colostomy, which we now called Rosie. Why Rosie? The opening to the colon was cute and looked like a rose bud. Rosie had a life of her own. She would surprise us and do whatever she liked whenever she liked. So we quickly got to know her. In the first week, a nurse would visit each day to teach us how to cut a pattern around Rosie.

Using the Internet, we discovered that not all colostomy bags are equal. The bags they gave us at the hospital were absolutely the worst. We found some beautiful "designer bags" online, with soft opaque materials and odor controls. So Rosie got a new wardrobe. Next, we bought Jeri some loose dresses that would conceal the bulge caused by Rosie's bags. We even found some two-piece bathing suits that covered Rosie. So Jeri was able to swim in the ocean. Yes, we could still make love. We discovered there was life after Rosie.

One year later, Dr. Terada was able to reconnect Jeri's colon during a second-look operation. We lost Rosie. Incredibly, it made us sad to see the old girl go. We fondly reminisced over her mischievous tricks. Of course, it was very liberating for Jeri to get rid of Rosie.

Tip: Giving the colostomy a name was very helpful. This personification turned Rosie into a third person. We would joke and say, "Rosie did this..." or "Here goes Rosie, again." With time, we got used to her constant tricks. For example, Rosie had a big mouth— especially around people. When Rosie became loud, Jeri would act like it wasn't her. She would innocently look in my direction, and I took the brunt of it. We could always get a good laugh out of Rosie, who became a running source of entertainment. Our friends all knew Rosie and became comfortable with her. This made Jeri feel good.

Dealing with Easy Problems: Instant Menopause

It happened the night after we got home from the hospital. I woke up in the middle of the night with a jolt. The bed was shaking badly. My first thought was, "Earthquake!" Jeri was lying next to me covered in sweat. She was shaking and gasping for air. My next thought was, "Heart attack!" I started to dial 911. Then I heard Jeri gasp, "Hang up. It's just menopause." I remember saying something like, "Menopause? No way, you're too young." Finally it hit me: she had surgically-induced menopause—her ovaries had been removed. I felt instant relief. It wasn't a heart attack. It was Jeri's first hot flash.

It took some time to cool her off. I got some wet towels and put the fan on high. As it turned out, hot flashes were no joy. The intense rush they produced made it very difficult for Jeri to go back to sleep. As the weeks went by, the frequency and intensity of the flashes increased. They kept us both awake, night after night. Insomnia was something neither of us had experienced before. It sapped our energy when we needed it to fight the cancer and recover from the operation. The immediate solution was for both of us to take sleeping pills. Of course, the pills didn't get rid of the hot flashes but they made it possible for us to resume our sleep after each jolt. The title of John Lennon's song says it best: "Whatever Gets You Through the Night."

Luckily, Jeri did not suffer from the other effects of menopause—such as mood swings and vaginal dryness. However, the hot flashes were a constant annoyance. At first, we tried many natural approaches to attenuate the flashes, but none worked. Jeri's cancer was tested to be 90% estrogen-receptive. As a result, Hormone Replacement Therapy (HRT) was never an option. In fact, whatever remaining estrogen her body produced was blocked by the Aromatase inhibitors she took for the rest of her life. Several years later, the flashes became weaker and less frequent but they never completely went away. Living in Hawaii made it easier to deal with the flashes. During the day, Jeri could dip into the ocean. At night, there was only one sheet of cover to pull away. Yes, the bed got soaked.

Now, the Hard Problem: Endless Chemotherapy

Chemotherapy was our hardest problem. To fight her cancer, Jeri would have to take chemo for the rest of her life. She died when the

Chapter 2: The Longest Chemo

various chemos stopped working. Chemotherapy is an awful and barbaric treatment. Coming from the world of computer science, I find it shameful that the medical community is still relying on chemo in the battle against cancer. After all, it was over 40 years ago that Nixon had declared "war on cancer." Our hope was to keep Jeri alive long enough for a real cure to show up. It didn't happen. There always seemed to be something on the horizon, but nothing ever materialized. Our choices were always: chemo and more chemo. So we had to find a way to live with this thing called chemo.

Tip: Very often, you will hear from well-meaning people: "You must try this...it really works." Typically, "this" refers to some natural cure, diet, or treatment in some far away place. It's always some alternative to chemo. Of course, the person taking chemo would love to hear of some alternative. Over time, we discovered that none of these alternatives worked. It was modern medicine that kept Jeri alive. So it's best to avoid all these detours and stick to what really works. Having said this, we found natural supplements to be useful for detoxification.

Jeri started chemo less than three weeks after she got home from the hospital. She was still very weak from the surgery when I drove her to her first session. I sat next to her for the next five hours while the chemo dripped into her vein. When it was over, she was very pale and incoherent. Her mind was in some kind of fog. I drove her home and put her to bed. She was soon in deep sleep. I decided that this may be a good time to go grocery shopping. Boy, was I wrong.

A half-hour later, my cell phone rang. It was Jeri. All I could hear was, "Help!" I drove back home as fast as I could to a very nauseated Jeri. She just kept vomiting. She would throw up any anti-nausea pill I gave her. And, it just kept going. In desperation, I called Dr. Terada's after-hour line. He said, "I don't want her to damage her throat. Take her to the nearest emergency room and have them call me." The emergency doctors were able to stop the vomiting. However, they managed to put

Jeri into a state of bad convulsions—she now had muscle spasms that would not stop. It turned out she was allergic to Compazine, the anti-nausea medicine they had injected into her. We spent most of that night in the emergency room. This is when it dawned on me that chemo was not going to be easy. I had to be better prepared the next time.

Chemo: Anticipate the Unexpected

What makes chemo so awful? The short answer: all the side effects. Some of these side effects are benign—like losing one's hair. Others can be deadly. For example, some chemos can irreversibly damage the heart or perforate the colon. Most chemos have nasty side effects such as fatigue, nausea, constipation, headaches, nerve damage, rashes, mouth sores, excessive bleeding (from low platelets), and so on. Finally, most chemos weaken the immune system around the middle of each cycle, which means that you're susceptible to every passing bug.

We found chemo to be totally unpredictable. No two chemo treatments are the same. In fact, the same drug may have varying side effects with each session. You must be prepared for anything to happen at any time; you just can't lower your guard. And you have to take it one day at a time. There are always good days and bad days. The trick is to be prepared for the worst, but hope for the best. I became Jeri's bodyguard—always on the lookout for anything that could go wrong. I learned how to be proactive. For example, I became good at detecting people with colds and keeping them away from Jeri. I also learned to react quickly to the various problems that came our way. Finally, I became Jeri's memory bank for past chemo problems and how to deal with them.

Living with Chemo: A Guide for Caregivers

Clearly, we needed a plan for how to deal with chemo. If Jeri stopped taking chemo, for whatever reason, she would die. There was only one choice: we had to make chemo work. This meant we had to contain the side effects, so that Jeri could have the maximum number of good days between chemo sessions. To achieve this goal, I came up with new roles. I told Jeri, "Your job is to do your best to enjoy every moment. My job is to worry about the cancer and the effects of chemo. By the way, you must also take the chemo for both of us." Surprise, Jeri didn't like that last part. In jest, she asked, "Why can't you take the chemo for both of us?" This was also the time when she came up with her three rules for survival: 1) fight the cancer very aggressively, 2) live every day to the fullest, and 3) leave the rest to the universe (and your caregiver). I just now added the caregiver part.

Based on these roles, here's a short list of caregiving practices that worked for us over the years:

- *Prepare ahead for each chemo session.* We carefully went over the side effects of each chemo treatment and then consulted with the chemo nurses on the best course of action. If this was a repeat chemo, I reviewed the diary to make sure we wouldn't repeat past mistakes. We also prepared some meals ahead of time.

- *Accompany her to the chemo sessions.* I always drove Jeri to and from chemo. In the beginning, I stayed with her throughout the chemo session to give her moral support. In later years, I left her with the chemo nurses and ran errands.

- *Stay with your chemo nurses.* The chemo nurses are an important part of the team. Jeri was fortunate to have the same chemo nurses— Sandy, Paul, Michelle, and Phyllis—during all her years of chemo. These nurses were extremely familiar with Jeri's history. Consequently, they could anticipate how she would react to a new chemo treatment. They were also a great source of advice when things went wrong.

- *Knock her out after the chemo session.* I would put Jeri to bed as soon as we got home. Typically, her mind was in a very bad place. We found that the best course of action was to put her to sleep for the next twenty-four hours using Ativan and sleeping pills. This let her get some deep rest. By the time she woke up, most of the chemo was out of her body.

- *Proactively deal with the side effects.* I tried to stay on top of the side effects before they got out of hand. For example, I would always give her the prescribed medicines on schedule. I also carried around some sublingual anti-nausea pills just in case. I did not want a repeat of the emergency room episode. Constipation was always a problem for Jeri. So we started a stool softener regimen before it developed. We quickly escalated the doses at the first sign of constipation.

- *Watch over her like a Hawaiian rainbow.* Hawaiian beach boy, Blue Makua, once told Jeri, "When you're out surfing, Robert watches over you like a Hawaiian rainbow." She loved that expression. I had to keep an eye on her even when she was having a good day. As I said earlier, chemo is full of surprises. For example, a chemo cocktail could have different cycles for each drug. Consequently, at any time Jeri could have a delayed chemo reaction while she was in the surf lineup. Occasionally, she would experience a very sudden drop of energy—we called it "bonking"—while surfing. She would sit out there, frozen on her surfboard, temporarily paralyzed. I would have to send the lifeguard to bring her back to shore. Then we would carry both Jeri and her surfboard up the steps. Jeri would bonk when she hit a low point in her blood counts. When that happened, I would either have to carry her or call a taxi.

- *Get that poison out of her system, fast.* Each time Jeri took chemo, it was as if she had received a dose of poison. My job was to detoxify her. What does this mean? First, I made sure she was always well hydrated. She drank lots of fresh-fruit juices that are rich in potassium and other minerals. Honeydew melon was a particularly good choice. Second, she followed a Mediterranean diet—lots of fresh fruits, vegetables, greens, and fish. She also had a glass of red wine with dinner. Third, she took high-quality daily multivitamins along with other supplements—calcium, CoQ10, iron, fiber, probiotics, and immunocal. Yes, these are many pills to swallow. Finally, she got eight hours of sleep every night, with the help of a sleeping pill.

Chapter 2: The Longest Chemo

- *Deal with the hair loss issues.* With the exception of Taxol, most chemos don't make you lose your hair. Jeri took Taxol during her first and ninth years of chemo. In both cases, she lost her hair shortly after the first session. The first time was quite traumatic. Women don't like to be bald. After recovering from the shock, Jeri decided she would go with the bald look—no wigs. Initially, she had a barber completely shave her head. Then I shaved it daily with my electric razor to keep it nice and smooth. Jeri had a nicely-shaped head with large, attractive green eyes. The bald look suited her. We found the loss of hair on the eyebrows and eyelids to be more of a problem—it gives a sick look. Jeri used a waterproof pencil to paint her eyebrows. Luckily, her eyeliner was permanently tattooed. She looked stunning, especially with large earrings which softened the look of baldness. At the time, it was fashionable for men to shave their heads, so they would stop her on the street and congratulate her on the cool look. The second time she lost her hair, Jeri decided to go the wig route. She said, "I don't want people to know I have cancer. I don't want them feeling sorry for me." I really liked her bald, but my role was to support her, not to argue. Soon, she compromised by going bald on the beach and wearing wigs in the evening. The wigs looked very good on her, especially after a hairdresser shaped them. Eventually, her hair started to grow back. She liked to dye her short hair with very exotic colors.

- *Keep up with the research, but don't invest in biotech stocks.* In addition to keeping up with the various chemos and their side effects, I was constantly researching the literature for new developments on the ovarian cancer front. I read everything I could find on the subject—including articles in specialized medical journals. I was especially interested in treatments that did not involve chemo such as vaccines, monoclonal antibodies, gene therapy, nanotechnology, and so on. Over the years, I followed the progress of several biotech companies with very promising new treatments. One of these companies conducted a massive Phase 3 clinical trial to get FDA approval. My hopes were raised so high that I bought stock in the company. Unfortunately, the product failed. It was heartbreaking. The lesson: keep up with the research, but don't get your hopes up too high—be realistic. Someday, there will be a cure. It just didn't happen in Jeri's time.

- *Stay on course.* You must trust your medical team—your doctor and chemo nurses. If you trust them, stay with them until the end. Don't go on endless doctor-shopping trips. The grass is not necessarily greener in the nation's largest cancer centers; it's just more experimental. Before you get into these last-ditch experimental treatments, make sure you've exhausted what is already proven to work. A good team will be able to give you all the standard treatments for your cancer.

Note: When Jeri first started chemo, we met a very intelligent young woman who also had ovarian cancer. Let's call her Judy. We soon discovered that Judy refused to take chemo, which she felt was poison. Instead, she went from one experimental treatment to the next. She had visited all the major cancer centers on the mainland to consult with various specialists. And she knew everything about alternative treatments. Unfortunately, none worked. Judy died within a year.

- *Make her happy every single day.* I tried to make Jeri forget about her cancer between chemo sessions. I told her, "Worrying won't make the cancer go away. Just let me do the worrying." I wanted her to focus on living every day to the maximum. We started each day with a cup of espresso, accompanied by a dark-chocolate Godiva truffle. That put a smile on her face. We never let a good day go to waste. As you will read later in this book, we were very lucky to live in Hawaii. Eventually, Jeri became a surfer and the waves kept her "permanently stoked."

- *Enjoy your new honeymoon.* I was very lucky to be with Jeri nearly every moment during her chemo years. It was a very romantic time. Before cancer, we had a beautiful life together. After cancer, it became even better. We were lovers on a permanent honeymoon. We lived each day as if there were no tomorrow. She felt very loved and it made her stronger. Jeri knew she would never be alone: she had me, her friends, and the ocean. It was a wonderful time for both of us.

Of course, there is a lot more to caregiving. In this chapter, I covered some of the things that worked for us. I hope that by the time you read this chemo will have become a barbaric relic of the past. Here is some food for thought: "Chemo, radiation and so on may represent state-of-the-art care today, but so, at one point in medical history, did the application of leeches."[2]

Grieving Note: Did I Let Her Down?

Remarkably, this is the question that haunted me in the months after Jeri's death. In the fog of grieving, the bad chemo days and the process of dying became one. It seemed like Jeri had been dying forever. It also felt like I had let her down; I had failed to keep her alive. Remember, I told her not to worry. You will read more about this in later chapters.

As I write this, my mind is much clearer. I can tell you that the chemo years were magical, and it seems Jeri must have felt the same. I was lucky to unearth an e-mail she wrote to her friend Kathy #2 on April 19, 2008—exactly 14 months before she died. Here's an excerpt from a long message in which she goes over her treatment options after learning the cancer had spread to her lungs:

Dear Kathy,

Warning—gushy, philosophical paragraph ahead: I've had an amazing, fulfilling life of which I would like more. The last 8 years have been absolutely wonderful—probably the best years of my life, even if I was sick. I'm so thankful for them. More quality time would be priceless to me. But, of course, I don't want to waste whatever quality time I have taking last-ditch treatments or

---

[2] Barbara Ehrenreich, *Bright-Sided* (Metropolitan Books, 2009).

chasing mirages. Forgive the analogy, but life is like surfing a wave: it's the quality of the ride, not the ending, that counts—but a nice kick-out would be good. I hope no one will ever say that I lost my battle with cancer: I know I've already won it by beating the survival odds by far, no matter what the final outcome is. And I've tried very hard to adhere to my three rules: Live every day to the fullest, fight the disease, and after that, leave the rest to the universe. Making the trade-off between rules 1 and 2 is not easy. I hope I'm granted the wisdom to make the right choice now.

Love,

Jeri

I tried to put words into Jeri's mouth ever since she died, so I was glad to have this confirmation. That note to Kathy says very clearly, in Jeri's very own words, what I've been trying to say in this chapter. From a grieving perspective, it was a gift to be able to read, in absentia, her views on the life and death issues she faced back then.

Jeri was a poster girl for chemo. She probably had three good days for every bad one, which is very good. She would be glowing with energy between chemo treatments. A new chemo patient once asked her, "Is this your first day?" She answered, "No, this is my ninth year." It gave the patient hope. To many of us, Jeri seemed to be getting younger and more beautiful with each passing year. I have pictures to prove it (see www.JeriOrfali.com). The detox must have been doing its miracle. Most importantly, her spirits were incredibly high. She had this radiant smile that people loved. On good days, you couldn't tell that Jeri was fighting cancer. She looked like the healthiest person in the room.

On a personal note, I owe Jeri my life. One year before she died, she became my caregiver for four months as I fought my own cancer. We took turns taking care of each other. I'm glad I lived. It enabled me to get her through the dying process that you will read about in the next chapter.

Chapter 3

The Making of a "Good Death"

"There is no easy way out of this world. It takes nine months and a lot of hard pushing to get people into it, and it usually takes at least that much effort to get them out. Dying is difficult work. It involves pain and grief, and it would be pure folly to imagine that it didn't or that we could avoid suffering altogether. When we talk about dying well or a good death, we have to remember that no death is truly good. We are always talking about making the best of a difficult, inevitable, and very human event."

—Virginia Morris[1]

Nothing had prepared me for Jeri's final days and I was completely taken by surprise. Everything happened very fast; it seemed that all I could do was react. After almost ten years of caregiving, I thought nothing could surprise me; I would just deal with each crisis as it presented itself. I was wrong. From a caregiving perspective, the last days are very different and extremely demanding. Luckily, we were able to give Jeri a "good death."

During those last days, many things could have gone wrong. Any blunder could have put Jeri in terrible pain. From a grieving perspective, I kept revisiting these last days over and over again, going into every little detail. Had I failed Jeri, the ensuing guilt would have overwhelmed me.

Why was I so unprepared, after all these years? The answer is that there is no step-by-step guide for how to deal with death by cancer—or

---

[1] Virginia Morris, *Talking About Death* (Algonquin Books, 2004).

death from any chronic disease, for that matter. I had to grope my way through the process. The only real guidance I had received was from Jeri, who had given me a very clear directive: "Please, make sure I do not suffer at the end. I don't want pain."

Consequently, I did a lot of research on pain management. Still, I did not understand the process that would cause the pain. For example, which organ would fail first? Also, I did not have a clue as to how we would manage the actual end-of-life process. Where would it happen? When would it happen? How would it happen? Yes, I was familiar with hospice care. However, I could never get a clear answer from them on how much they were prepared to do. In Hawaii, there is no physician-assisted death. So how would a hospice deal with final-stage cancer pain? Would it be better to just get palliative care at the hospital? And how far would they go? As Jeri's soulmate, I had to navigate her through this death maze to ensure that she would not suffer at the end. I was a death virgin—I had to feel my way across this strange landscape we call the "end of life" while weighed down by the extreme anguish of seeing my partner go.

In this chapter, I will go over Jeri's last days and the decisions that we faced along the way. Jeri did have a good death. She died with relatively little pain, surrounded by friends and at peace with herself and the universe. It wasn't easy, but we did it. I will also cover the lessons we learned in the process of giving Jeri this good death. Why does a book on grieving include a chapter on dying? The answer: to grieve well we need to understand how our partner left this world. Jeri's death was my first close encounter with the process of dying. I experienced a double shock: Death and the loss of Jeri. Needless to say, these last days haunted me for a long time. You must read this chapter to understand the grief it later triggered.

The Cancer Has Spread

We got the first piece of bad news in late March, 2008—about 15 months prior to Jeri's death. A routine CAT scan revealed that the cancer had spread outside the abdomen and some of it was now in her lungs. This was very bad news. The good news was that the cancer spread did not seem to affect Jeri's quality of life. On the outside, she looked fine. She would say, "Look, I'm very healthy except for a small problem—cancer." She continued her chemo regimens followed by good surfing days.

As the months progressed, the various chemos seemed to be getting less and less effective. We could tell that the cancer was spreading from the rising CA-125 counts. We stopped counting when the cancer marker rose to 547—the norm is below 35. Outwardly, Jeri was still doing fine. These were very good months for her. She learned how to walk on her surfboard. She even managed to get me through my operation and other health-related issues. We took turns at caregiving. It was a very sweet time.

By February, 2009, Jeri had exhausted all chemos. After more than nine years, none seemed to work. The cancer had become chemo-resistant. Dr. Terada told us, "I didn't think I'd ever run out of chemos." A new CAT scan showed that the cancer had spread much further. She had a new tumor on her bladder, and the ones in the lungs had become bigger. It looked like the end was near. Of course, no one could tell by looking at Jeri. She was beautiful and strong. Her friend Kathy would say, "She's a force of nature." Outwardly, Jeri looked like a surfer—an athlete. Inside, the cancer was ravaging her.

I Can Surf Till I Die

No more chemo. I was stunned. I felt that same sunken feeling I had when I first learned of Jeri's cancer. I heard myself asking Dr. Terada, "Does this mean we should start hospice now?" He was taken aback by the question. He reflected for a second and then answered, "No, not yet. You can go talk to them if you like, but it's not time yet. If you're in hospice, we can't do further treatments like radiation. We may need to radiate to manage the pain."

In contrast to the rest of us, Jeri had a big smile on her face. On the way to the car she told me, "Now that chemo is over, I can just surf every day until I die." It seemed like a great plan. I was all for it, but I still didn't have a clue about what would happen next and when. I didn't want to share my fears with Jeri. Instead, I replied, "Yes, keep surfing." Jeri did spend the next two months surfing. She had a small problem with back pains, which was quickly resolved with exercises from the Egoscue *Pain Free* book.[2] An MRI revealed her spine to be clear of cancer.

The Right Leg Went First

I always thought that Jeri's death process would start with a failed organ. After the latest CAT scan, I expected either the bladder or a lung to go first. Instead, the first thing to fail was a limb. In mid-April, her right leg started to hurt.

Note on lymphedema: The leg problem took us by surprise. It just crept up on us, seemingly out of nowhere. In January, the right leg started to swell. At that time, it didn't hurt. Dr. Terada sent Jeri for an ultrasound to rule out a blood clot. When it came back negative, he decided that it was just lymphedema—meaning that the lymph nodes were not draining the leg properly. Typically, this happens after lymph nodes are removed during surgery. It may also be a sign of cancerous lymph nodes. In both cases, the treatment is to re-route the flow of lymphatic fluids around the failed nodes. Three times a week, Jeri would go for a 2-hour lymphatic drainage massage. Thank you, Ann and Luanne. We also discovered—by way of an obscure paper on the Internet—that Kinesio taping could be used to re-route the flow of lymphatic fluid. This method is very convenient and it works.[3] Check it out if you have this problem.

The timeline is now two months before her death. Jeri is taking Tylenol for her leg pain. The lymphedema treatment helped reduce the

---

[2] Pete Egoscue, *Pain Free* (Bantam, 1998).

[3] Kenzo Case, *Kinesio Taping for Lymphedema and Chronic Swelling*.

swelling but not the pain. She went out surfing every day. Then things started to fail quickly. A week later, she was out swimming when the leg pain jumped through the roof. I had to rescue her out of the ocean. It was her last swim. She could hardly walk to the shore. My friend Mike helped me get her back home in a taxi. The next day, she was in a wheelchair. This was the first of a series of heartbreaks.

Pain Management: The Delicate Balancing Act

Dr. Terada responded by prescribing Vicodin—her first narcotic painkiller. He also started Jeri on radiation. The hope was that it would shrink the tumors enough to diminish the pain. Perhaps, she would even regain the use of her leg and surf again. We had high hopes. The Vicodin kept the pain under control for about a week. During that time, Jeri could move around in her wheelchair and go places. But it didn't last long. The pain baseline started to shift upwards again as the cancer spread. The growing tumors were pushing on nerves and causing more pain. In response, Dr. Terada kept escalating the pain treatments. Jeri started taking large doses of Oxycontin, augmented by Celebrex and steroids. She was in good spirits when the pain did not break through. We had to keep her leg in comfortable positions at all times.

Note on breakthrough pain: This is pain that comes on suddenly for short periods of time. It is common in late cancer. Typically, the baseline (or background) pain is kept under control by painkillers. However, some pain periodically "breaks through" the medication. The trick is to manage this breakthrough when it occurs.

By the end of April, Dr. Terada had Jeri hospitalized for pain-management treatment. She went to Queen's Hospital—the home of a world-class team of palliative care specialists headed by Dr. Daniel Fischberg. Conveniently, Jeri's radiation treatment was also in the same hospital. So all the doctors she needed were under the same hospital roof. Again, the hope was that this dream team would find the right combination of treatments to get Jeri back in the surf lineup.

Note on palliative care: Over the last ten years, palliative care has become a recognized subspecialty of medicine with its own fellowships, hospital departments, and medical school courses. It's now standard practice in hospitals across the U.S. Its practitioners provide pain management, symptom control, and counseling for people with advanced disease.

It didn't take us long to discover that pain management is not a hard science. It involves a lot of tweaking. The doctors had to keep twiddling the knobs to find the right combination of painkillers for Jeri, as each person is different. In the hospital, they attached Jeri to an infusion pump, which delivered the pain medicine—now Fentanyl—directly into her veins. The machine was programmed to deliver a base level of painkiller. In addition, Jeri could give herself a bolus (a small dose) of medicine whenever she needed it. This allowed her to control her breakthrough pain. She could avoid the peaks and valleys of intermittent dosing.

This was all very good; Jeri's pain was now under control. However, there was one little problem: It took a huge amount of Fentanyl to keep her pain down. She was consuming the equivalent of 100 Vicodins a day. Dr. Fischberg had to find a combination of non-opiate drugs that would reduce the Fentanyl and still keep the pain under control. After ten days of tweaking, it seemed that he had found the right combination. Somehow, he managed to keep the pain under control while still allowing Jeri to remain lucid. So I was able to take her home with Fentanyl patches for her base pain and an array of other medicines to deal with the breakthrough pain. In the hospital, they also taught Jeri how to use a walker so she was more mobile than when she first came in.

During the next nine days, the pain was mostly under control. I would wheel Jeri around Waikiki when she felt well. When she experienced breakthrough pain, we would elevate her right leg and she would take whatever pill was prescribed. By the ninth day, however, the breakthrough pain became more intense and frequent. That night she experienced her first hallucinations. She didn't recognize me. Instead, she appeared to be in deep conversation with a doctor from Botswana (she had been watching a TV program that took place there). The hallucinations must have been quite pleasant; she laughed a lot. But then, she started to walk in her sleep. That night, I woke up to find her on the balcony. We live in a high rise, so this last development was not very good. Clearly, the medicines needed to be readjusted. The next day, we were back in the hospital.

Once again, Dr. Fischberg did his usual magic and brought the pain and hallucinations under control. In addition, he switched Jeri over to Methadone and Dilaudid, which she could take in pill form when she was discharged. Dr. Terada visited Jeri every morning to examine her leg and swollen abdomen. She was quite bloated, and her friend Deborah got her a new wardrobe of loose-fitting clothes. The upper leg was now covered with lumps. Some of the younger doctors thought it might be shingles. They wanted to take a biopsy. Dr. Terada did not think a biopsy was necessary. He knew it was the cancer spreading to her leg.

Finally, I found enough courage to ask Dr. Terada the dreaded question, "How much time does Jeri have left?" He gave me the straight answer, "Well, I don't exactly know, but it's less than six months." Jeri was on the bed listening very attentively. When he left the room, she said, "Thank you for asking the question. I needed to know. It makes me feel better." In contrast, I felt like I had just been stabbed in the heart. I had to ask her, "Why does knowing this make you feel any better?" She answered, "Now I know what to expect." I was very sad.

Where to Die: Hospice, Hospital, or Home?

With less than six months to live, Jeri became a candidate for hospice care. Dr. Terada signed a paper that allowed representatives from hospice to talk to us in the hospital. Because of where we lived, the choice narrowed down to a single hospice, St. Francis. Tracy, the palliative-care counselor, encouraged us to take the hospice route. She wanted Jeri to be released from the hospital to the hospice. I was not convinced. Here's my best recollection of the exchange that took place that day:

Tracy: Hospices do a much better job than hospitals for end-of-life care. All the surveys show that.

Robert: I'm not convinced. I know, for a fact, that in this hospital you can keep Jeri's pain under control. We could just stay here until she dies. Her insurance covers 365 days of hospital stays. We have Dr. Terada and Dr. Fischberg here. Why would we go anywhere else?

Tracy: Hospices provide excellent pain management. Dr. Terada will still be Jeri's primary physician. In addition, they have their own doctors. Jeri will be much more comfortable there. Probably the most important thing is that they can also help you take care of her at home. She can be at home instead of in a hospital. Besides, you can always return to this hospital if things don't work out. All it takes is one signature.

Robert: But she won't have access to all the hospital equipment. What if she needs an EKG or blood transfusion?

Tracy: Yes, it's a different philosophy. Jeri can always come back to the hospital if she needs special treatment. You should talk to the hospice representatives directly and hear what they have to say. I can arrange for an interview tomorrow.

Tracy's most compelling argument was that I could have Jeri back home. The hospice people would provide round-the-clock support for pain management, which I felt we really needed to make it work from home. Later, I turned to Jeri and asked, "Where do you want to be? The choices are: hospital, hospice facility, or home." She had a very clear-headed answer, "Let's first talk to the hospice people and see what they have to say."

Note on end-of-life care in hospitals: Hospitals are not in the business of nursing the chronically ill. They're not set up to provide end-of-life nursing. Typically, you get admitted for a specific condition. You are then released as soon as you get treated. In Jeri's case, she was admitted and released several times to deal with her shifting pain. I believe that most insurance companies require that you get released from a hospital after the treatment is completed. You just can't say, "I think I'm going to die sometime, and I'd like to spend my remaining days in the hospital." Of course, they'll take you in if you need prolonged acute care. In this case, you may end up dying in the hospital's Intensive Care Unit (ICU) intubated with all sorts of life-support equipment. In fact, about 50% of all patients with chronic illness die in hospitals. Most of these deaths are unplanned.[4] Hospitals may provide comfort care when they think a patient has just hours or days left to live.

The next day we got a visit from the hospice representative. We wasted no time getting down to the issues that concerned us. Again, this is my best recollection of what was said that day:

Jeri: I don't want to die in pain. When I need it, will you give me enough pain medicine to make me fully unconscious? How do I know that with a name like St. Francis you just won't end up sprinkling me with holy water and giving me last rites, instead of inducing a coma?

Hospice representative: You'll just have to trust your doctors to do what's right for you. Dr. Terada will still be there with you. We also have our own doctors who'll be managing your pain at all times.

Jeri: So how would we manage the pain at home? What happens if I get breakthrough pain that suddenly gets out of control in the middle of the night? How do we get the pain meds?

Hospice representative: We provide all your pain meds free of charge. Unlike regular doctors, our doctors can fax pain-medication prescriptions directly to a 24-hour pharmacy where you can pick

---

[4] David Feldman and Andrew Lasher, *The End-of-Life Handbook* (New Harbinger, 2007).

them up. Our volunteers can also pick up the meds and bring them to you.

Robert: What happens at the brink of death when things start to break down all at once? If it really gets bad, can you guarantee her a room in the hospice facility?

Hospice representative: We'll always guarantee her a room when she gets into the active death process. We set aside a number of rooms for these type of situations. Just don't call 911.

Jeri: So, how will you determine that I'm actively dying?

Hospice representative: We will assign you a registered nurse (an RN) who will track your progress. Your RN will be visiting you at home on a regular basis—three times a week, or more if you need it. We also have an RN on duty at all times. Just call us when you need help.

Jeri: What other services do you provide at home?

Hospice representative: We'll provide—free of charge—all the equipment you'll need for home care. The list includes hospital beds, bathroom chairs, oxygen tanks, commodes, bronchodilators, bedside tables, and so on. We don't provide the actual home care. Your caregiver, Robert, will take care of you. Of course, he may need to hire help. I'll provide you with a list of agencies that specialize in home care. If Robert needs relief, you can stay in our facility—provided we have space. It will cost you $300 per day.

Hospice representative: We're fully booked right now. Would you like me to put you on our waiting list? You can stay in the hospital until a room frees up.

Jeri: Yes, please put me on the waiting list. But Robert and I will need to research this some more before we sign up.

The meeting was very informative. Now Jeri wanted me to visit the hospice facility and report back to her. The next morning, my friend Spinner and I drove up the Pali highway to visit the hospice facility. The landscape was stunning—green forests and steep cliffs with waterfalls, as far as the eye could see. I got off at Queen Emma's summer palace. The hospice was in a beautiful mansion that stood right across from the palace gardens. Inside, the place was immaculate. There was a nice courtyard with tables and chairs. The rooms were superb and the staff seemed very friendly. It felt like we were at a bed-and-breakfast in the Napa Valley wine country. Spinner liked it, too. She said, "Jeri is going to love this place. It's so pretty."

Hospice It Is

I went back to the hospital to report to Jeri on what we had just seen. I had also talked to many people who said the hospice was really excellent. The ratings were, unequivocally, good. Here's my best recollection of the conversation I had with Jeri that day concerning hospice:

Robert: Where do we go from here? What are your thoughts?

Jeri: I like this hospice stuff. Perhaps, that's the way to go.

Robert: But I want you at home. Of course, I don't want you to suffer. Your comfort should always come first.

Jeri: It will take a lot of effort to take care of me at home. Why do you want to put yourself through this ordeal?

Robert: Because I love you. I'm really happy to be able to do this for you. I'm glad you saved my life last year, so that I can be here for you today. Last week, you told me you wanted to die near the ocean, looking at Diamond Head. The hospice is in the mountains. Of course, it's beautiful there, too. If I could provide you with the same care, would you prefer to be at home?

Jeri: Yes, I would prefer to be at home. Listen, I have a plan that may work. What I want to do next, is to get released to the hospice facility. I can spend a few days there and get to know the doctors and nurses. I also want to see if this hospice stuff works. In the meantime, you can get the apartment ready for me. I'm sure the hospice people will tell you what you'll need for home care. It's part of what they do. You can take me home when you're ready.

Robert: Yep, it's a very good plan. Let's make it happen.

The next day, Jeri was released from the hospital to the hospice. It was on May 28, three weeks before she died. There were many tears as she said goodbye to the team that had taken her this far, but she was excited about going to the hospice. I wheeled her to the car, and we took the short drive up the hill to the hospice. For the next six days, this was her new home. It certainly beat the hospital room.

Jeri really loved the hospice facility and staff. The nurses were exceptionally good. She also liked and trusted Dr. Lee, her new hospice doctor. From her bed, Jeri could see emerald-green mountains. But most of the time, she was not in bed. Instead, she was in her wheelchair exploring the grounds and visiting with her friends. She felt very alive. Unfortunately, the people in the adjoining rooms were all in the process of dying. Sometimes, Jeri could hear sounds of death. In the mornings, she was the only patient who could enjoy breakfast on the outside patio overlooking the mountains.

Jeri felt very alive in a facility for the dying. This turned out to be a good thing because she got to meet the people who would later help her die. They all got to know her before she was on the brink of death. A few days later, she told me, "I don't belong here, yet. Take me home."

Turning Home Sweet Home into a Hospice Suite

Meanwhile, I was working at full speed on getting our apartment ready for Jeri's homecoming. I made a very good decision: I hired Spinner on a full-time basis to help me with the "remodel" and to offload me in general. I needed all the quality time I could get with Jeri. As you can tell from her name, Spinner (as in Spinner Dolphin) is very fast. In no time, she moved the living-room furniture to storage to make room for the hospital bed. Then she moved everything around to make the entire apartment wheelchair accessible.

As promised, the hospice delivered the equipment Jeri would need. Spinner and her husband, Mike, put together a box of drawers on wheels to give Jeri accessible bed-side storage. Our friend Deborah bought some beautiful blue sheets and pillows for the new bed.

It took us a total of five days to turn the apartment into a beautiful hospice suite. During that time, I was also able to enjoy some very long visits with Jeri at the hospice—including some romantic dinners on the patio. On Thursday, June 4, Jeri was back home overlooking the ocean and Diamond Head. She was so happy to be back. Mike helped me wheel her up to the apartment. I'll never forget the look on her face when she saw her beautiful new suite. She was very pleased with what we had accomplished. She smiled and said, "Now, let the games begin." The timeline is 14 days before her death.

Pre-Active Dying: Let the Games Begin

The next ten days were filled with fun and laughter. The "girlfriends" turned this time into one big party. "We're going to bring Jeri to the ocean," became their battle cry. They were joined by Nicole, our home-hospice RN. And they enlisted the help of some very muscular Waikiki beach boys, who vowed they would carry Jeri into the ocean and then tow her to the surf lineup. Of course, poor Jeri was not exactly ready for the ocean or the surf lineup. I was later to find out that she was in the pre-active phase of dying. But none of us noticed any signs of approaching death. Instead, we just kept the festivities going at full speed.

A Typical Day

During her pre-active death period, Jeri's day started with breakfast on the lanai veranda followed by a shower. Nicole would then show up to examine her and fine-tune her medicines. The girlfriends—Deborah, Kathy, and Spinner—would arrive a bit later. Sometimes, they were accompanied by their husbands. Everyone laughed and joked a lot. Jeri was slowing down, but she didn't seem to miss a beat. She was the heart of the party. She would soon tire though, and take a short nap. This is when we planned the outing of the day. For example, we organized shopping trips to Nordstrom and Macy's to buy her new clothes. She would try them on with three of us helping her in the changing room. Several times, we took her out to dinner at some of her favorite restaurants. Jeri enjoyed her outings. She would put on makeup and get all dressed up for the occasion. Even though it made her tired, she was always ready to go.

Bring The Ocean To Jeri

Eight days before Jeri died, I rented an ocean-front room at the Moana Surfrider for a ten-day stay. It was right on the beach directly overlooking her favorite surfing spot. For the next five days, the hotel room became our outing destination. We would leave home for the Moana each day at noon and return later in the evening. It was only a five-minute drive, but it took much preparation.

From the lanai of her hotel room, Jeri had a perfect view of what turned out to be the biggest swell of the year. She would wave at her surfer friends. Some of the better surfers would wave back while riding a wave. Typically, Jeri would rest a bit on the hotel bed before the girlfriends and other friends would arrive. Then the fun would begin again. In one gag, the girlfriends decided to bring the ocean to Jeri, so they showed up one day with a big container of ocean water with sand at the bottom. Jeri could then immerse her feet in ocean water while looking at the waves outside.

Maestro, This Is My Last Haircut

In the evenings, we would all eat dinner in the room overlooking the ocean. Spinner would organize the nightly dinner feast. At this point, Jeri would eat very little, about 25% of normal. She would say, "I'm not exercising, so I don't need to eat that much." Jeri liked the celebration of life that these feasts represented—the sharing of good food with good friends. She would sit in her wheelchair at the head of the table. Her attention would alternate between the waves outside and her friends inside. She had a say in all that was happening around her. She seemed keenly aware, but she would also withdraw inside her mind for short spells.

One evening we wheeled her down Kalakaua Avenue, Waikiki's main drag. Jeri would stop and hug friends—mostly fellow surfers—she met along the way. Our first destination was Mario's, where she got a haircut. I briefly stepped out to make dinner reservations. When I was out of earshot, she told Mario, "Maestro, this is my last haircut." They were both in tears when I returned.

That night, we had a nice dinner at her favorite sushi restaurant. We were seated on an outside terrace from which we could watch the constant procession of life down Kalakaua. Jeri seemed to absorb it all. Occasionally, she would withdraw deep inside herself. Later, when I grieved, I kept asking myself: "What was she thinking then?" Now, I think I know the answer: She was starting to withdraw from life to prepare for death. It's all part of the pre-active phase of dying.

Pre-Active and Active Phases of Dying

During the last stages of Jeri's life, there were many unfamiliar changes which I did not understand at the time. As I found out later, there are signs of dying that are observable, although not everyone follows a predictable sequence of events. Health professionals speak of *dying trajectories* that suggest how persons with specific diseases will die. For example, those with a terminal illness, such as advanced cancer, will show a steady decline toward death. Those with serious chronic illnesses may have peaks and valleys that sometimes give the impression of recovery. At the end, each person's death is unique.[5]

According to the *Hospice Patients Alliance,* "There are two phases prior to the actual time of death: the *pre-active* phase of dying, and the *active* phase of dying. On average, the pre-active phase may last approximately two weeks, while on average, the active phase lasts about three days. We say on average because there are often exceptions to this rule." [6]

The Signs of Pre-Active Dying

The signs of the *pre-active* phase of dying include:

---

[5] Source: Hawaii Hospice and Palliative Care Association.

[6] Source: Hospice Patients Alliance, *Signs and Symptoms of Approaching Death.*

- Increased restlessness, confusion, agitation, inability to stay content in one position, and insisting on changing positions frequently. It is exhausting for the family and caregivers.

- Withdrawal from active participation in social activities.

- Increased periods of sleep and lethargy.

- Decreased intake of food and liquids.

- Pauses in breathing, known as *apnea*.

- Increased swelling of either the extremities or the entire body, known as *edema*.

As David Kessler eloquently describes it, "Dying is like shutting down a large factory filled with engines and assembly lines and giant boilers. Everything does not suddenly go quiet when the *off* switch is pushed. Instead, the machinery creaks and moans as it slows to a halt. Unless suddenly felled by an accident, a heart attack, or other sudden trauma, most of our bodies are like those factories, creaking and moaning as they shut down. It can be difficult to remember that the winding-down process is natural. We do not go gently into death. No matter how prepared we think we are for death, we do not let go of life easily."[7]

The Signs of Active Dying

The signs of the *active* phase of dying include:

- Going in and out of semi-coma or even coma.

- Extreme restlessness, confusion, and agitation. You may see the dying person pulling at their clothing or bed sheets, over and over. They may also seem confused about the time or place. These behaviors occur as a result of less oxygen to the brain, medications, and chemical changes in the body. This condition is called *terminal restlessness*. Kübler-Ross believes that it's caused by the dying

---

[7] David Kessler, *The Needs of the Dying* (Harper, 2007).

person's "fear of immobility."[8] In any case, do not try to restrain your loved one. Just talk calmly and softly about whatever comes to mind.

- Dramatic changes in breathing patterns as the body continues to shut down. A person who is dying may take as many as 50 breaths per minute, or as few as six. We normally take 12-18 breaths per minute. Sometimes, the person may appear to be gasping for air—they may feel like they're suffocating. This frightening condition, called *dyspnea*, can sometimes be successfully alleviated with oxygen and opiates such as the ones used for pain. Opiates tend to expand the arteries in the lungs, easing the passage of air.

- Severe respiratory congestion and fluid buildup in the lungs. The person may make gurgling sounds, sometimes referred to as the *death rattle*. These sounds are due to the pooling of secretions because the person forgets to swallow. At this point, the person is unable to cough up the secretions. The air passing through the mucus causes the gurgling sound. Thankfully, this condition is not painful.

- Inability to swallow foods or fluids.

- Breathing through wide-open mouth that some doctors call "the O sign."

- No longer being able to speak.

- Urinary and bowel incontinence in a person who was not previously incontinent.

- Blood pressure can drop dramatically and the pulse rate can double.

- Extremities—such as hands, arms, feet, and legs—may feel very cold to the touch. They may also feel numb.

- Changes in skin color—especially on the hands and feet. They may look blue and blotchy. The cause is low blood circulation. The blood goes to the brain and the more vital organs. It's part of the body's process of shutting down.

---

[8] Elizabeth Kübler-Ross, *On Death and Dying* (MacMillan, 1969).

- Person's body looks rigid. It stays in unchanging positions. The eyes may look glassy and teary as they stare open but unseeing. It is common to see a little bit of foaming at the mouth.

- Occasional bursts of energy and life. Sometimes, quite unexpectedly, the person may become alert and talkative. At this point, they're simply letting go of what is left of their physical energy; they're not getting better. Use this window to say what you need to say to reach closure.

These symptoms are just signs of a body shutting down; circulation stops, tissues do not get enough oxygen, the brain starts to flicker, and organs fail. The order of failure depends on the underlying disease and other factors. Eventually, the vital center is destroyed and the person dies.[9] It's all part of the labor of dying—it's the reverse of birthing. In a hospice setting, none of these symptoms are treated as medical emergencies. The goal, at this point, is to keep the dying person as comfortable as possible.

Caregiving in the Pre-Active Phase of Dying

Caregiving during this pre-active phase was a beautiful and tender experience; it was also very exhausting. With Spinner's full-time help —and the hospice's part-time help—we had the situation under control. Here's a quick list of what we did for Jeri:

- *Provided memorable meals:* It's important to have good food till the very end—any meal could have been Jeri's final meal. We also wanted to present the food well. We often had feasts with our friends to celebrate life. The hospital food was so terrible that I had to provide all the meals. The hospice food was a bit better, but I still provided dinners—mostly takeout from her favorite restaurants. I found it much easier to provide meals at home. Spinner handled the feasts at the Moana.

---

[9] Sherwin Nuland, *How We Die* (Vintage Books, 1995).

- *Helped her move around:* In the last days, Jeri had the use of only one leg, so we always had to do a little dance to get her from one place to the next. For example, she would put her arms around my neck, get up on her good leg, and then I would swivel her to-and-from a wheelchair, bed-side commode, hospital bed, bathroom chair, or car seat. This dance was very loving, especially in the middle of the night. I felt a total sense of merger with her. She would ring her bell to wake me up and I would help her get to-and-from the commode by her bed. During the day, I had help from Spinner and Deborah. They both knew the routine very well. We had to cover Jeri round-the-clock. I was so glad to let her use my limbs to get around.

- *Stayed on top of the medications:* Spinner helped me get the meds. Later, Nicole would bring them. I had to make sure Jeri took all her meds on schedule. Jeri had no problem swallowing her meds during this phase, which made it easy.

- *Kept her leg comfortable at all times:* We always had to find the right position for her bad leg. What seemed to work one day wouldn't work the next.

- *Enjoyed her every moment:* It was a very tender time. We felt so happy to have her with us. We knew that she would only be with us for a short time, so we wanted to savor every moment. Of course, none of us thought that she would die so soon.

As you can see, some of the items on this list are very specific to Jeri's final days. Each one of us will depart from this earth in our own unique way. For caregivers, this is a time of intense giving and loving. For a soulmate, this is the most intense form of bonding two people can experience. You really understand what it means to be intimate. It's the purest form of love.

Active Dying: It Wasn't Easy

Jeri started to die on Sunday night on the way home from the Moana. She was gasping for air and wheezing all the way home. That night, she had a hard time swallowing her meds. After several attempts, she finally swallowed them and then fell into a deep sleep. Her breathing was still irregular. After an hour, she seemed to be getting better so I fell asleep, but not for long. In the middle of the night, she rang the bell. As usual, I rushed over to get her to the commode. This time, however, nothing happened. But when I tucked her back in bed, something did happen. She turned to me with a very cute smile and said, "Like a baby." She had become incontinent. I said, "Oops! Don't worry. We'll take care of it." So I gave her a shower in the middle of the night, while she gasped for air. I changed the sheets, kissed her, and put her back to sleep. Then I called the hospice to ask for advice.

Does This Mean I'm Being Grounded?

The next morning, Nicole called to say she was on her way. She walked in at 8 a.m., accompanied by Dr. Lee. They were followed by the girlfriends. Thirty minutes later, the medical supply people showed up with oxygen tanks. Jeri made a face when she saw them. She turned to Deborah and asked, "Does this mean I'm being grounded?" Dr. Lee must have overheard Jeri. She answered, "You'll need the oxygen. It will help you breathe better." She then adjusted the meds and said something about a Foley catheter. She also told me to put Jeri on a liquid diet and to give her some soft food with her pills. Dr. Lee was a very caring doctor. That morning she spent an hour with Jeri.

For the rest of the day, Jeri seemed to be okay as long as she inhaled her oxygen. She didn't seem to care for the oxygen nozzle on her nose. She kept pulling it away, which sent her gasping for air. The girlfriends thought she was getting hot flashes, so they would turn up the fan.

Making It Through the Night

Monday night was pretty bad. Every half hour, Jeri would sit up, pull away the oxygen nozzle, and then gasp for air. I would respond by soothing her and then gently putting the nozzle back on her nose. This went on all night long. Several times, I called the hospice for advice, but they had none. I was tempted to call 911 to have Jeri put on a respirator, but this was not what she wanted. She definitely did not want to end up on life support in a hospital. So I just held her hand and calmed her down to help her get through the night.

The next morning (it's now Tuesday) Nicole called to say she was on her way. But I now faced a new problem: Jeri couldn't swallow her pills. Luckily, we still had some liquid morphine from a previous treatment. So I gave her morphine, with Nicole's permission. But, we had an even more serious problem. After listening to Jeri's lungs through her stethoscope, Nicole had a very worried look. She said, "I think her lung may have collapsed. She's going to die today. We must take her back to the hospice facility, now."

I was totally stunned. All I could mutter was, "But, she wants to die at home." Nicole just said, "Robert, she's going to be much better off in our facility. You must do what's best for Jeri. I have a room waiting for her. Our transporters are on their way." All I could say was, "OK, but if she gets better I want her back home."

Back to the Hospice

One hour later, Jeri was back in a hospice bed. Dr. Lee had prescribed a heavy dose of liquid morphine. Jeri had a hard time swallowing, so I requested that they put her on a morphine pump. Unfortunately, the pump didn't arrive until early the next morning. Jeri's girlfriend Kathy volunteered to pick it up herself. Dr. Lee had to intervene to have the delivery of the pump expedited by courier.

Later that Tuesday, Jeri briefly came out of her semi-coma. She pointed her finger at me and then gave me a very loving smile. My heart melted. She also beamed when she recognized the girlfriends. Then she asked, "Where am I?" When she finally realized that she was back at the hospice, she pulled away her sheets and said, "I want to go home. I want to go home."

I felt terrible. I had let her down. All I could say was, "Baby, please trust me. You're better off here." Luckily, the girlfriends were able to distract her and they talked about something else.

It's OK to Let Go

A little later, I heard Spinner whisper, "Now is a good time for you to tell her it's OK to let go." I knew she was right, but I just couldn't utter the words. Spinner kept prodding me. So I finally heard myself say, "Baby, it's OK for you to go. I'll be OK. Just take care of yourself. I love you." I was crying like a baby. A few minutes later, Jeri lapsed back into a state of semi-coma.

Later, I told the girlfriends, "Look, we can't all be here at the same time. Jeri won't die tonight. She's too strong—she's an athlete. She may live for many weeks. So we'll need to break down into teams to have one of us stay with her at all times—day and night." Deborah and Kathy took the late-night shifts—from midnight till 9 a.m. Spinner and I would cover the rest. This gave us a chance to take showers and get some sleep. Kathy would do the first late-night shift.

That evening, I left Jeri in Kathy's hands. Kathy came trotting in at midnight full of energy and ready to go. She started playing Jeri's favorite CDs. I was exhausted. I hadn't slept for two nights. So I drove home, took a shower, and went straight to bed.

Her Last Words

The next morning (it's now Wednesday) the phone woke me up at 8 a.m. It was Kathy. She said, "Quick, come over. Jeri is wide awake and having a great morning." I was so excited and was at the hospice 40 minutes later. I walked into Jeri's room to find her surrounded by five girlfriends—Annette and Dee had joined the party. Jeri was wide awake, laughing, and having a great time. She gave me her most beautiful smile. I gave her a very wet kiss. I noticed her lips were dry, so I kept moistening them with kisses. I called Jeri's sick mom in California and put Jeri on the phone.

After their conversation ended, Dee, who has a beautiful voice, sang a few songs for Jeri. The party went on till 10:15 a.m. Dee and I were both holding Jeri's hands when she said, "I'm so tired. I need to rest." These would be her last words. She then fell into deep coma.

Chapter 3: The Making of a "Good Death"

Of course, we all thought Jeri would come back again after she got some rest. During the chemo years, Jeri always bounced back. But this time she didn't. We kept the vigil going, waiting for Jeri to wake up. She slept peacefully all through Wednesday. At midnight, I left her in Deborah's hands. I went home for a shower and some sleep. I expected to find Jeri wide awake the next morning.

Can You Hear Me?

Unfortunately, the next morning came—it was now Thursday—and she was still in a deep sleep. I spent the whole day holding her hand. Friends kept coming and going, but all I could see was Jeri's serene face. Her big green eyes were wide open. She looked so beautiful, but I missed hearing her voice. For some reason, I started thinking about the funeral. Then it struck me that I needed to talk to her about it. I knew that she wanted to be cremated and have her ashes scattered in the ocean off Waikiki. But I had so many questions about how she wanted her funeral done. Typically, Jeri liked to choreograph these type of events. She was very creative.

I called Spinner over to Jeri's bedside and we started planning the funeral. We were hoping Jeri could hear us and jump in with her ideas. Eventually, we came up with a great plan for a surfer's funeral. It was going to be wonderful. We were both getting very excited. Spinner said, "Jeri's going to love it." I desperately wanted to go over the plan with Jeri. So, I slowly went over each detail of the funeral with her. I then told her, "Squeeze my finger if you can hear me." I did not feel a squeeze. Spinner was insistent, "I know she can hear you. Just repeat the story." I must have repeated the story at least three times. She looked like she heard it, but still no squeeze.

That evening—around 9 p.m.—Jeri started to make loud gurgling sounds as she breathed. I was terrified. I called the nurses. They tried to clear her throat, but the sounds didn't stop. The gurgling continued for the next two hours. The nurses kept reassuring me that she was not in pain. I still wanted them to do something. Later, I was to find out that this was the infamous "death rattle." The sounds were caused by her inability to cough up the fluids that she had accumulated, but she was not in pain.

Death Came in the Middle of the Night

That night Kathy arrived shortly after midnight. I stayed with her for an hour to make sure Jeri was OK. She seemed to be extremely calm. At 1:00 a.m., I decided that I should go home and get some sleep. I went home and took a shower. Then I called Kathy, before taking my sleeping pill. It was 1:30 a.m. Kathy said, "Jeri's doing fine. The liquids seem to have cleared up. She's breathing very calmly. Get some sleep." I took my sleeping pill and quickly fell asleep.

Less than an hour later—at exactly 2:25 a.m.—the phone rang. It was the nurse from the hospice. I heard her say, "I'm sorry to tell you that your wife, Jeri, just passed away." I was stunned. But all I could say was, "Thank you. I'm coming right over."

After the nurse hung up, I had three immediate reactions: Why wasn't I there? How did it happen? Did she suffer? I called Kathy from the car on my way to the hospice. She told me that Jeri's heart had just stopped beating. Apparently, Kathy was holding her hand and was surprised by the slowing heartbeat. So she started timing the intervals between beats. Then, to her surprise, Jeri's heart seemed to have just stopped. She told herself, "Perhaps, I'm not doing this right." So she called the nurse, who then pronounced Jeri dead.

I arrived at 3 a.m., followed by the girlfriends. Jeri looked very much at rest and seemed to be smiling peacefully. She appeared to be merely asleep and was, as always, very beautiful. All I could do was kiss her and say goodnight. I must have been feeling the effect of the sleeping pill I had taken earlier. I told the girlfriends, "We all need to get some sleep, too."

As we left the hospice together, there was a profound feeling of sadness. At the same time, we were relieved that Jeri had died peacefully and relatively quickly—she had not slowly starved to death. It was all very surreal.

Grieving Note: Did She Have a Good Death?

The events described in this chapter had a huge impact on my grieving. I must have replayed the scenes from the last days over a hundred times in my mind. In part, I had to deal with the idea that Jeri was gone, forever. I also felt traumatized by the scenes of my beloved Jeri dying. Additionally, there were questions that kept nagging me: Did she have a good death? Had I let her down at the very end?

How do you define a good death? Clearly, Jeri died surrounded by friends and family. She seemed at peace with the universe. But did she suffer too much at the end? Could we have done better?

In other words, could the timing of her death have been better? To answer this question, I will present a hypothetical scenario. Let's assume for a moment that, as in Oregon, Hawaii had legalized physician-assisted dying for the terminally ill. Jeri was a staunch proponent of euthanasia in such circumstances. So the question is: What time would Jeri have picked for her departure? Jeri had told me many times that, ideally, she would want to go when her life was more bad than good.

If she had a crystal ball, Jeri would have probably picked Sunday evening as the right time to go. It was the cross-over point from good to bad. She would have had dinner at the Moana with her friends and me as we overlooked the ocean she loved so much. We would have all said our goodbyes. Then, we would have had a final toast celebrating Jeri's life. This is the time when she would have taken her final cocktail. She would have died peacefully a few minutes later. Obviously, this is the perfect scenario for a good death, but it assumes she had a crystal ball—that is, the knowledge of hindsight.

Of course Jeri did not have a crystal ball. None of us have. So the question becomes: Given the information Jeri had, what time would she have picked to die? Most probably, she would have picked Monday morning when the oxygen tanks showed up. Let's assume that Jeri was being treated by a fictitious doctor who was licensed to perform euthanasia in Hawaii. Jeri would have said, "Doctor, I've had a good life. Now, I want to die with dignity. Please give me an injection and put me to sleep." Why an injection? By then she wouldn't have been able to swallow her cocktail.[10] We would have all said our goodbyes and made a toast to Jeri's good life. The doctor would have given her a shot, and she would have died peacefully within minutes. Obviously, this scenario is not too bad, but it's still not as good as the first one.

Let's get back to reality. The state of Hawaii does not support physician-assisted death. With the best hospice care available, Jeri died on Thursday night, instead of on Monday. And, she died in a hospice instead of at home. We missed the optimum target by a few days. In all fairness, she was in a semi-coma most of Tuesday. After Wednesday morning she was in a deep coma—which is like being dead. By terminating her life, Jeri would have avoided the suffering of Monday night and Tuesday morning—a total of 16 hours. However, she would have missed out on the two beautiful moments we had on Tuesday afternoon and Wednesday morning. In conclusion, Jeri did not experience the best possible death for her situation, but she came very close. We were just 16 hours off the ideal time.

Of course, those 16 hours ended up haunting me for a long time. When it comes to grieving, a painful death that lasts even a few seconds can haunt you for a very long time. Today, after much soul searching, I can unequivocally say that Jeri had a very good hospice death. Since physician-assisted dying is not a legal option in Hawaii, we gave her the best possible death.

Caregiving During the Active Phase of Dying

I'll be the first to admit that my caregiving failed during Jeri's active-dying phase. What happened? The answer is that it all happened too fast. It caught me off guard. I now believe that I handled the events of Sunday night extremely well. It was, by far, the most tender and loving

---

[10] Note: The Oregon *Death with Dignity Act* requires that the patient self-administer the medication. Jeri would have had to inject it into her catheter.

care-giving moment I had ever experienced with Jeri. I was so much in love with her that night. It's impossible to imagine two people being more intimate and close. However, by Monday, I should have hired an RN full time. Maybe, I should have hired two full-time RNs, if we were going to use the morphine pump. In any case, I couldn't find an RN in time for Jeri to die at home. I did try. In hindsight, I should have hired an RN earlier.

However, even if I had hired three full-time RNs, I don't think I could have done a better job than the hospice did. Why? The answer is that they understand death better than anyone else. The nurses and RNs in the hospice provide end-of-life care every single day. In contrast, a typical RN-for-hire does not know much about death. Why is this important? Because the hospice people also understand the emotional needs of the dying. They are gentle, compassionate, and caring. They talk softly to the dying and treat them like people till the very end. So Nicole was absolutely right—Jeri was much better off dying in the hospice.

Preparing for Death: Lessons Learned

As Dr. Ira Byock eloquently reminds us, "We are, each one of us, at every moment, a heartbeat away from death."[11] Most of us will not leave life the way we choose. However, this doesn't mean we shouldn't be prepared. The diseases that once killed us swiftly have been replaced by the Big Four—heart disease, cancer, cardiovascular disease, and lung disease. Typically, these diseases are chronic, long-term, and degenerative. Dying in the age of chronic disease is an extremely complicated process. The lucky few will go suddenly. The rest of us will die in small steps. We'll find ourselves navigating through a labyrinth of confusing end-of-life choices. Here are some of the lessons on dying that I learned through trial and error:

- *End-of-life caregiving is not a solo act.* Home care for the dying requires an enormous amount of effort and time. It takes a team

---

[11] Ira Byock, *The Four Inner Things That Matter Most* (Free Press, 2004).

effort, a village. Caregiving for the actively dying can be incredibly complicated and expensive. For example, RNs typically charge $50 per hour. In some cases, you may need round-the-clock RN support. Do the math to see if your finances can handle it. *Warning:* Long-term care could easily be the wild card that wipes you out financially. You should consider buying long-term care insurance while you still can.

- *Learning more about death won't kill you.* Most of us are death virgins. We go out of our way to avoid the topic of death and especially its details. As a result, we're totally unprepared when end-of-life confronts us. We're all going to die, so the least we can do is spend a few hours learning about death. The knowledge will make us better navigators and more informed consumers when the time arrives. I tell my friends that they should all read *Talking About Death* by Virginia Morris. Check the references in this chapter for additional reading.

- *Hospice care is not for everyone.* Hospice care certainly beats sudden and repeated trips to the emergency room, followed by lengthy hospital stays. However, to be eligible for hospice care, a doctor must declare that a person has fewer than six months to live. Doctors can predict cancer deaths with some confidence. It's much harder to predict deaths from other chronic diseases. So, you may have to hire a team that provides hospice-like care using home agencies. Of course, it's very costly.

- *Manage the pain aggressively.* As I pointed out in this chapter, pain management is a delicate and tortuous balancing act. It may take a lot of tweaking to get it right. "Enough" narcotics is whatever works to alleviate your pain. Narcotics can be safely administered for months—or even years—before death. Don't worry. You won't turn into a drug addict, even if the doses seem terrifically high. However, there are other side effects that need to be managed. Also, don't underestimate the effort it takes to acquire narcotic-based meds. Be sure to fill the prescriptions before you leave the hospital.

- ***Know that extreme pain may require extra procedures.*** Some of the extreme pain conditions (for example, nerve and neuropathic pain) may require high-tech procedures, such as *epidural catheters,* that deliver the narcotic directly to the spine. Typically, the hospice does not provide such procedures. You may want to have these done at the hospital before you sign up for hospice. In addition, *morphine pumps* are an added expense for most hospices. Consequently, they won't provide one unless you ask for it. In the final days, these pumps are needed to provide a steady supply of narcotic into the bloodstream. Make sure your proxy knows all of this.

- ***Get your advanced directives in order.*** You'll need a *Living Will* that specifies the type of life-support care you would want in various situations. For example, "if I become terminally ill or injured" or "if I become permanently unconscious." Because you can't anticipate every situation, you'll also need a *Durable Power of Attorney for Health Care.* This document lets you appoint your health-care *proxy* —the person who will make health-care decisions for you.[12] Be sure to pick a proxy who you can trust to navigate the health-care system on your behalf. At the end, your physician may issue a *Do Not Resuscitate (DNR)* order. Typically, this medical order is kept in your hospital charts. You'll also need an *at-home DNR* to keep paramedics from resuscitating you in case someone dials 911.

- ***Write a goodbye letter.*** Remember, it is a pretty complicated terrain out there. Death can be quite chaotic. For example, you may have specified "no intubation," but what if you need a ventilator for a short time? This is where your choice of proxy becomes important. It's also a good idea to write a *goodbye letter* that provides additional guidance to your proxy. For instance, you could write, "Don't continue treatments if there is no hope of recovery to my normal lifestyle." You can then specify what "normal" means for you. The

---

[12] Every state has its own versions. The *National Hospice and Palliative Care Organization* (www.caringinfo.org/stateaddownload) has all 50 state forms available for free download.

letter can also include your instructions on cremation (or burial) and the memorial service. Bottom line: Make sure your proxy knows the system well and understands your wishes.

- *Physician-assisted dying must be made an option.* Terminal patients must be given that choice. For some, it may be the least painful, most humane, and dignified final exit. Knowing they have that choice may greatly reduce their terminal anxiety and fear; it provides insurance, just in case. It also keeps them from committing suicide prematurely, while they still can. Note that without assisted dying the only way to control unbearable suffering today is through *unconscious sedation.* Patients are given a combination of narcotics, barbiturates, and anesthetics to induce coma. Death comes slowly from either the progressing disease, pneumonia, or starvation if artificial nutrition is withheld. I now know that Jeri was extremely lucky. She may have died rapidly from a blood clot that penetrated the lungs. In any case, she had a very soft landing. Most of us won't be that fortunate.

- *Work on legalizing assisted dying in your state.* Gallup polls consistently indicate that Americans overwhelmingly support physician-assisted dying, Oregon style. When asked the question: "When a person has a disease that cannot be cured, do you think doctors should be allowed by law to end the patient's life by some painless means if the patient and his or her family request it?" In the 2007 poll, 71% were in favor while 27% were opposed. Make sure your legislators get the message. In fairness, I should point out that there are two sides to this story. The modern hospice movement, for which I have a great deal of admiration, provides the most compelling position against assisted death. Their alternative is to provide *comfort care* for the dying. It's that wonderful care Jeri received at the end of her life; but there was still some suffering. You should carefully weigh both sides of the argument and draw your own conclusions. In any case, you must let your legislators know if assisted dying should be added to our current repertoire of final options. It's a decision that greatly impacts the way we die.

Chapter 3: The Making of a "Good Death"

- *End-of-life support can be the ultimate love experience.* This is a very precious and intimate time for lovers. It's incredibly sad to see your lover go, but it's also an incredible bonding experience. It is the culmination of your love. Note: Your lover may sometimes hang on to life just to be with you (or, because she worries about what will happen to you without her). It's important to let her know that it's OK to let go. In the words of Kübler-Ross, "She should be allowed to detach herself slowly from all meaningful relationships in her life.... She dies by separating herself step-by-step from her environment and relationships."[13]

- *Avoid care-giver burnout.* Caregiving at the end of life is more like a marathon than a sprint. This is especially true for diseases—like dementia—that have a long and tortuous death trajectory. It's important that you take care of yourself, so that you can take care of your loved one. I tried to block three hours each day for exercising, showering, and grocery shopping. I also tried to get enough sleep.

- *Here's an idea that could help you:* Jeri died with a smile on her face. Could something good be happening at the hour of death? Dr. Kenneth Ring, author of *Heading Toward Omega,* is the leading authority on *Near Death Experiences (or NDEs).* According to his research on NDE, "The most common words used to describe it is an overwhelming, absolute peace." The peak experiences of near death can be explained by an assortment of physiological reasons. For example, the release of endorphins near the end numbs all pain and gives a feeling of deep euphoria. Some researchers attribute the visual sensation of "a tunnel with bright light at the end" to random firings of the optic nerve when the brain starts to shut down. In addition, electrolyte imbalances and oxygen deprivation can cause psychedelic-like hallucinations (like a so-called good LSD trip). According to Dr. Daniel Dennett, author of *Consciousness Explained,* "These experiences we call NDEs can all be explained by the physical effects of the dying brain—they are the brain's

---

[13] Elizabeth Kübler-Ross, *On Death and Dying* (MacMillan, 1969).

biochemical way of dealing with traumatic stress." In any case, it doesn't seem like a bad ending.

Breaking a Taboo: The Privacy of the Deathbed

In our society, the deathbed experience is private. What happens in the deathbed stays in the deathbed. You rarely see in print the gritty details of how a death really plays out.[14] Doctors and nurses don't talk about it. Families rarely discuss it in public. Funeral obituaries gloss over it. Of course, the dead can't talk. And from Hollywood all we get are endless scenes of instant death.

I found during my grieving that it helped me immensely when people would share details of a death they had closely witnessed. I kept drilling them for more detail, as much as they were willing to share without breaking down in tears. Why? I wanted to compare notes with them. It helped me understand that other people also go through the end-of-life process. Jeri was not singled out by the forces of the universe. The specifics helped me understand that the death process—not just death itself—is a universal experience. Of course, we will each die in our own way.

After some hesitation, I decided that Jeri would not mind sharing her end-of-life experience with the rest of the world—especially if it could be of some benefit to others. Her death is a textbook example of a good hospice death, so there are definitely lessons to be learned here.

Conclusion

This chapter shows that dying can be a long and messy affair. As the surviving soulmate, the death you witnessed can leave you with deep feelings of guilt and remorse that can haunt you throughout your grieving. Why? Because most of us have a sanitized view of death, which is really a messy organic process. Because death is messy, you will blame yourself for not having done something or other better.

---

[14] The exception is: Marilyn Webb, *The Good Death* (Bantam Books, 1997).

Chapter 3: The Making of a "Good Death"

You'll always wish you could have done more for your dying lover. You will go through endless sequences of "what if" and "if only" ruminations revisiting every aspect of the death. Again, the problem is that most of us are death virgins. The better we understand death, the less pain we will experience during grieving. The level of detail that I provided in this very long chapter is essential for understanding some of the grieving chapters that follow.

Chapter 4

A Surfer's Funeral

"You live your life with a person, you grow up with that person, it's 25, 35, 45 years, and when that person dies, somehow you see their entire lives through the prism, through the lens, of those last months, those last weeks. You can't get that out of your mind."

— *Dr. Sherwin Nuland*

The next morning, I woke up to a terrifying world without Jeri. I just couldn't fathom what had happened. Jeri was gone, forever. My mind went numb. I started getting ready to visit Jeri at the hospice. Then it dawned on me that there was no more Jeri. She was no longer at the hospice. Her body was now in a funeral home, ready to be cremated. They were waiting for me to sign the papers. I couldn't believe that Jeri would just go up in flames. Then it dawned on me, once again, that she was already gone. There was no more Jeri. There was just a body waiting to be cremated. It was all beyond my understanding.

Then I began to hallucinate. The scenery wasn't pretty. It was a landscape of devastation and desolation, as far as the eye could see. It was like black-and-white footage from Hiroshima the day after the bomb was dropped. It felt like the earth was going to open up underneath me and swallow me. I was sweating and shaking in a state of panic and fear. Then I looked outside and the world seemed intact. It was just another beautiful Hawaiian day. The sun was up and the blue ocean was glimmering. I looked in the mirror and I was still whole, even though I felt ripped apart. So, it was all happening in my mind. The devastation was in my mind. It was my own private holocaust—all in my mind.

The next moment I began to sob. Then, I kept on sobbing—or more likely wailing—for what seemed like an hour. Eventually, the sobbing stopped and my mind totally cleared up. I was still alive and I could think again. I knew some huge cosmic event had just happened, but I had work to do. I would deal with the cosmic stuff later. It was all too huge for me to digest right then. So just like that, I put my grieving on hold. My real grieving was to start the day after Jeri's funeral.

I was once again in task-oriented mode with my adrenaline still pumping at full speed from the previous days. Again, I had to take care of Jeri. There was a funeral to plan and a body to cremate. I called Spinner to work on the schedule. I was back in the real world, at least for now. That was how I survived the first few days after Jeri's death.

In this chapter, I'll go over Jeri's surfer funeral and the events that preceded it. I also cover the important role her website memorial played in my immediate and future grieving. It's a nice piece of technology that can help people mourn better. It also provides a modern—and much more complete—version of a tombstone for people who are cremated. Surprisingly, it turned out to be more than just a visual place where Jeri's memory lives forever; or, more likely, as long as the Internet exists. Later, it helped me recreate my own identity, which was an important part of my grieving process.

The Mother of All Grief Bursts

The pain I just described was my first *grief burst* after Jeri's death. It was also my most intense grief burst ever. During my grieving, I experienced hundreds of these bursts—all horrible. The rest of this book is about how I dealt with these bursts and, finally, got rid of them. But this first one was very intense and dangerous, so I want to spend some time dissecting it.

For now—more on this later—a grief burst is an unexpected wave of grief. It's a sharp stab of emotional pain and anxiety that lasts about two minutes and is relieved by deep sobbing (or just crying if you're in a public place). The bursts come in waves; each wave brings a dose of pain. These bursts are an outward expression of some inner pain. In this first grief burst, I was overwhelmed by a brew of primal feelings and deep emotions triggered by Jeri's death the night before:

- *I felt very angry.* I was mad at a killer. Mother Nature? Invading cancer cells? A killer had murdered the love of my life. What had she done to deserve such a fate? She was a beautiful, caring person who had never hurt anyone. All she wanted was to surf a little longer. The killer, in an act of mad destruction, had taken everything that mattered to me on this earth. I was devastated and angry.

- *I felt guilty.* I had told Jeri it was OK to go. When she died, I expressed relief that she had not gone through a long starvation cycle. Had I wished my soulmate dead? Did this make me an accomplice to her murder? I also felt guilty to be still alive, while she had died.

- *I felt powerless.* I was unable to protect Jeri from that killer. Did I fail her?

- *I felt fear and anguish.* The killer was on the loose. I was badly wounded; it felt like there was a big hole inside me. I felt the killer would soon return to finish me off. I was about to die at any moment. I was in fear, waiting for the next blow.

- *I felt alone in the universe.* I lost Jeri—my life companion and soulmate. How could I continue alone without my partner? The world was a lonely and desolate place. I was now condemned to live in a world without Jeri.

As you can see, I was facing a deep ontological crisis. I felt the world had become a scene of destruction. It felt very insecure. If you have experienced the death of your soulmate, then you will know exactly what I mean. For the rest, perhaps an analogy may help. Think of an 8.5 earthquake. People who survive such devastating quakes report that they can't trust the ground beneath them. They're terrified of the aftershock that may get them next. They're terrified of being swallowed by the earth, and they're surrounded by widespread destruction.

Suicide Watch: To Be or Not to Be?

I believe this first grief burst can be very dangerous. If someone were to commit suicide after the death of a soulmate, this would be the time. Think of *Anthony and Cleopatra, Romeo and Juliet,* or the thousands of modern-day suicide pacts. Why is suicide so attractive at this point? The answers: 1) It makes a very romantic double-ending—the lovers can be buried together; 2) The grieving pain can be unbearable—it can make you temporarily insane; and 3) It's an act of protest against the killer or, if you prefer, the capriciousness of the universe. Suicide may also tempt those who believe in an afterlife. Why wait in miserable pain if you can join your lover now? Of course, the concept of hell can help dampen that temptation.

Luckily, the thought of suicide never crossed my mind. I believe in physician-assisted dying for the terminally ill, but in this situation suicide did not make any sense for me. Why? I had seen how much Jeri valued every moment of her life until the very end. She was a life-affirming force who made me appreciate the value of my own life. For me, the romantic answer is to live well and as long as I can so that the memory of Jeri can continue to live inside my heart. And when I die, Jeri will continue to live in the search engines of the Internet—our new matrix.

Jeri Experienced the Mirror of My Pain

Actually, it was Jeri who gave me my grief-survival strategy. One month before she died, she called me over and said, "Babe, do you remember that night, last year, when you were sick and about to die?" I didn't particularly want to remember that night but I said, "Yes." She then gave me a great parting gift, which turned out to be the best high-level guidance on grieving I ever received. Here's what she said:

"Well, that night when it looked like I would lose you, I remember going through the worst pain I've ever had in my life. It was

terrifying. It was a deep existential pain that I can't exactly describe. It was totally mental—not something Dr. Fischberg could fix. I'm so sorry, Babe, but you're going to have these same horrible pains after I die. But I want you to know that it's all in the mind. You're a great conceptual thinker. This stuff is really up your alley. If anyone can deal with that mind stuff, you can. So deal with the grieving pain. After you figure it out and beat it, you'll find that life is worth living again. It will be more good than bad. You can then continue to live for both of us. But, first you must bring the pain down. I'm so sorry to put you through this."

There is no pain greater than the loss of a soulmate. It's beyond comprehension. My analyst later told me, "No two people suffer the same grieving pain. Everyone is different." Actually, there is one person who could have felt my exact pain: My dead soulmate. In theory, my soulmate would be able to experience the exact mirror of my pain—she's my other half. Of course, your soulmate at this point is dead. In my case, Jeri had experienced the mirror of my pain while she was alive. She was able to warn me about what was yet to come. It was a very rare gift.

The Days Immediately After

That first grief burst took place around 7 a.m. the morning after Jeri's death. Had I slept a little longer, I probably would have avoided it. From 8 a.m. onwards, I was surrounded by a beehive of activity. The medical supply company showed up, bright and early, to remove the hospital bed and other equipment. They were followed by Deborah and Spinner, who wanted to know how they could be of help. I said, "Please take away all of Jeri's stuff—jewelry, clothes, blue bed sheets, surfing stuff, everything. Just leave me the pictures and her surfing sunglasses." They asked, "Are you sure?" I replied, "Absolutely, I don't want to turn this place into a mausoleum."

Then the phone started ringing and it just kept ringing for the next ten days. The first to call were the hospice people: Nicole, Dr. Lee, and Father George. It felt good talking to them—they understood what I had been through. Dr. Lee said, "Robert, now is the time to take care of yourself." Then came the condolence calls—from relatives, far-away friends, closer friends, and people I didn't even know. There were calls from people on airplanes who were coming for the funeral. And, for the next month, I was flooded with condolence cards. It was all very heartfelt and touching.

This early outpouring of support and love was extremely soothing. I felt that people shared my pain. They all missed Jeri and felt some of my loss. I was not alone. Of course, I was in a state of numbness and confusion. I didn't really understand what people were saying, but it still felt good and reassuring.

Visiting the Crematory

The first order of the day was dealing with the issues surrounding Jeri's body. I drove with Spinner to the crematory to sign the papers, order a whole bunch of death certificates, and specify how I wanted the cremation done. I wanted the ashes placed in a bio-degradable container made from Hawaiian leaves, so that they could be tossed into the ocean. I also told them to ship a small amount of ashes to California so that Jeri's mom could have a little ceremony of her own. (Part of Jeri's ashes are now scattered in her garden.) Lastly, I arranged for a 30-minute viewing of Jeri's body before the cremation.

The viewing took place three days later. A group of us—the girlfriends and their husbands—drove to the crematory, a beautiful place in the hills above Honolulu. We were joined by Jeri's girlfriend, Deborah #3, who had just flown in from California. Again, Jeri's body looked beautiful and very peaceful. It was still Jeri, but without the life energy. I kissed her, cried, and said goodbye. On the way out, I saw two men who seemed to be waiting for us to leave. They were the cremators. They had come for the body—that same body I had loved and cuddled all those years. Suddenly, I felt guilty. I had signed the papers to have my loved one burned into ashes. But, this is what she wanted. It's also what I want for myself. Of course, I had no control over the emotions I felt that day. You don't have control over your emotions when there is grief. It's the nature of the beast.

Funerals Are a Wonderful Invention

Grieving deals with internal pain. Mourning, on the other hand, is about the external part of loss—the rituals and traditions that help sustain us in the days that immediately follow the loss. Nothing beats a good funeral when it comes to mourning. It's the ultimate antidote. It's exactly what society has prescribed, from time immemorial, to suspend pain during the immediate period that follows a death.

My entire attention during the next ten days was focused on the funeral. It involved an endless amount of planning and preparation. Luckily, I had help from the girlfriends, who were now joined by their husbands. Brian, Kathy's husband, flew in from London; Mike, Spinner's husband, flew in from Oregon; Rich, Deborah's husband, had not left the island. And we had help from more girlfriends—both local and from the mainland. The latest girlfriend to arrive was Kathy #2, Jeri's oldest friend from California. She came with her entire family. So I had a small army to help me with the funeral. For some unknown reason, I kept calling it a wedding, perhaps because it felt like a big celebration.

Now, How Do We Get the Ocean to Cooperate?

I was faced with an immediate problem: I had to pick the day of the funeral. People were flying in from all over and they needed to know the date. I also had to write an obituary for the newspaper, which required a firm date. However, this was a surfer's funeral, so I had to deal with the ocean conditions. The forecast for the next 30 days was back-to-back swells. Remember the swell at the Moana? Well, it just kept on going and going. It's as if the ocean was sending out these huge waves to say goodbye to Jeri. The surfers at the funeral were in for a big treat, but that was not necessarily so for the rest of us.

The problem was: How do I get Jeri's ashes out to the scattering site? The canoes and catamarans were not going out—the ocean conditions were just too rough. The impasse was finally broken by my friend Garvin, the lifeguard captain. He said, "Robert, just pick a day. It's Jeri. We'll get her out. We can put you and her on the jet ski and get you out there. The surfers and the lifeguards will be there." Now, I could pick the day. Hopefully, the swell would die down a bit so that I could get the non-surfers out on canoes and catamarans. Of course, I knew that Jeri would want big waves for her funeral. It's as if she had planned it.

After I picked the date, everything started to move very fast. I wrote the obituary for the paper. I also wrote the words for the posters and leaflets we would hand out and post in the surfer areas. Jeri's girlfriend Jayne did the layout. Spinner was able to hire Mauna Lua, Jeri's favorite Hawaiian band. We had played their CDs during Jeri's last moments. Spinner also hired the helicopter service that would drop flowers in the middle of the ring of surfers. There were countless other details. We met each night at dinner to strategize. In a sense, it was like planning and executing an elaborate wedding, in ten days or less.

The Making of "My Jeri"

I wrote Jeri's obituary and then e-mailed it to the Honolulu paper just in time to meet their publication deadline. But something felt terribly wrong. My writing was stiff, formal, and rigid. I tried to liven it up with a picture of a smiling Jeri carrying her surfboard, but it still didn't do the trick.

Obituaries just make the dead look deader. They're as lifeless as a dead body in the morgue. An obituary is the formal announcement of a person's death. It's the nails in the coffin. Typically, it focuses on how the person died and on the funeral arrangements. The short biographical description tends to be dry and lifeless. (You can read what I wrote on Jeri's website.)

Clearly, I had to do better for Jeri. She was more than just a dead body or a "fallen hero" in the war on cancer. She was a person who had lived and then died in this world. As the surviving soulmate, I was left with the task of giving meaning to her life and death. As the young dead soldiers in Archibald MacLeish's poem tell us:

They say, We were young. We have died. Remember us.
They say, We leave you our deaths: give them their meaning
They say, Our deaths are not ours: they are yours: they will mean
what you make them.[1]

So two days after her death, I turned off the phone and wrote "My Jeri." The words came from deep inside my heart. I cried with each word. Finally, I had something that began to capture the meaning of Jeri's life and death. What I wrote that day was to become my eulogy for the funeral.

"My Jeri"—Written Two Days After Her Death

Here, I include "My Jeri" exactly as I wrote it. (It is also on Jeri's website.) It should give you a feel for my state of mind at the time. This is what I wrote on June 21, 2009:

We're here today because we were touched by Jeri, usually in some very special way. It never took too long for people who met her—even briefly—to realize that this was a very special woman. She was lively and lovable with a great sense of humor. But you could also sense her inner strength—she was one tough cookie. Like you, I was touched by this beautiful person. I met her in 1979. I was a happy thirty-year old bachelor then, but I knew I had found a gem. So after our first encounter, we became totally inseparable for the next thirty years. It's almost like we were fused together—she was my lover, coauthor, partner, and best friend. Early on, we decided not to have children. We wanted to live for one another "till death do us part." We were very possessive of our time together. I can't tell you how much I miss her. She's left a huge hole in my heart. But, I also think I'm the luckiest man to

---

[1] Archibald MacLeish, *The Young Dead Soldiers Do Not Speak* (1941).

have lived on this planet because of the thirty blissful years I had with her—what a gift she was!

The Early Years

I would like to share a few things about Jeri to give you a better sense for who she was. Jeri was born in Los Angeles in 1952. She was adopted when she was four days old by a relatively poor family. She faced some very big challenges in her early life but somehow managed to bootstrap herself out of it. She became a born-again Christian and even went on a mission in El Salvador—I guess, to convert the Catholics there. She was so poor, that at times she didn't have a nickel to take the bus to her work as a file clerk for the IRS in downtown Oakland. There was a lot of pressure for her to get married early to get out of her predicament. Instead, Jeri managed to work her way through school. By the time I met her (in a bookstore/coffee shop), she had earned a B.A. in psychology. Luckily for me, she was also dating guys and was not into religion any longer. I found out she was a great belly dancer, which was her hobby then (but I didn't know it when I met her). She made her own costumes and danced at clubs accompanied by some very talented musicians and bands.

The Silicon Valley Years

We were both in the computer industry in the early Silicon Valley days. After we teamed up, Jeri got her master's degree in cybernetic systems. I helped her work on her thesis for the next two years, and it became the basis for everything we accomplished later in our professional lives—we had developed a model for computer software to communicate intelligently over networks. We spent the next twenty years developing this vision into a reality—it is now part of the Web. No, we did not invent the Internet. In Silicon Valley, Jeri joined many exciting startups—including Rolm, Tandem Computers, and BEA Systems. She was a good techie, who at one time managed hundreds of the best programmers in the Valley. These highly individualistic and talented people learned to respect Jeri and accept her leadership—even though she was a woman in what was then, mostly, a male-only industry. She was a natural leader because of her great personality. She really cared about people and knew how to turn out some great products. She also knew how to market her products. In my opinion, she was a genius—very smart, well-rounded, and multi-talented. I wasn't the only one who thought this: she was named Silicon Valley Executive Woman of the Year in the early 1990's.

The World-Tour Years

At one point, Jeri and I decided we would give back some of the knowledge we had gained. We would write books that explained our vision and help a new generation of programmers understand this esoteric technology. She became my coauthor along with Dan Harkey. Jeri insisted that we write in a very friendly style to make the technology accessible. We used cartoons of Martians and simple terminology to explain some very difficult stuff—like the mission-critical software that runs the banks, stock markets, and telephone companies. These are programs that can't fail.

To my surprise, our books became bestsellers. Our Client/Server and Java books sold over a million copies. In the last two years of our professional life, Jeri and I went on two world tours promoting the technologies in our books. We were surprised by how famous we were everywhere—our books had been translated into 27 languages. We had a great time on the road with the "Jeri and Robert Show." And, as you would expect, Jeri was a very articulate and expressive speaker—the audiences loved her from Beijing to Stockholm.

The Cancer-Fighting Years

At the end of our last world tour, we decided that Hawaii was the most beautiful place on this earth. (We also loved the Greek Islands where we did a lot of our writing, but only in the summers.) Because of what we did, we could move anywhere, so we decided to make Hawaii our home. We knew we could write here because we had worked on several books while on the ocean-front at Waimanalo. In July 1998, we packed our stuff and moved to Kailua on the island of Oahu. We were in heaven. Unfortunately, Jeri got diagnosed with ovarian cancer shortly after.

Most of you here met Jeri during her heroic fight with cancer. I can tell you that we were very lucky to be here in Hawaii during this trying time. We had three things that helped Jeri live nearly ten years after her diagnosis when the average for her specific type of cancer is only two:

- First, there was a great medical team—including Dr. Keith Terada her world-class oncologist (with help from Kim); her very caring nurses—Paul, Michelle, Sandy, and Phyllis—who helped her through chemo; and later the hospice people at St. Francis— Dr. Lee, Nicole, Judith, Jeff, Danny, and many others.
- Second, Jeri discovered the healing power of the ocean in Hawaii.
- Finally, she loved the people of Hawaii and she became a Hawaiian at heart. She constantly studied the history, music, literature, and the ocean culture of Hawaii.

Early on, Jeri decided to fight the cancer using three principles: 1) Fight the cancer very aggressively—she had three operations and nine years of chemo (a world record), 2) Live every day to the fullest, and 3) Leave the rest to fate.

The Surfer-Girl Years

The ocean was very good to Jeri. At first, she tip-toed her way into the water by walking the beach and then swimming, snorkeling, and canoeing. Next, she discovered body boarding and became a "wall rat." Finally, she graduated to surfing. Jeri was always very passionate about whatever she did and surfing became her greatest passion. She loved her board, surf locker, and the local surfers at Canoes. Jeri had many teachers who taught her how to surf— including most of the beach boys and lifeguards of Waikiki and the people at the surf rack. Thank you Tommy, Robert, Daniel, and Auntie Pat for carrying her board when she was too weak. Thank you Kealihi for towing her after a bad chemo. Jeri always wanted to know more and she was not afraid to ask questions. I thank many of you here for teaching her. You helped her become a good surfer at the age of 50. She was even able to win fourth place in China's contest for her division. Most importantly, it helped her fight her cancer and maintain that incredible spirit that we all loved.

The Final Days

Jeri lived long enough to see the first summer swell in mid-June, 2009. We rented a room in the Moana from which she could say goodbye and wave to many of you, while you were catching these big waves (her girlfriends—Kathy and Deborah—even kept her feet dipped into ocean water they brought into the room). Now, Jeri wants you all to keep on surfing for her. Her ashes will be with us forever in the waters of Waikiki. We will be with Jeri when we swim or surf. Also, Jeri will be in very good company in this sacred spot of ocean—she will be with the great surfers and beach boys of the past. So please, let's take her ashes to the ocean where she belongs.

Grieving Note: The Significance of "My Jeri"

Writing "My Jeri" was a very cathartic experience. It was also an important grieving milestone. The final days were now less than 10% of her life-story narrative. Before, they totally dominated the narrative. All I could think about was the dying Jeri. My memories were skewed by the haunting imagery of the final days, the silence at the end, and the inert body at the crematory. Clearly, I needed a fair and balanced narrative of Jeri's life, which is what "My Jeri" helped me accomplish.

"My Jeri" seemed to magically bring my partner back to life. Jeri had a very beautiful life, of which death was a very small part. Now I could recognize my Jeri again. The fog of the last days had temporarily lifted. Of course, I knew she was dead; I had seen the body. I was not trying to resurrect her. I was simply trying to reclaim her life story. I was trying to re-balance my memory of Jeri. She was so much more than the dead body I had seen at the crematory. She had lived a good life and she had a good death.

My Jeri: The Grieving Soulmate Problem

In a subtle way, "My Jeri" was my first attempt to come to grips with the existential significance of my soulmate's life and death. There was a complete life story here with a beginning and an end. Jeri had completed the circle of life, while mine was still unfinished—a work in progress.

One of the big challenges for grieving soulmates is how to disentangle the interlocked identities. As a soulmate, your identity is totally fused with that of your partner's. It's the nature of soulmate love. We tend to complete each other's thoughts. We feel our pain together; when one hurts, the other hurts. We share a common history. We grow up together, so we have a shared bank of memories. And we would gladly take a bullet for our soulmate. Our separate egos have fully bonded and we are one.

Instead of being two separate "I's," soulmates fuse into an entity, called "we." Instead of two single atoms, soulmates become a single molecule. This explains why soulmates can experience total, non-egotistical, and unconditional love. So what happens when death does us part? The answer is: The surviving soulmate becomes an "I" again —a single atom.

Find Her First, Then You'll Find Yourself

The work of grieving is to make that new-born "I" become whole— you heal when you become a self-contained individual once again. As the surviving soulmate, a big part of your healing process centers on re-balancing your identity. You must become whole again, which means you'll have to re-create your identity without the physical presence of your loved one. The memories, however, live forever in your heart. They become an important part of your support system—especially if they are happy memories.

So what does this have to do with "My Jeri?" I later discovered that the best way to reclaim my own identity was by first making my partner whole again. In other words, first do the partner and then you'll find yourself. Why? Because the dead partner has a completed narrative with a beginning and an end. You can see the boundaries—the contours—much more clearly. In contrast, your own boundaries are much harder to untangle. You are still alive and mired in grief. So you'll have a very hard time finding your inner "I" when all you can feel is the pain of loss. On the other hand, it's much easier to think about your lost partner during these painful times.

So my insight was to work on my partner's "I" first. If I could fully situate her existentially, then what remains behind is me—with my existential life still a work-in-process. This simple insight really works. After I discovered it, I was able to heal fast. Of course, there were also other things that I had to discover before that happened.

I Still Needed to See Her

The prose version of "My Jeri" was nice, but I felt an intense visual hunger—I needed to see her again. I needed visuals to accompany the narrative. The individual photos were just too still. I needed animated sequences of pictures organized in life threads to recreate my Jeri visually. There were no videos of the earlier years and all we had were old pictures stored in shoeboxes. Jeri and I had never looked at these old pictures. We always lived in the present.

Where would I house these visual threads? I was a geek in my previous life, so there was only one answer that came to mind: The Internet, of course. I needed to put together a website so that Jeri could live in the matrix. Instead of an inert tombstone, she would have a very lively website. It would become my repository of memories of a life well lived. I could share memories of my Jeri with others, such as her mother. Now that I had a plan to take "My Jeri" to the next level, I hired Jayne and her husband, Al, to help me make it happen.

The Website Story

I wrote this testimonial on August 1, less than two months after Jeri died, to promote a new business started by the people who helped me put together Jeri's website, Jayne and Al. I'll include my testimonial "as is" because it explains the process that led to the development of Jeri's website. The writing is still raw. It conveys some of the grief I then felt. Here's what I wrote:

> In the days that directly followed my beloved Jeri's death, I found myself in a complete daze with a seemingly compulsive urge to collect pictures of Jeri during happier times. I needed something to help me immediately forget the last few days of Jeri's battle with cancer. In my grief, I had to recreate Jeri as she was most of her life. I needed to erase the memory of the last few weeks—the sick person in a hospice bed and the body I saw at the crematory. In other words, I needed Jeri minus the last week. I had a hunger to visually reconnect with my Jeri.

The Visual Life Story

> During one of my more lucid moments, I decided that the hodgepodge of pictures I had collected needed some structure. They had to be organized in a life story with threads (or chapters) that told Jeri's life. I also felt that I needed to make this story widely available to Jeri's friends and family to help them in their grief wherever they were—in Hawaii, on the mainland, and beyond. In another moment of lucidity, I decided to hire Jayne and Al to put together a memorial website to help tell her story.

> Jeri's funeral at sea took place about ten days after her death. During this extremely sad period all I did, every day, was work with Jayne and Al on Jeri's story. It was my daily grief therapy. I wrote "My Jeri" to help release my pain and tell Jeri's story from my perspective. This became the narrative around which we

organized the entire website (www.JeriOrfali.com). The boxes full of old pictures were transformed into major threads that brought the narrative to life. In time, they became beautiful slideshows that helped me visualize the Jeri I knew and loved over the last 30 years.

On the day of the funeral, we used the material from the slideshows to create posters of Jeri's life. The narrative in "My Jeri" was my eulogy. Al did a great job making "My Jeri" into a video by filming the oratory. With the help of Jeri's surfer friends, he was also able to capture on film the rest of the funeral events, including the surfers paddling out and the scattering of Jeri's ashes in her favorite surf spot off Waikiki. A few days later, the video of the funeral was incorporated into the website, along with a picture gallery of the event. This video was very helpful to Jeri's friends who could not make it to the funeral. It made them feel as if they were there.

In the days after the funeral, the guestbook on the website helped me communicate with people who were grieving Jeri's death and, at the same time, learning more about her life. Most people knew a little bit about Jeri but very few were familiar with the whole picture. Many were amazed at the multiple facets of that wonderful woman—belly dancer, Silicon Valley executive, author, and later surfer girl. What a beautiful story. Thank you, Jayne and Al for helping me bring it to life.

It's Helping Me Grieve

Today (nearly two months after Jeri's death), the website is helping me in my grieving. I miss Jeri very much. I find the memories captured on the website healing. Every morning, I have my coffee with Jeri on the website. Regardless of how sad I feel, I can always get a smile on my face by playing the slideshows of the two of us on the Greek Islands or of Jeri belly dancing or surfing. Jeri was an amazing woman, so I will always have amazing memories. Whenever there are happy memories, there will always be love. As

I play and replay "Love of My Life," I know that I can never lose what I once enjoyed. Jeri will be part of me as long as I live. Consequently, I'm starting to realize that I cannot be alone as long as she's part of me. This is the key to my recovery. So the website is helping me heal and it also tells Jeri's life story. "Every life is a compilation of stories," and the website does this very well.

Three Things We Could Have Done Better

Now the regrets. In hindsight, there are three things I would have done differently:

- First, I would have loved to have seen Jeri participate in the creation of her website. I think she would have had so much fun seeing those old pictures come to life. She could have recorded her story in her own words. I know she would have had a blast creating the narrative and then playing it on her website. She would have sent links to her friends and gotten back a lot of feedback and good laughs while she was still alive.

- Second, I wish I had some footage of Jeri talking about her life. After she died, I really missed her voice and hearing her talk (she had been in a coma-induced silence for the last two days on her deathbed). Now, her voice only exists on a greeting message she recorded for our phone. I find myself calling our phone over and over again just to hear her voice.

- Finally, I would have liked the project to have been developed on a more leisurely schedule. I can't tell you how hectic it is to put together a website in the crunch that follows a death. We should have done it earlier for all these reasons.

Because it was so helpful to me, I subsequently encouraged Jayne and Al to offer this service, including the hindsight observations, in the form of a business. I am in no way involved financially. My only interest at this point is that it will help other people as much as it has helped me. I read somewhere, "The universe is made of stories not atoms." I hope you will have fun telling yours.[2]

Back to the Surfer's Funeral

The night before the funeral, I got a call from Ted, a legendary canoe captain. He told me, "Robert, you can count on me tomorrow. Jeri is one of us. We'll make sure we take her out where she belongs. I've been doing this since I was a kid. I know every reef and channel. I can take you out, regardless of how big the waves are." I was really touched. The day before a canoe had capsized and broken in the big waves. I was depending on Teddy to keep us dry.

The next morning, besides Teddy, two other big-wave captains—Virgil and Tommy—showed up with their canoes. So we had three canoes that day. Luckily, the waves died down a little around the time of the funeral, which made it easier to go out. As a result, 15 friends were able to accompany Jeri in the canoes. The surfers didn't need a ride— they had their surfboards. The rest of our friends stayed on the beach.

The funeral on the beach was picture perfect. Many old friends showed up. In addition, Jeri's surfer friends were there. The band played her favorite Hawaiian songs, and Mike and I gave short obituaries. It was another beautiful Hawaiian morning on the beach. The canoes and the surfers went out for the send-off. We formed a circle in the ocean, just beyond the break. Then, the helicopter flew over us and dropped thousands of plumerias that were hand picked by Jeri's friends—thank you, Dee. The plumerias landed in the middle of the ring of surfers and canoes. It was like magic. This is when I put Jeri back into the ocean, where she belongs. I jumped into the ocean with her and finally let her go.

Jeri is in the company of great surfers from the past. Hopefully, she's catching her share of waves for eternity. At least, her ashes are in a very beautiful spot in the middle of the cosmic ocean. And I can visit her every day when I go for my swim.

---

[2] This testimonial appears in www.talkstoryfilms.com.

Jeri's surfer funeral was a beautiful and moving event. The scene in the ocean was very intimate and sweet. Luckily, there were three surfers with video equipment on the scene. They were able to record the entire at-sea experience. Al was able to produce a breath-taking video of the entire ceremony. It is now on Jeri's website for all to see. Seven months later, Al's video was broadcast on Hawaiian TV. Too bad Jeri couldn't attend her own funeral. She would have enjoyed every moment. It was exactly the way I had described it to her as she lay on her deathbed.

Mourning: Lessons Learned

Here are some of the grieving lessons I learned at this point in time:

- *Focus on the narrative.* It's important that you provide the narrative that gives meaning to your soulmate's life and death. No one can do it better than you. Jeri's death was the end of her life. I'm her designated storyteller. I am the witness to her life. I can help validate it at the existential level. When I finally get Jeri's entire story out, I will be able to see her as a complete person—a finite "I" separate from me. That will help me heal and become whole again. I won't feel that I died when she died, which is typically what a surviving soulmate feels when their partner dies.

- *Beware of the day after.* The day after the death is probably the time when you experience your biggest grief burst. It's also the period when you may feel most suicidal. Make sure someone is always with you during that time.

- *Create the website.* Jeri's website is where I go when I need to replenish my visual memories. It's always there for me, as well as for others. I also downloaded the slideshows and videos onto my iPhone, which gives me very portable access at all times. I always carry cards with the link to Jeri's website. I hand them out to returning visitors to Waikiki who ask me, "How's Jeri?" Typically, they are in shock when I give them the news of her death. The website helps them get closure and keeps me from having to go into all the details again. I tell them, "You can visit her website and watch the funeral. We'll talk later."

- *Funerals are a wonderful invention and a team effort.* I don't know how I would have survived without that funeral. It kept me very busy and focused during those dangerous days after Jeri's death. The funeral was a high point in my grieving experience. That day, I was joined in my grieving by many friends. They shared during those moments some of my grief. Hopefully, the funeral gave them closure and enabled them to say their final goodbyes to Jeri.

- *Visit the body.* You'll need to take a box of tissues with you. It's a sad but necessary ritual. Later, it will help give you closure. You may want to take some photos of your soulmate's body—especially, if it looks peaceful. I kept revisiting my pictures of Jeri's dead body during my grieving. It helped me accept the fact that she was really dead.

At this point, I'm just at the beginning of my grieving journey. This short list covers the lessons I learned during those early days. Unfortunately, there's a lot more to come.

Chapter 5

The Grief Burst Explosion

I'm walking through streets that are dead
Walking, walking with you in my head
My feet are so tired, my brain is so wired
And the clouds are weepin

Could you ever be true? I think of you
And I wonder

Just don't know what to do
I'd give anything to be with you

— Bob Dylan, "Time Out of My Mind" [1]

The grief bursts returned with a vengeance right after the funeral. They started to hit me all at once and from every direction. This time they did not stop. So what is it about "after funerals" that triggers such a reaction? Perhaps it's that funerals represent the *grande finale* of a life. They signify the final passage from which there is no return. They drive home the idea that your loved one is gone forever. Maybe it's because everyone starts to leave after the funeral. They go back to their lives, families, and jobs and you are left alone to face your loss. Maybe I had more time to reflect after the funeral, and I could more clearly see the enormity of my loss. Maybe it's all of the above. In any case, this is when it all started to sink in. It was time to face my loss head on. I couldn't avoid it any longer.

In this chapter, I'll first go over what it means to lose your soulmate, the deepest loss a person can experience. Then I'll cover the explosion

---

of grief that is triggered by the realization of the loss. The mind tries to forget these grief bursts from hell. Typically, we develop some kind of amnesia to make us forget pain we previously experienced. Luckily, I kept a collection of e-mails from that period. They cover some of my pain in gory detail. It's first-hand documentation of that horrible stuff that plays out in your mind. I'll be able to share it with you. My grief bursts went on for four months. In the chapters that follow, I will tell you exactly how I got rid of them completely. With the knowledge I have today, I think I could have extinguished those grief bursts in half the time—maybe, even less. Keep this thought in the back of your mind when you read some of the gory material that follows.

Surveying My Loss

I did a quick survey of my loss. Thirty years of my life had just vanished into thin air. When my lover died, she took everything that mattered in my life with her. This could explain the scenes of devastation in my mind. Jeri played so many roles in my life. There were the major roles—lover, partner, life witness, coauthor, caregiver, intellectual companion, and so on. Then there were all those everyday life roles—clothes matcher, TiVo technician, home decorator, news commentator, espresso maker, gourmet chef, confidante, holiday organizer, back scratcher, and many more. She was my ever-present companion in life's more mundane activities—breakfasts, dinners, movies, walks, travel, sunset watching, whale spotting, shopping, and the list goes on. She was the love of my life and the person I grew up with. She was the person I woke up to every morning of my life.

The grief bursts were proof that the enormity of my loss had started to sink in. I was grieving for all these primary and secondary losses—so many roles left with holes that needed mending. That's why it felt like I had such a huge hole inside of me. I had lost such a big part of me. How could I ever recover?

Additionally, there were two very subtle losses that seemed to effect my immediate situation:

- ***Besides my soulmate, I had also lost a child.*** Yes, I know it sounds irrational but let me explain. The caregiving during the end-of-life period created some very tender and nurturing bonds between us. I felt so incredibly in love with Jeri at the end. It was as if our love had reached a new plateau. Why? The answer is that the death process is just like birthing but in reverse. I felt like a mother who was nursing a child. When Jeri died, I lost my child, too. It was an additional source of deep pain.

- ***I also lost my grieving mate.*** Your soulmate is probably the one person in this world who could have helped you through your entire grieving process. If she hadn't died, Jeri could have been my grief counselor. She could have helped me navigate the existential issues of life and death. She would have helped me absorb the constant shock of grief bursts. She would have given me a shoulder on which to cry, night and day. She would have held me when I was trembling in fear. Of course, she could not be here to help with my grieving, just as she couldn't attend her own funeral.

Death snatched Jeri from my arms. I will never be able to hold her again. It is a huge and devastating loss. I relied on her for much more than I ever imagined.

The Loss of a Soulmate Is Unmatched

The loss of a soulmate is unmatched for the emptiness it leaves in its wake. The grief will vary according to the strength and length of your relationship. The more you've loved, the more you'll grieve. The pain now is the flip side of the happiness you once had with your lover. Of course, not all spouses are soulmates—love is not necessarily alive in all marriages. I'm describing the pain of losing your lover and partner in life.

Grieving a Parent

Unfortunately, much of the grief literature does not differentiate between the different types of grief. I believe that the loss of a soulmate—whether from sudden or anticipated death—generates the deepest type of grief a person can experience. People sometimes tell me they understand my grief because they experienced the death of a parent. They're wrong. The loss of a soulmate is completely different from the loss of a parent. It's a different type of grief. I loved my father very dearly. When he died prematurely at age 55, I hardly cried. I grieved for a day or two and then decided I should be celebrating his life instead. In contrast, my soulmate's death just tore me apart for months. What's the difference?

The answer is that the lives of the partners in a soulmate relationship are totally intertwined and fused. This is the nature of the bond. It's why they are soulmates. In contrast, the early parent-child bond is meant to be broken. The passage into adulthood requires that they separate—the young adults must eventually find their own paths in life. So when death comes, the identities are already separated. (The exception is young children who are still in a dependent relationship with their parents.) In any case, as adults we can adjust to the death of a parent. We expect our parents to die first. Of course we grieve, but we also recover quickly.

Grieving a Child

On the other hand, parents have a much harder time grieving the death of a child, especially one who is still dependent on them. Typically, parents are not supposed to outlive their children, so there is intense grieving to be done. It's probably as intense as the grief from hell that I experienced after the death of my soulmate. However, the parents can grieve together for their loss. They share their loss equally. If the loss is not equally felt, it may lead to a divorce. The death of a child can also be mitigated if there are more siblings. But, it's never easy. There will always be deep grieving when a child dies.

Grieving a Non-Soulmate Spouse

Losing a spouse is very painful, but the pain is attenuated when the spouses are not also soulmates. The relationship isn't as tight; it's more loosely-coupled. So they may have more resources to draw upon when their spouse dies. In other words, if you're not soulmates in your marriage, then your relationship tends to be more diversified. You're drawing some support from other sources. When you are a soulmate, you have all your eggs in one basket, so to speak. This is wonderful when the two partners are alive, but it is completely devastating when one dies. Jeri was lucky to be the first to go. My grief counselor tells me stories of surviving spouses who complain: "I don't feel any pain. Yet people expect me to be grieving. Is there something wrong with me?" Typically, these people were married, but not soulmates. Yes, there's a big difference.

Grieving a Divorce

What about divorce? Doesn't it show that separation is not the end of the world? Yes, divorce is the de-coupling of a relationship, but there is a big difference. The two parties make it happen; death is not the culprit. It's a voluntary separation. Unlike soulmates, the partners in a divorce are not fulfilled in their relationship. Their relationship is more bad than good. So they gradually separate and re-identify themselves during the divorce process. Typically with a lot of help from lawyers, therapists, and supporters on both sides.

For soulmates, it's the exact opposite. They do not choose to separate; it is forced upon them by death. The surviving soulmate is in the middle of an active and very engaged relationship when their lover dies. The relationship can get even stronger and more intimate during the last days. It can be the ultimate form of bonding. Of course, this type of end-of-life bonding can happen when nursing dying children or parents. It may even strengthen a loosely-coupled marriage.

Back to the divorce issue. Certainly, there are cases where the divorce is unexpected. For example, one spouse may unexpectedly decide to dump their partner. In that case, the dumped partner may not be prepared; the divorce was not by choice. The surprised partner may end up going through a long grieving process. They may even wish their spouse dead. Some may believe that separation through death would be more acceptable. Of course, they're wrong. Death is more than just separation. It creates a whole slew of existential problems that become part of the grieving process.

Grieving a Soulmate

This discussion is not about "my pain is bigger than yours." I'm simply trying to make the case that soulmate-grieving must be given special consideration. The grief associated with the loss of a soulmate is especially devastating because so many adult-to-adult bonds are destroyed all at once. The deep fusion in the relationship results in a very complicated form of grieving. It will take a lot of work to untangle the selves, as you'll read in the next chapters.

To summarize, not all grieving is the same. Grieving a soulmate is not the same as grieving a child or grieving a parent. Each of these griefs has specific characteristics that must be dealt with accordingly. Having said that, these different griefs also have much in common, as you will discover throughout this book. The magnitude of a grief is also a function of the level of bonding between the dead person and the survivor. The more the bonds the greater the grief. Finally, the burden of grief can be somewhat alleviated if the survivor does not have to carry it all alone. This could happen in relationships that leave in their wake multiple survivors who equally share the grief load. Friends and family can help you grieve your soulmate, but only to a certain point. By definition, their relationship with your soulmate is more loosely coupled than yours. The important point here is that grieving a soulmate is typically a solo act; that means solitary, unmitigated, and big-time grief.

Complicated Grief

The death of a soulmate is an extremely brutal experience. The survivor becomes a very good candidate for what psychologists call *complicated grief*. It's a situation where the grief does not resolve itself with the passing of time. The survivor simply withdraws from the world and barely functions. According to psychiatrist Dr. David Peretz, complicated grief could develop when the survivor and the deceased are highly dependent on one another for "pleasure, support, or esteem." Ouch!

Grieving, then, becomes what Dr. Katherine Shear, professor of psychiatry at Columbia University, calls "a loop of suffering." Simply put, it can wreck a person's life. Its chief symptom is a yearning for the loved one so intense that it strips a person of other desires. Life has no meaning.[2] Other symptoms of complicated grief include: anger and bitterness over the death, recurrent pangs of painful emotions, and distressing intrusive thoughts related to the death. It's no fun.

Complicated grief requires professional intervention. It afflicts an estimated 15% of the bereaved population in the U.S. This means that about one million new grievers each year will suffer from it. With all the grief bursts exploding in my head, I was afraid of becoming a prime candidate for this type of grieving. It felt like I was headed for a perfect storm and that I would never recover from Jeri's death.

"I'm in Pain"

I sent this e-mail on July 15, 2009—nearly a month after Jeri's death. It describes a typical day of grief bursts as well as my frame of mind during that period. Note: Each crying bout consists of multiple waves of grief—or grief bursts.

Dear Friends,

I'm a walking blob of pain—a scary sight. Here's what my typical day is like:

- I cry when I wake up every morning and do not find her in bed or in the apartment (about 10 minutes of deep sobbing).
- I have my coffee, logged on to her website. I watch the same slideshows every morning. Then, I call poor Jayne (the webmaster) and have her add a picture or modify something, almost daily.

---

[2] Fran Schumer, "After a Death, The Pain That Doesn't Go Away," *New York Times*, September 28, 2009.

- I cry when I fix brunch because I know she's not going to be eating with me.
- I'm mostly OK when I perform tasks throughout the day.
- I cry when I visit hospitals or drive by the hospice. I cry when I go grocery shopping. Sometimes, I cry spontaneously when I'm driving.
- I cry after my swim when I'm in the shower (about 5 minutes of sobbing).
- I cry before I go to sleep and until the sleeping pill takes effect (about 5 minutes).
- I dream of her every night. I wake up two or three times a night, but go back to sleep crying when I realize she's not next to me.

Mostly, I miss her and can't believe she's gone. I feel guilty that she's not with me enjoying her morning coffee, the ocean, and the joy of being alive. I feel a lack of purpose in life without her. I'd be ready in a second to take care of her in a wheelchair, under chemo, or whatever. I go over and over the events of the last two months of her life trying to figure out if I missed something or could have done anything differently. I have examined in extreme detail all of the events leading to her death (the last five days). Did I do something wrong? I fret over whether she should had done more chemo and less radiation at the end. Did I let her down? The answer is no, based on the best info I had then (but, not now).

Yes, I understand that I must now find a new identity without her presence (while keeping the memories). The problem is that I don't know if I want to do this. My identity with her "as is" may be just fine. I want to be like her: Live one day at a time and then see what the next day brings—no big identity quests.

I need to better understand this grieving process: When do I know I've reached the peak of my suffering and pain? When will I be less raw? Will the pain ever go away? Also, all this crying gives me sinus problems, headaches and neck pains. I want it to stop, but it only seems to get worse every day.

I have fond memories of our life together. The website puts a smile on my face and reminds me of all the good times we've had together. We had a wonderful life. With these happy memories, there will always be love. But there's just too much pain now. My memories of Jeri's last days are just too raw and painful.

Aloha, Robert

Excerpt from "The Witness"

This e-mail was sent on September 12, 2009—almost three months after Jeri's death. I call it "The Witness." You can read the full text of the e-mail in the appendix at the end of the book. Here, I just want to illustrate what a grief burst feels like. I'll explain how I dealt with this burst in later chapters.

Dear Friends,

In the last few weeks, I was able to identify a new source of grief bursts—meaning the surfacing of a new emotion within me. Unlike my other flashbacks that are bursty, this one is more movie-like. It's more like a reel than a snippet. It typically starts with Jeri appearing very vibrant in some previous phase of her life. It then moves to her sick bed and then her dead body at either the hospice or the morgue. And it ends with some deep void that represents Jeri's absence from her surroundings. Obviously, this new flashback represents a replay of Jeri's death. It feels like a knife going through me because I'm reliving her death each time. It's a big ouch! on the grief-burst meter.

I know exactly how vibrant and alive Jeri had been while on this earth. And now I can see exactly the void she left behind. She's gone—Pouf! I am her life-witness (and also her death-witness). It feels like I witnessed a crime in slow motion with both my hands tied behind my back, unable to do anything about it. A human being was annihilated in front of my eyes. I am a witness to this crime against humanity and I have nowhere to report it. I look around me and life just keeps going on, as if nothing happened.

Yet, Jeri has just "disappeared" from this earth. She is erased from each scene in my daily life. I am left deeply traumatized.

Aloha, Robert

Grief Bursts: One More Time

If you've lost a soulmate, you'll know exactly what a grief burst is. For everyone else, the e-mails should give you a feel for what it's like. They're obviously hard to explain in words. However, it's important to understand these grief bursts so that we can keep track of them and later zap them away.

You may be able to tell from the e-mails that a grief burst is a red-hot emotion (like molten lava) accompanied by some discomforting imagery. Luckily, it is released—or dissipated—by sobbing. Sobbing is like wailing—it comes from your inner core. It's a healing aid. The grief bursts come in waves or bouts. In between, there are long pain-free intervals, sometimes filled with sadness. A wave consists of one or more grief bursts.

I read somewhere that if all the bursts came at once, the totality of the pain would probably kill you. Fortunately, the pain is doled out in small doses that let you absorb it. Grief bursts seem to be associated with some recurrent themes. For example, "the last days." Typically, these bursts are an outward manifestation of some deep inner feeling or emotion. They can also be triggered by traumatic memories.

For those of you who know traditional pain, you can think of a grief burst as breakthrough pain—a spike or spasm. In this case, the baseline pain is typically sadness. During the sad periods, I had many inner conversations that went on forever. They were a bit like what Jeri seemed to be experiencing just before her death.

Living with Grief Bursts

I was starting to feel that life was hopeless and that there was no point in anything. But, somehow, I also managed to maintain a daily routine.

Here is how I described this period in an e-mail excerpt I sent on August 14, 2009:

Dear Friends,

Eight weeks have passed since we lost Jeri. The "presence of her absence" seems to be everywhere in my world. I feel a terrible void. How can she be so alive one moment (just look at her surfing videos on the website) and then be so dead the next? Yes, that the "dead stay dead" is a constant surprise. According to the literature, my primary task in grieving is to "fully recognize my own loss in its entirety to clear the deck for growth." So, I'm trying to comprehend and make some sense out of the incomprehensible. However, what's the alternative? To avoid the pain of loss, I would have had to avoid the life and love Jeri and I shared. In C.S. Lewis's words, "The pain now is part of the happiness then."

During most of the last eight weeks, I felt like a blob of pain wandering aimlessly in a mental wilderness, with no destination. It was a time of intense feelings—from terrifying to numbing. However, even as an aimless blob, I did manage to eat solo in some of our favorite restaurants, swim every day, read voraciously, and carry on with everyday life routines. And, most incredibly, I survived these last eight weeks.

In conclusion, the last eight weeks were incredibly painful and nothing had prepared me for this level of pain. When Jeri first got diagnosed with cancer, I was in pain but she was next to me. Last year, when her cancer progressed, I felt extreme pain but she was next to me. She was even next to me during the last week of her life—so the pain was intense, but still under control. The pain I felt in the last eight weeks is unique and frightening, and I must face it alone.

Aloha, Robert

The Pain of Grief: Lessons Learned

Here are some of the grieving lessons I learned during that period:

- ***Take stock of your loss.*** Typically, the full impact of your loss hits you right after the funeral. It's a scene of devastation. You were dependent on your soulmate on so many levels: physical, emotional, and intellectual. Your soulmate was the anchor of your everyday life activity. Take an inventory of your loss. Later, you'll discover that some of this loss can be salvaged. For example, the memory of Jeri still lives inside of me. This means I cannot be lonely. Her love can continue to sustain me. All is not lost.

- ***Recognize your grief bursts and keep track of them.*** Grief bursts can strike at any time and in any place. At this point, there's nothing you can do to stop them, and there's no place to run away. The grief will follow you wherever you go. So just go with the flow and absorb the shock as well as you can. If you can, cry—it's your best release mechanism. What you can do is record each grief burst in a diary. Jot down the emotion, feeling, or thought that may have triggered the burst. In the next chapters, you'll learn how to deal with these grief bursts and zap them out of existence. Until then, absorb the hits.

- ***Take care of yourself.*** You're under high stress and your immune system is not at its best. Grieving can sap your energy so you may experience fatigue. This is the time to eat healthy meals and get your daily exercise. You may also want to get a medical checkup. Dying from a broken heart is real.

- ***Friends can help you, but only so much.*** Try not to overwhelm them with your grief. The sad truth is that your friends cannot bring your lover back to life, however much they would love to. Most of your friends are probably couples and they haven't experienced the death of their soulmate, so you may frighten them with your grief. In any case, there's very little they can do to help you grieve. You'll need the type of help I cover in the next chapters. However, there are some things that you can do with your friends on the grieving front. First, send them monthly updates, by way of e-mail, to keep them abreast of your progress. You don't want to keep revisiting old territory with them. Second, use your time with them wisely. Go over specific grieving issues that concern you, but don't ramble on. Finally, your friends can help you get back to a normal life. Join them for regular activities. Remember that your friends are not grief counselors, but they do want to help you within their limits.

- ***You'll be slowing down and going inside yourself for a while.*** Grieving will bring sadness, which is a signal for the body to slow down and retrench. You'll be living in slow-motion mode. You will be spending time inside your mind. Your attention will focus inward. It's a time of meditation and reflection. You can take stock of your loss and learn how to adjust. During that time, you'll be thinking a lot about the meaning of life and death—yours and your partner's. Make sure you don't ignore your outside needs. If at all possible, don't let the grief consume every single moment of your waking hours. Try to set aside a fixed time slot each day for grieving. In the next chapters, we'll use this slot to get rid of the grief bursts. Note: If it weren't for the grief bursts, this reflective and melancholic time could be rather pleasant and nourishing. It's a time of regeneration. Enjoy it if you can.

- ***You can still have a life.*** Yes, you can be lonely in the presence of people during this period, but don't let that keep you from venturing out of the house. Try to maintain a regular daily routine. I maintain my list of chores on my iPhone (otherwise, I'll forget). I try to do a few each day. Baby-step your way through the chores—don't try to do everything at once. And it doesn't all have to be perfect. Remember, you now have more time on your hands. So you can do more. Multiple small accomplishments can help you regain your independence and self confidence. Don't start big projects. And, you can't escape by traveling; the grief will chase you wherever you go. Finally, try to enjoy life's little pleasures—such as sunsets, walks, swims, and good food with friends. Let these small pleasures spoil you.

• *Grieving a soulmate is very painful, but it can also be a beautiful experience.* You must actively work on resolving your grief. There's much work ahead of you, but eventually the pain will go away. The grieving will then become a loving experience, something that you can enjoy.

At this point, you're probably asking: How do I get these grief bursts to stop? Is there a grief-burst cure? This is the topic of the next chapters.

Chapter 6

The Grief Burst Cure

Walk out of any doorway
feel your way, feel your way
like the day before
Maybe you'll find direction
around some corner
where it's been waiting to meet you

What do you want me to do,
to do for you to see you through?
A box of rain will ease the pain
and love will see you through

Such a long long time to be gone
and a short time to be there

— *Grateful Dead, "Box of Rain"* [1]

The grief bursts were getting more intense by the day. It was scary. I was especially fearful when people would tell me, "You'll never recover. That's just how it is." The more optimistic ones would say, "Oh, it's going to take years to get over this." Or they would attempt to mitigate it by saying, "You two had such a strong relationship; you'll never be the same." Ouch! I was a condemned man. I would be tortured—by grief bursts—for the rest of my life. It was absolutely ridiculous. My soulmate had loved me. Our love was sweet. Jeri would never have wanted me to go through a life of pain on her behalf. She had even warned me of the pain. She said: "*If anyone can deal with that mind stuff, you can. So deal with the grieving pain.*" I had to do

---

[1] Lyrics by Robert Hunter, copyright *Ice Nine Publishing Company*. Used with permission.

something, that's for sure. But, where to start? I needed a clue, a direction.

In this long chapter, I'll retrace the steps that eventually brought me to my destination: the grief-burst cure. When you're in pain, you act out of desperation. So I grabbed onto any lifeline that could help—self-help books, grief theory, and counseling. I started with Freud and just kept moving down the line to the latest findings in grief theory. Along the way, I consumed the vast self-help literature on grieving. In this chapter, I provide a concise and up-to-date review of the best grief theory has to offer us. Unfortunately, there was not enough out there to get me through my pain. I had to improvise to fill in the missing pieces. I even had to resort to old tricks from my computer science days and apply them to grieving. In the end, it all came together. I discovered the elusive *grief-burst cure*. Most importantly, it worked.

Here's the roadmap for what lies ahead. In this chapter, I'll tell how I stumbled onto the grief-burst cure. Mostly, it was a discovery process. You'll need to read the entire chapter to understand what the cure entails. In the next five chapters, I'll tell you how I used this cure to zap my grief bursts into oblivion. My definition of healing consists of two parts: 1) zero pain and 2) happy memories of Jeri. I achieved both in record time.

What Kind of Help Did I Need?

First and foremost, I wanted the pain to stop. Obviously, it wouldn't stop on its own—at least not in the foreseeable future. So there was grief work to be done. Here's what I was looking for:

• *A finite cure that would quickly get me to zero pain.* I did not want an open-ended cure. The cure method had to provide answers to these questions: How long does the pain last? What's the timeline to recovery? How do I measure progress? The following answers were totally unacceptable: 1) it will take forever; 2) it depends; 3) it will never go away; 4) let time heal you—humans are resilient; and 5) it will take a very long time—years. I wanted a timeline that would not exceed four months, maximum. During that period, I wanted the frequency of grief bursts on a steep downward slope that edged towards zero—the end point.

- *A natural cure.* I did not want to be on medications—that meant no antidepressants or other meds to numb the pain. I would not resort to recreational drugs or excessive drinking. I wanted my mind to be lucid during the day. I was ready to make one exception: I'd take a sleeping pill—or whatever would get me through the night.

- *A non-workaholic cure.* I did not want to postpone the pain by drowning myself in some big work-related project. If I did that, the pain would probably return with a vengeance at a later time. In addition, the suppressed emotions could lead to psychotic disorders. "Stay busy to forget her" was not for me.

- *A cure that would not kill Jeri a second time.* "Forget and detach" was not an acceptable cure. I needed to preserve the memories of my soulmate and feel her comforting presence. I did not want to obliterate her memory. On the contrary, I wanted her memory to continue to live within me. I wanted the painful memories gone or, perhaps, morphed into good memories.

- *A cure that would not require a religious conversion.* I did not want a born-again experience that involved some new-found faith in paradise and an afterlife. For example, "Jeri is in heaven waiting for you" was not acceptable. Of course, the definition of heaven could be sweetened to mean "Hawaii." In that case, the proposition could become, "Jeri's self is out there in the ocean waiting for you to join her." It would be even sweeter if I could also get her body back—preferably, without the cancer. Yes, I could be very tempted—if I were to see proof. Please, no reincarnation as a shark! Remember, I swim with her every day. But, I wasn't going to hold my breath waiting—not when I had grief bursts exploding in my head.

That's it. I was not really asking for much. You would expect such a cure to be readily available. After all, people have been dying since the beginning of time. So where is the Dr. Fischberg of grief?

C.S. Lewis's *A Grief Observed*

I got off to a painful start. The first book I stumbled upon in my search was *A Grief Observed* by C.S. Lewis.[2] This book, by the well-known Oxford theologian, is the all-time classic of grief literature. Reading it was not easy on my emotions—it felt like being in an echo chamber. Lewis was going through grief-burst hell. He had just lost to cancer his soulmate, Joy Davidman, whom he referred to as "H." Much of Lewis's journal is the diatribe of a devout Christian who almost loses his faith after the death of his soulmate: "Where is God?... Go to him when your need is desperate, when all other help is in vain, and what do you find? A door slammed in your face." Personally, I was more fascinated by the super-eloquent description of his grief pains. They seemed to mirror mine. In his words:

> "Grief is like a bomber circling round and dropping its bombs each time the circle brings it overhead.... Tonight all the hells of young grief have opened again. For in grief nothing stays put. One keeps emerging from a phase, but it always recurs. Round and round. Everything repeats. Am I going in circles, or dare I hope I am on a spiral? But if a spiral, am I going up or down it? How often—will it be for always?—how often will the vast emptiness astonish me like a complete novelty and make me say, 'I never realized my loss till this moment?' The same leg is cut off time after time. The first plunge of the knife into the flesh is felt again and again."

Ouch! I could get a grief burst just by reading this. I felt his grief. It was just like mine. However, at that point, I was looking for a cure, not more pain. Unfortunately, C.S. Lewis did not have the faintest inkling of what a cure might entail. Here's what he wrote:

> "We were one flesh. Now that it has been cut in two, we don't want to pretend that it is whole or complete. Therefore we shall still ache. Sorrow turns out to be not a state but a process. I not

---

[2] C.S. Lewis, *A Grief Observed* (Harper, 1961).

only live each endless day with grief, but live each day thinking about living each day in grief."

Eventually, Lewis returned to his faith: "She's in God's hands. Turned to God, my mind no longer meets that locked door." For me, this diatribe with God wasn't too helpful. I was about ready to give up on Lewis when I came across this nugget:

"For as I discovered, passionate grief does not link us with the dead but cuts us off from them. It is just at those moments when I feel least sorrow that H. rushes upon my mind in her full reality, her otherness.... For me at any rate the programme is plain. I will turn to her as often as possible in gladness. I will even salute her with a laugh."

Bravo! I learned something. C.S. Lewis reinforced that I could find comfort in my memories of Jeri, but only if the pain subsided. All was not lost. Of course, I had already discovered this from the website experience. The good memories were very helpful. However, at this point the memories of Jeri's final days were just too overwhelming. I had to re-balance my memories.

What Does Freud Have to Say?

Next, I decided to read what the psychologists had to say—grieving seemed to be right up their alley. Everything in psychology seems to start with Sigmund Freud. In 1917, Freud published *Mourning and Melancholia*, which to this day remains a dominant influence on grief theory. In this short work, Freud proposes that grieving requires the breaking of all affectional bonds with the deceased. His "Forget and Detach" theory has become the basis for most writing on grief. In his work, Freud comes up with two important clinical observations:

- *Grieving is a normal process that must take its course.* Of course you will suffer. You will eventually recover when you accept your loss. In Freud's words: "When you let reality pass its verdict—that the object no longer exists." Normal grief is not a typical illness, and it shouldn't be treated as one. However, grief exhibits the symptoms of the illness called *melancholia*—severe depression, guilt, hopelessness, and withdrawal. Freud explains, "In grief the world becomes poor and empty; in melancholia it is the ego itself." So grief is like melancholia, but it shouldn't be treated. You must suffer through it.

• ***You must do the required "grief work" to confront the reality of your loss***. Freud emphasizes that during mourning you must first reconcile yourself to the new reality, and then work on breaking all your ties with the object of your grief. Time alone does not heal all wounds. The "work of mourning" takes time: "it's a task carried out bit by bit" and it involves suffering.

Freud's "Work of Grief"

My apologies: This section contains some heavy Freudian jargon— please bear with me. Freud's theory of grief attempts to explain what happens during the "work of mourning." His main idea is that we have vested libidinal ties with the deceased. For example, we feel for them love, desire, and other emotions. So grieving consists of severing all these emotional links—every single one of them. At the end, we will be able to reclaim our libidinal investment, meaning the emotional energy we have put into our lost loved one.

In Freudian terminology, *cathexis* is the formation of attachments—the concentration of emotional energy on an object (like Jeri). The work of grief is about letting each memory run its course. During "the work of mourning" Freud writes:

> "Each single one of the memories and hopes which bound the libido to the object is brought up and *hyper-cathected*, and the detachment of the libido from it is accomplished."[3]

Freud calls this a "compromise." In exchange for abandoning our libidinal investments in our lost soulmate, we'll regain life and be able to love again. In Freud's words: "When the work of mourning is

---

[3] Peter Gay (editor), *The Freud Reader* (Norton, 1989).

completed the ego becomes free and uninhibited again." We can now reinvest the freed libido in a new object.

What if we decide not to break the ties? According to Freud, bad things will happen. We will remain attached to our lost love, separated from reality and from life. As Freud puts it, "…by taking flight into the ego, love escapes annihilation." Freud warns us that this inward "narcissistic identification with the object" is very harmful. The loved object will end up sucking the life out of our ego, which is now infected with the dead object. As a result, we will suffer from melancholia, which Freud writes, "behaves like an open wound, drawing to itself cathectic energy from all sides…and draining the ego until it is utterly depleted."

I'm Not Going to Let Jeri Die Again

Yikes! This is horrible stuff. Freud's detachment theory was a total nonstarter for me. Of course I did not want to be consumed by my loss; my pain had to stop. However, I was not prepared to let Jeri die a second time by destroying my memories of her. I believe that I can still be in love with someone who has died. What I wanted was to be able to maintain my memories of Jeri, but without the pain. Obviously, I wasn't going to get this from Freud. I believe that Freud's approach only leads to endless grieving. I mean, let's get real. Do you have any idea what it takes to undo "each single one of the memories and hopes?" Typically, soulmates share thousands of memories and their libidinal ties are very strong.

Surprise, Freud Couldn't Detach

Not surprisingly, Freud turned out to be clueless when faced with his own grieving. When his daughter, Sophie, died from influenza in 1920, Freud continued to remain attached to her. As a result, his later work registers the "endlessness of normal grieving." He even brings into normal mourning the violent characteristics of melancholia. In 1929, Freud wrote a letter to his friend, Ludwig Binswanger, acknowledging the endurance of bonds to a loved one:

"My daughter who died would have been 36 years old today.... Although we know that after such a loss the acute state of mourning will subside, we also know we shall remain inconsolable and will never find a substitute. No matter what may fill the gap, even if it be filled completely, it nevertheless remains something else. And actually, this is how it should be. It is the only way of perpetuating that love which we do not want to relinquish."[4]

In real life it seems, Freud's *Forget and Detach* does not work. It didn't work for the master himself. At the end, Freud leaves us without our love, our memories, or a path to recovery. What a deal!

OK, We'll Let You Keep Some Memories

Some of Freud's later disciples tried to relax the theory to make it work. In 1989, Julia Kristeva published *Black Sun*, which supplements Freud's description of mourning and melancholia with a theory of the "imagination and sublimation."[5]

Unlike Freud, Kristeva offers the possibility that our loved one may find a permanent place in our life. Rather than repress, you can give your loss another form. That is, you can *sublimate* your love energy into proxy objects for your loved one—creating a work of art, setting up a foundation, building a memorial, writing a book, composing a poem, and so on. You remember your loved one via the proxy object. In some cases, you may even try to immortalize your soulmate with some big endeavor.

Jonathan Lear extends Freud's theory with a different approach built on "being able to tolerate her absence." [6] Then there's Megan Craig's idea of a "strange love" that inhabits anyone who has loved and lost. I'll let her explain that new relationship with your dead soulmate:

[4] Ernst Freud (editor), *The Letters of Sigmund Freud* (Basic Books, 1975).

[5] Julia Kristeva, *Black Sun* (Columbia University Press, 1989).

[6] Jonathan Lear, *Happiness, Death, and the Remainder of Life* (Harvard Press, 2001).

"It is a love in reserve, a love reserved. You may not find a place for it ever again, or its place may be just that, in reserve.... It will not be the same, nor will it entail a clean return to an earlier self. You are no longer here where I am. Rather than try to join you where you are or fasten an image of you where I am, I am going to keep you in reserve. That is, I'm going to let you go and hold onto you nonetheless. I'm not sure if that is a form of depression, mourning or melancholia, but I think it is a way of living with a memory that keeps us both intact."[7]

Nicely said. This strange love compromise is certainly a step in the right direction. Unfortunately, Freud's original detachment theory is still the predominant view among mental health professionals—you must let your soulmate go. Luckily, there is now a significant minority that disagrees with this view. Instead, they believe that we may form a different relationship with our deceased loved ones. It involves feeling their comforting presence kept alive by pleasant memories and internal dialogs with them.[8]

I took time to cover Freud's work in some detail because it has so much influence over everything related to grief. His ideas are still very much in vogue. They include his requirement that we detach from our lost love, his emphasis on the work of grieving, and his insistence on the obliteration of all memories of our loved one. And melancholia is just a fancy name for the complicated grief I covered in the last chapter. We'll be revisiting these issues from a more modern perspective. Again, Freud provides the foundation for all grief work, even if some of it is just plain wrong.

Bowlby's Attachment Theory

"Loss of a loved person is one of the most painful experiences any human being can suffer. And not only is it painful to experience but it is also painful to witness, if only because we are so impotent to

---

7 Megan Craig, *Strange Love* (www.sunysb.edu/philospohy/faculty/mcraig).

8 John Archer, *The Nature of Grief* (Routledge, 1999).

help. To the bereaved nothing but the return of the lost person can bring true comfort; should what we provide fall short of that, it is felt almost as an insult. Through so much of the older literature, there is a tendency to underestimate how intensely distressing and disabling loss usually is and for how long the distress, and often the disablement currently lasts. There is a tendency to suppose that a normal healthy person can and should get over bereavement not only fairly rapidly but also completely. Throughout this volume I shall be countering those biases."

— John Bowlby [9]

British psychologist John Bowlby wrote these words to introduce *Attachment and Loss*, his ground-breaking trilogy on grieving. At the time it was published, this epic work on grief—1,500 pages long—became the most thorough treatment of loss to appear in the literature. It was a modern treatment of grieving that made use of the latest research in cognitive thinking, biology, and behavioral systems theory. Jeri was quite familiar with Bowlby's work. She used some of his attachment theory in her master's thesis in cybernetics. She adapted some of his work on dependency to inter-computer communications. So, we have some indirect history with this man who was described in his obituary as "one of the three or four most important psychiatrists of the twentieth century."[10]

I will cover two areas of Bowlby's work which I found to be very useful. First, his *attachment theory*, which is much more understandable than Freud's libidinal ties. Second, his *stages theory* of grieving, which was the precursor to Kübler-Ross's subsequent work.

The Cybernetic Self

In the first volume of *Attachment*, Bowlby sets out to develop a new theory of motivation and behavior control built on up-to-date science.

---

[9] John Bowlby, *Attachment and Loss Trilogy, Vol. 3* (Basic Books, 1982).

[10] Jeremy Holmes, *John Bowlby and Attachment Theory* (Routledge Press, 1993).

It replaces Freud's model, which is based on psychic energy. In Bowlby's words, "As my study of theory progressed it was gradually borne in upon me that the field I had set out to plough so light-heartedly was no less than the one Freud had started tilling sixty years earlier."

Bowlby observed that complex organisms have goal-oriented behaviors with continual on-course adjustments. For example, an eagle uses feedback to adjust its flight pattern to track the movements of its prey. Bowlby then set out to apply these ideas to human behavior. His cybernetically controlled behavioral systems were to replace Freud's concepts of drive and instinct. In Bowlby's model, survival and procreation guide the functions of human behavioral systems for attachment, parenting, mating, feeding, and grieving. His key idea is that all complex organisms maintain an internal working model of the environment that surrounds them. They then adjust their actions accordingly. However, adds Bowlby, if the working models of the environment and self are out of sync—for example, after a death—then "pathological trouble" may ensue. This is where loss and grieving come into the picture.

Separation and Alarm

According to Bowlby, we possess a complex representation of our loved one stored in our brain. With death or separation an alarm is raised. The signals we receive from the outside world do not match our inner representation. On the outside, we stop receiving feedback from our loved one—there's a huge void in the environment. This sets off a major alarm reaction, aimed ideally at regaining contact. Of course, this is not possible if our loved one is dead. Consequently, we have a futile alarm reaction that continues and continues. The alarm bells just keep ringing as we continue the restless search for our loved one. Bowlby calls it "separation distress."

So, with the death of a loved one, we lose an essential part of our inner experience of self. In other words, there is a mismatch between the outside world and our inner model of the world. According to Bowlby, our inner representation of the lost lover must now change through a process of adaptation. Our inner identity must gradually adapt to the changes in the external world caused by death. However, it takes time for this to happen. Our inner experience of our lover remains intact and cannot quickly change to adapt to the new environment. Also, we tend to selectively filter out messages which we do not like.

Over time, we must go through a long grieving process to change the inner ideas we hold of our identity. So grieving brings about a gradual change in a person's identity. Bowlby's emphasis on a gradual change of identity complements other features of grief such as separation, distress, and depression. The bottom line is that we must mentally come to grips with the new version of reality.

Bowlby and Parkes: Stages of Grief

Bowlby's work attracted the attention of Colin Parkes, who set out to study a non-clinical group of widows in their homes. He wanted to chart the course of adult grief, about which little was known at the time. The findings led to a joint paper with Bowlby, published in 1970, which covers the way adults respond to separation. In their paper, they describe the response as an orderly progression through four distinct stages of grief: 1) shock and numbness, 2) yearning and searching, 3) disorganization and despair, and 4) reorganization. This was the first *Stages Theory of Grief*—it is built on attachment theory. Unfortunately, it did not receive much attention at the time.

I read, somewhere, that Parkes had visited Elizabeth Kübler-Ross in Chicago, who was then gathering data for her influential book, *On Death and Dying*. In 1978, Kübler-Ross adapted the Bowlby and Parkes stages theory to describe a 5-stage response of the terminally ill when faced with impending death. This model became the basis of the *Stages Theory of Grief*, which I cover later in this chapter. Bowlby also introduced Parkes to the founder of the modern hospice movement, Cicely Saunders. Together, they used attachment theory to meet the emotional needs of the dying and bereaved. They built on the concept of grief as a process toward attaining a new identity.

Like Freud, Bowlby believes that some form of detachment is the ultimate goal of grieving. Unlike Freud, he does not advocate the "forget" part. Bowlby's idea of grieving is that our system will make continual on-course adjustments to reach a new state of inner equilibrium. That is, we become whole again by readjusting our inner world view to absorb our physical loss. We need to rebuild the support system we had relied on. In the process, we develop a new identity.

Bowlby's idea of detachment is also less rigid than Freud's complete separation. In Bowlby's model, adults do not need to detach totally from a lost attachment figure. Instead, they can rearrange their representation of self so that the deceased can continue to serve as a symbolic source of protection, comfort, and love. I did not have to break my emotional ties with Jeri or end my love. All that "libidinal severance" nonsense was gone.

Is Bowlby's Model Useful?

Bowlby does not tell us how to get to the other side of grief. His model simply describes a system in disequilibrium, but does not explain how to recover from it. Even his stages model does not explain how to move from one stage to the next. So Bowlby takes a *laissez faire* approach when it comes to the actual work of grieving. In this case, the invisible hand appears to be the passage of time. Perhaps, he believes that the human system is self-correcting and will naturally find its path to a new equilibrium. It's a bit like economics—markets find their own equilibrium via supply and demand. But unlike Adam Smith, Bowlby does not have a law of supply and demand. He simply describes the workings of a complex system as it reacts to a huge external loss. He offers no remedy.

Bowlby's systemic ideas make it easier to understand the nature of grief. Once you understand the nature of the beast, it becomes easier to conceptualize a cure. I found it much easier to deal with the mechanics of a system in disequilibrium than with libidinal glue. Bowlby's work on attachment remains very influential to this day. For example, his work was extended to analyze different types of attachments in relationships and then apply them to grieving outcomes.[11] Yes, the work of Bowlby is useful.

Ernest Becker's *The Denial of Death*

After Bowlby, I seemed to hit a brick wall in my search. I was trying to research the latest neo-Freudian theories when I ran into Ernest Becker's book *The Denial of Death*, which was awarded the Pulitzer Prize in 1974.[12] It's a terrifying book that still has adherents among social psychologists who have developed Becker's views into a testable theory called the *Terror Management Theory (TMT)*.

According to Becker, we are the first animals to control nature, and also the first animals to understand that death is our collective destiny. Consequently, we live in terror about the end of life—"death is man's peculiar and greatest anxiety." A person's character is "a defense against despair; a structure built to avoid the perception of annihilation, an attempt to avoid insanity." So the fear of death becomes the mother of all fears and anxieties. Psychology's role is to help us live with this fear. It must provide evasions, death-denying strategies, and defenses for our "trembling" selves. Listen to what Becker has to say:

> "To see the world as it really is is devastating and terrifying: it makes routine, automatic, secure, self-confident activity impossible. It makes thoughtless living in the world of men an impossibility. It places a trembling animal at the mercy of the entire cosmos and the problem of the meaning of it."

Becker's adversarial stance with nature does not bode well for grieving. In our grief, we need to come to grips with our mortality. We need to accept death as a natural ending to life. There is a need to think about death, but it has to be non-adversarial. It's not us against nature;

---

[11] M. Stroebe et al. (editors), *Handbook of Bereavement Research and Practice* (American Psychological Association, 2008).

[12] Ernest Becker, *The Denial of Death* (Free Press, 1973).

it's not nature against us. When I asked my grief counselor, "Why Jeri?", she answered, "Why not Jeri?" Her blunt reply took me by surprise. But she's right—none of us is coming out of this alive. There's a lesson to be learned here. We must come to grips with our own mortality. Of course, reading Becker is learning it the hard way. Becker can be an excellent read, if you're not in the midst of grief pains.

My Grief Counselor, Christa

The time was five weeks after Jeri's death. My grief bursts were increasing with each passing moment. My research had come to a dead end. Becker was the final straw that broke the camel's back. My mood had become as somber as his. I was at a dead end. It seemed hopeless. Then, out of the blue Hawaiian sky, I received two phone calls that helped me go on with my quest for a cure. The first call was from the hospice grief counselor—her name was Christa. She was throwing me a lifeline. Here's how the conversation went:

Christa: Hello, Robert. I'm a grief counselor with the hospice. Are you OK?
Robert: No, I'm not OK. I have these terrible grief bursts.
Christa: Do you need help?
Robert: Yes, I need help. But can you make it stop?
Christa: The pain is part of grieving. It will take its time.
Robert: I don't have time. I want it to stop now.
Christa: Well, we can offer you three counseling sessions for free. We also have a support group. Would you like to set an appointment?
Robert: No, not now. I really need to think about it.

A grief counselor? That was a new twist. What could she do for me? I had read Freud and Bowlby; it looked like the psychiatrists couldn't do anything for me. I didn't want their meds. If I went the psychotherapy route, I could end up with someone like Becker. What did they know about grief? What did they know about the end of life? I was going to say no to Christa. It would just be a waste of my time and hers. She mentioned something about a support group. I didn't want to do that.

Why would I want to be in the presence of strangers who did not know Jeri? Just "sharing grief" was too vague. I really wanted a cure. None of this seemed very helpful.

The next morning I was in grief burst hell. That is when I decided that I would take Christa up on her offer. Maybe she could help. After all, she had been with the hospice for ten years; she understood death. She would also know quite a bit about grieving, and it would come from the heart. She was not just another clinical therapist who built on Freud. She had the right experience and I sensed it in her voice. Later, I would discover that Christa had lost two of her sons in an accident. She divorced her husband over her grieving. To better understand what had happened, she went back to school and became a grief counselor. I was lucky to have found her.

A Typical Session With Christa

My meetings with Christa went on for over nine months. At first, we met each week. As time progressed, we met once every month just to talk. In a typical meeting, I would start by giving Christa a copy of my progress report that included the daily number of grief bursts and their type. Then we would go over issues that concerned me. She was a good listener and always supportive. Occasionally, she would give me a pep talk to lift up my spirits:

"Your 30 years with Jeri were a tremendous gift. You both experienced a realm that few people ever reach. You must build on this gift. From the death-bed pictures, you can see that Jeri had a smile at the end. She acknowledged that she had a great life and accepted the inevitable."

Christa did not have a grief burst cure, but she understood them well. She knew my pain. She had been there herself. Here's how she walked me through grief bursts:

"You were soulmates, so you feel more pain. The grief has a will of its own. It comes when it wants and leaves only when it is ready. Acknowledge the bursts and treat them like unwanted guests.

You've been there, you know them. Set aside some time each day for grieving and then be prepared for your visitor. Try to deflect the red-hot stuff. It's the pits. You don't want to revisit the same stuff over and over again. You've been there, done that. Enough is enough. Now move on. Confront your fears. Remember, you cannot be in this state of pain forever—you won't be able to live. Something innate makes us move on."

Christa was not a Freudian when it came to the preservation of my memories of Jeri. No, there was no need to break my ties with Jeri. Here's what Christa had to say:

"You want Jeri to be in your heart and mind in a loving way but not with the pain. You need to rearrange things and still have her support you emotionally. Put your memories into action. Incorporate them into your life. You're still together. Jeri is a source of advice. She can help you deliberate. You know she's been there, so you can now enjoy life's pleasures for both of you. She has a soothing and affirming presence in your life. You can draw on your memories day and night."

Christa felt I would recover on my own someday, but she wouldn't give me a time frame. In any case, I felt thankful that I was not a candidate for complicated grief.

Six Months Later, I Interviewed Christa

Many months later (when I was writing this book), I asked Christa to explain her plan-of-action. How had she evaluated me when I first came in? What was her plan for dealing with my pain? Here's what she had to say:

Christa: I first try to assess if that person wants to get better, or if they want to live in a state of "poor me." Some want to grieve for the rest of their lives. They don't want to get out of it. They can't deal with life any longer. Their grief is complicated.

Robert: Given my strong bonds with Jeri, how did you know I wasn't a candidate for complicated grief?

Christa: You came to me for help. You were reaching out. You seemed to be looking for a hook—you were doing all this reading. You were in bad shape, but you wanted out.

Robert: So what was your plan of action?

Christa: I had some tasks for you: 1) you needed to accept Jeri's death; 2) you had to accept that you were still alive and wanted to go on; 3) you needed to deal with the pain—it takes a lot of energy; and 4) I needed to track your progress to see if you got better. You had to meet these goals.

Robert: Did you think I'd get through this?

Christa: Yes. Early on, I did a strength-assessment on you. You had a keen analytical mind. You could analyze your situation. You were actively trying to get better.

Robert: Did you have a cure?

Christa: No, you had to go through this. It takes time. Here's what I did to help you: 1) I tried to divert your pain to give you some reprieve—a mini-vacation from pain. So I told you to give yourself permission to grieve at certain times of the day; 2) I encouraged you to find your own resources to deal with the pain. You did very well— much better than I expected. I even learned a lot from you. Your book will be of help to so many people.

Robert: You said something about relying on my own resources. Isn't that a given?

Christa: No. Many people require a lot of hand-holding. They come to rely on me. They call me all the time. I tell them, "Call your own cell phone. You need to find your own inner strength." Sometimes, I have to terminate my relationship with them. I really have nothing more to offer. I've become their crutch.

Robert: Tell me more about these complicated grief cases.

Christa: Typically, they can't function on their own. They're stuck: Why her? Why now? It's not fair. They can't accept the fact that death happened. They can't go on with their lives.

Robert: So who takes care of them when they become chronic?

Christa: Usually, I get a family member involved. Often, I have to refer them to a psychiatrist for the meds.

Robert: Do the meds help?

Christa: They're better than they used to be. All are sedatives, so they also need to give you something to pick you up. So, you get a drug cocktail. You go through life in a stupor. You do not feel pain or joy—they both get masked by the meds. But for some people, it's the only way out. Did I answer all your questions?

Robert: Yes, thank you. Your answers were very helpful.

Christa: I've been doing this for 11 years.

I was lucky to have connected with Christa. The lesson learned here is that a grief counselor can help. However, you must find the right counselor. My advice to you is to find someone from a hospice. They intimately know death and therefore can feel your pain. If you get the wrong counselor, you may end up with a dose of Freudian psychobabble. Also, I would avoid going on meds. If you can, try to find a natural cure, perhaps along the lines I describe in this book.

Help from Dr. Joyce Brothers

Yes, you read this correctly, "The" Dr. Joyce Brothers. How did I hook up with her? Remember, I told you two good things happened to me. First, I got the call from Christa. Second, I got another call, this time from my stockbroker, Susan. What does a stockbroker have to do with grief theory? She gave me a "hot tip." Here's how the conversation went:

Susan: I miss Jeri so much. I can't even imagine what you must be going through. Jeri was your life.

Robert: It's no fun.

Susan: Listen, I have one piece of advice for you. Get a copy of *Widowed* by Joyce Brothers. Then read it today, from cover to cover.

Robert: What? She's a TV pop-psychologist. You want me to read a book by an advice columnist? I just finished reading Freud and Bowlby. What could Dr. Joyce possibly add to the mix?

Susan: Just get the book and read it. You'll thank me for it.

Robert: OK, I'll do it. But I just don't see the point.

It Was a Very Good Tip

I trusted Susan. So I drove over to Borders and bought a copy of *Widowed*.[13] It was a skinny little book that I read in one afternoon. And, it was simply wonderful. Susan was right. This little book was more helpful than Freud. Let me tell you why. Unlike Freud, this book was written from the heart. In 1989, Joyce Brothers lost her husband of 42 years to bladder cancer. Dr. Milton Brothers died at the age of 62. Joyce and Milt were true soulmates. When she described Milt's end-of-life struggle with his cancer, it reminded me of Jeri's. It made me cry. As a caregiver, Joyce experienced the same intense love I had for Jeri. She wrote, "We were so close at these times. I used to feel overwhelmed by my love for him." I really understood.

Like C.S. Lewis, she had felt the terrible grieving pain. She wrote, "I spent the first six or seven months after he died in one long wail of despair." One night while driving home, she even considered suicide:

"Why go home? There was no one there. No one to care. There was no point in going on. There was no point to anything any more. The highway was deserted. Why not end it all? Crash into a tree? They would think I had simply lost control of the car. My suffering would be over."

Unlike C.S. Lewis, Dr. Joyce Brothers was a noted psychologist. She brought some knowledge to the pain of grief. She could analyze her grief and write about it. She relied on an earlier version of the stages theory of grief—the work of Bowlby-Parkes and the earlier Kübler-Ross theory of death and dying. I will go over Kübler-Ross's later work in the next section; but, for now, here's what Dr. Joyce Brothers had to say about the stages:

"I had often lectured and written about the course of grief, explaining that each bereaved person goes through a series of stages of grief. The stages may be predictable, but there is very little that is orderly about a widow's emotions in the weeks and

---

[13] Joyce Brothers, *Widowed* (Ballantine Books, 1990).

months—sometimes years—following her husband's death. She is caught up in a passionate and painful maelstrom. The first reaction after her husband's death is almost always shock and then merciful numbness. The second stage, suffering, is a compound of emotions —longing, panic, helplessness, loneliness, anger, resentment, depression, self-pity and denial. It can be a time of intense psychic misery. The third stage is that of acceptance."

The Doctor Knew Her Grief

As you'll read next, Kübler-Ross proposes five stages instead of three. On the duration of pain, Dr. Brothers had some interesting numbers to share. The first stage, numbness, seems to wear off after the funeral. However, the second stage, pain, can go on forever:

"The second stage may last four months, six months, a year, two years, four years. It varies from woman to woman. And all of this is normal. There are no rules for grief. There is no timetable for grief. Nor do all women experience all these reactions. Nor do they experience them with the same intensity. There is nothing unloving about the woman who copes with her grief in a matter of months; there is nothing weak or hysterical about the woman who takes several years to reach the third state, that of acceptance."

This is all scary stuff. The grief reactions can vary all over the place. Even Dr. Brothers was caught off guard:

"Even though I knew all the reactions I would probably experience as I mourned for Milt, I was not prepared for their intensity. I was completely overwhelmed by my grief. Every morning I woke up and hoped it would be less, but it was not. That was the strange thing—it was not getting any less. I worried because everything in my life still referred back to Milt. It was like having a non-stop conversation with him in my head. I was afraid that I would never be able to adjust to his death, afraid there was something wrong with me.... Crying became almost like breathing or blinking."

As you can see, grief can be terrifying even for a trained professional. Eventually, Dr. Brothers got to the acceptance stage. It took her over a year to get there:

> "It had been a hard year, a terrible year, but I had survived. I was still lonely, but not all the time. I still cried, but less and less. I still compared every man I met with Milt, and of course none of them measured up."

One year was much too long for me. I would not be able to survive the daily onslaught of grief bursts.

But, How Did She Deal with Her Grief?

I could not see myself doing better than Joyce Brothers—she really knew her grief. Then I began to ask myself questions: What exactly did she do to deal with her own grief? What was her cure? I went back through her book, carefully looking for answers. Here's what I found:

- *Work on the memories:* "Each time you remember, a healing film grows on the memory until eventually it is no longer a raw wound. You are healthy again."

- *Crying helps:* "The memories and the tears they provoke are partners in the healing process. The more a widow cries and eases the pain of her loss with tears, the more she becomes conditioned to her loss. There comes a time when she can think of her husband without pain, without tears."

- *Make your soulmate part of you:* "Milt was part of me, and if he was part of me, how could I be lonely? I cannot tell you how much this memory helped. I am not saying that I went from loneliness to happiness in a day, but from that time everything began to get a little bit better."

- *Things seem to get better with the passage of time:* "I have learned that recovery comes in fits and starts, that for every two steps ahead, you fall back one. My life is so much better now than it was eighteen months ago, twelve months ago, six months ago, that I know it will continue to get better. Most widows discover that there is an end to grief and that life is full of promise again."

I can't tell you how much this helped me. Thank you, Susan, for the tip. However, it was still not enough. I could not wait a year or longer to recover. I had to do much better. I was thankful for the insights—especially, the "building on your memory" stuff. It was certainly better than Freud.

If you think about it, Dr. Joyce Brothers' theory of grief looks like this: After the initial numbness comes the pain. You will feel a slew of emotions, triggered by some memory, and then cry. The memories and the crying together help heal the pain. With enough time, you will be able to have fond memories of your lover, which will then help you overcome loneliness. At the end, you will be okay.

As you can see, it's really another *laissez faire* approach to grieving—no "grief work" is required. Just go through the pain and cry your heart out. Then wait for the tears and time to heal you. It's a bit fatalistic. Clearly, my search for a cure was still on. My next stop is Elizabeth Kübler-Ross. However, before I go there let me tell you something about the grief literature.

The Self-Help Grief Literature

Widowed opened my eyes to a different genre of books, which for lack of a better name, I will call the grief literature—or the self-help grief books. I went on Amazon and bought every book with widow, widower, or grief in the title. I ended up reading dozens of self-help books, written by practitioners who have either felt grief or are working with the bereaved. Typically, these books contain a ton of useful advice that covers almost everything a widow or widower will face in everyday life.

You get advice on how to deal with finances, anniversaries, married friends, support groups, loneliness, bed pillow arrangements, redecorating the house, disposing of the clothes, grief, sex, masturbation, praying, exercise, home repairs, dating again, and so on.

Some of these books are useless. Others provide very good advice. Mostly, I found them to be soothing—they kept me company during my grief. They were a lot more comforting than reading Freud, Bowlby, or Becker.

Widowed was one of the first books to appear in this genre and it still remains the finest. It stands out in a class by itself. In Chapter 10, I will summarize some of the best advice from these books. For now, I want to keep our train of thought focused on grief theory and my search for a grief cure.

What do all these books have to say about grieving pains? Almost unanimously, they build on the Kübler-Ross stages. Typically, they will describe each stage and then tell you that you will go through most of them as part of your grieving. None of these books tell you how to transition from one stage to the next, or even what to do when you're in a stage.

With the exception of *Widowed*, none of these books tells you how long a stage lasts, but it always seems to be a very long time. Most books tell you that you will eventually get to the other side. It's inspirational stuff: "Trust us, you'll get there, but it takes time." None describes the actual work of grieving. Again, the most I got was from *Widowed,* and it wasn't much.

In addition to stages, many grief counselors rely on a *task-theory* of grief developed by William Worden, a Harvard psychologist.[14] In 2003, Worden identified four basic tasks of mourning: 1) we must accept the reality of our loss, 2) we must experience the emotions connected to our loss, 3) we must adjust to life without our lost loved one, and 4) we must relocate our loved one in our mind so that progress is possible. You may notice that these "tasks" are more like long-term processes. Worden didn't anticipate that his theories would give rise to an industry of professional grief counselors. Later, he remarked, "I don't know what I've spawned."

---

[14] William Worden, *Grief Counseling and Grief Therapy* (Routledge, 2003).

I want to reemphasize that these books are very comforting when you are grieving. Even mechanical descriptions of stages and tasks are better than nothing. Sometimes the advice is quite useful. You feel that you're not alone while going through your ordeal. Others have been there before you.

Kübler-Ross: The Stages Theory of Grief

In grieving theory, all roads lead to the work of Dr. Elizabeth Kübler-Ross—the giant in this field. We're finally at her door step. It all started in 1969, with the publication of her book *On Death and Dying*.[15] It single-handedly changed the entire discourse on dying—a previously taboo subject. Kübler-Ross observed that her own terminal patients went through five emotional stages from the time they received their diagnosis: denial, anger, bargaining, depression, and acceptance. Each stage involves specific emotional tasks.

Kübler-Ross' life work was to help people traverse the passage from health to illness to death. Her stages of dying had a huge effect on medical schools, hospices, psychologists, counselors, social workers, and even the general public. We owe her big time. This woman should have received the Nobel Prize for her seminal work. In her 1974 book, *Death: The Final Stage of Growth*, Kübler-Ross added two more stages at life's end: finishing old business and discovering total truth (or universal transcendent love).[16] We won't go there.

Personal note: Again, I feel that I'm retracing some of Jeri's intellectual footsteps. On our first date, Jeri mentioned the work of Kübler-Ross on death and dying. It was part of her research in psychology. I also think she was grieving her father's recent death. I had never heard of Kübler-Ross. In those days, my theory of death came from Woody Allen. Early on, I told Jeri: "We're all going to die.

---

[15] Elizabeth Kübler-Ross, *On Death and Dying* (MacMillan, 1969).

[16] Elizabeth Kübler-Ross, *Death: The Final Stage of Growth* (Touchstone, 1986).

So let's focus the rest of our days on living life." We put aside Kübler-Ross and focused on fun things—like enjoying life and computer networks. Ironically, here I am revisiting Kübler-Ross after all these years. I guess death has a way of catching up with you.

What does this have to do with grieving? The answer is that for thousands of counselors and practitioners, the five stages of dying also became the five stages of grieving. It was a familiar model which they could apply in their work with the bereaved. And, after reading Freud, Bowlby and Becker, who can blame them? They were desperate for something practical they could latch onto. The bereaved were crying for help and the grief counselors used the familiar 5-stage model to help them.

Stages with Caveats

Unfortunately, most of the grieving literature misinterprets the Kübler-Ross stages. Most expect these stages of grieving to come in lock-step sequence. Instead, Kübler-Ross saw them as fluid—one stage does not inevitably lead to the next. And she did not believe that everyone must go through every stage. People can also swing back and forth between stages.

In 2005, Kübler-Ross and David Kessler published their own book on grieving. It's called *On Grief and Grieving*.[17] Now, we have the five stages of grieving straight from the source. Here's what they have to say:

> "The stages have evolved since their introduction, and they have been misunderstood over the past three decades. They were never meant to help tuck messy emotions into neat packages.... They are tools to help us frame and identify what we may be feeling. But they are not stops on some linear timeline in grief. Not everyone goes through all of them or goes in a prescribed order."

---

[17] Elizabeth Kübler-Ross and David Kessler, *On Grief and Grieving* (Scribner, 2005).

Now that you've heard the caveats, let's explore each of the five stages of grief: denial, anger, bargaining, depression, and acceptance.

Stage 1: Denial

Denial is the stage of numbness and disbelief that hits us right after a death. It gives us a temporary retreat from reality. Our internal forces use this time to regroup and regain strength before we deal with the loss. Here's what Kübler-Ross and Kessler have to say:

> "This first numbness helps us pace our feelings of grief. It's nature's way of letting in only as much as we can handle. To fully believe the loss at that stage would be too much. Denial means you come home and can't believe that your wife isn't going to walk in the door at any minute.... The denial is often in the form of our questioning of reality: Is it true? Did it really happen? Are they really gone?... As denial fades, it is slowly replaced with the reality of the loss. Now you turn inward as you begin the search for understanding. You explore the circumstances surrounding the loss: Did it have to happen? Did it have to happen that way? Could anything have prevented it? The finality of the loss starts to sink in. She is not coming back. This time she didn't make it."

The fact that you lived through your loss may be surprising to you. Accepting the reality of the loss is the beginning of the healing process. But as you continue in your grieving, all the feelings you were denying start to surface.

Stage 2: Anger

Anger makes its first appearance when you are feeling safer. It means you are progressing; you are allowing painful feelings to come out. You are no longer disconnected, "lost at sea." You are now angry at something or someone. According to Kübler-Ross and Kessler:

> "Anger is usually at the front of the line as feelings of sadness, panic, hurt, and loneliness start to appear, stronger than ever. You may be angry at yourself that you couldn't stop it from happening. You may be angry that you did not see it coming. You may be

angry with the doctors for not being able to save someone so dear to you. You may be angry that bad things could happen to someone who meant so much to you. You may be angry that you're left behind and you should have had more time together. Maybe you are angry that God didn't take better care of your loved one."

The more anger you allow, the more inner feelings you will find underneath. Note that guilt is anger turned inward at yourself. According to Kübler-Ross, you must be willing "to feel your anger, even though it may feel endless. It is a necessary stage of the healing process. Anger is a natural reaction to the unfairness of loss. Don't let anyone diminish the importance of feeling your anger fully."

Stage 3: Bargaining

After a loss, we really crave for life to return to what is was; we want our loved one restored. "Please, God," you *bargain*, "can I wake up and realize this was all a bad dream?" According to Kübler-Ross and Kessler:

"Bargaining can help our mind move from one state of loss to another. It can be the way station that gives our psyche the time to adjust. Guilt is often bargaining's companion."

In this stage, we become lost in a maze of "if only..." and "what if..." statements. "We want to go back in time: find the tumor sooner, recognize the illness more quickly, stop the accident from happening...if only, if only, if only..." As we move through the bargaining process, the mind alters past events while exploring all these "what if" and "if only" statements. "Sadly, the mind inevitably comes to the same conclusion—the tragic reality is that our loved one is truly gone."

Stage 4: Depression

After bargaining comes *depression*. As we come to realize that our loved one is not coming back, grief enters our life "on a deeper level than we ever imagined." Typically, this stage goes on for a very long time. Normal depression is natural and shouldn't be treated. However, long-term excessive depression must be treated: "in this case anti-depressant medications may be useful." Living with depression is a balancing act; we must accept some sadness without letting long-term depression destroy our quality of life. Here's more detail on what Kübler-Ross and Kessler have to say about this stage:

"This depressive state feels as though it will last forever. We withdraw from life, left in a fog of intense sadness, wondering perhaps if there is any point in going on alone. Why go on at all? This is what the bottom feels like. You wonder if you will ever feel anything again or if this is what life will be like forever.... But in grief, depression is a way for nature to keep us protected by shutting down the nervous system so that we can adapt to something we feel we cannot handle."

This stage allows us to explore our loss in its entirety. It serves as a cleansing process:

"It allows us to take real stock in the loss and clears the deck for growth. It takes us to a deeper place in our soul that we would not normally explore.... The sadness will leave as soon as it has served its purpose in your loss. As you grow stronger, it may return from time to time, but that is how grief works."

Stage 5: Acceptance

Acceptance is about learning to live in a world where our loved one is missing. We may not like this new reality, but we learn to live in it. We put the loss in perspective, learning how to remember our loved one as we begin to live again. Here's what Kübler-Ross and Kessler have to say about this final stage of grieving:

"Acceptance is often confused with the notion of being all right or okay with what has happened. This is not the case. Most people don't ever feel okay about the loss of a loved one. At first we may want to maintain life as it was before a loved one died. In time, through bits and pieces of acceptance, we see that we cannot maintain the past intact. We must readjust. We must learn to

117

reorganize roles, reassign them to others or take them on ourselves. The more of your identity that was connected to your loved one, the harder it will be for you to do this."

Next, they provide details on what happens during this process:

"We start the process of reintegration, trying to put back the pieces that have been ripped away. As we heal, we learn who we are and who our loved one was in life. In a strange way, as we move through grief, healing brings us closer to the person we loved. A new relationship begins. We learn to live with the loved one we lost. Finding acceptance may be just having more good days than bad. We start to form new relationships, new interdependencies or put more time in old ones.... A different life appears before you, one in which your loved one will no longer be physically present."

Finally, they emphasize that we can begin to live again, "but we cannot do so until we have given grief its time." We must go through the stages of grief.

What Do the Empirical Results Tell Us?

In 2007, a slightly modified five-stage theory of grief (with yearning replacing bargaining) was tested for the first time on a sample of 233 bereaved individuals over a period of 24 months after their loss.[18] The study only looked at death from natural causes (approximately 94% of U.S. deaths). Excluded were deaths from unnatural causes such as car crashes and suicide. Also excluded were individuals who met the criteria for complicated grief—for example, most soulmates. The study's focus was your every-day "normal" griever. What do the results show?

The results seem to support the stages theory, at least partially. According to the authors, "Each grief indicator appears to peak in the sequence proposed by the stage theory." The results show denial to be highest initially and then declining after the first month. Anger peaks

---

[18] P.K. Maciejewsky et al., "An Empirical Examination of the Stage Theory of Grief," *Journal of the American Medical Association* (February, 2007).

after 5 months and then starts to diminish. Yearning rises during the first 4 months and then starts to decline. Depression peaks at approximately 6 months and then starts to slowly decrease in the period between 6 and 24 months. Acceptance increases steadily throughout the study period ending at 24 months.

Had she been alive, Elizabeth Kübler-Ross would have felt quite vindicated by these results. Today, Kübler-Ross's theory is taken as "the definitive account of how we grieve. It pervades pop culture...and it shapes our interaction with the bereaved."[19] The stages theory of grief is now taught in medical schools, espoused by physicians, and almost universally applied by grief counselors in the field.

What Did I Learn?

Personally, I did not go through stages of grief. Instead, I experienced a period of initial numbness followed by a cluster of painful emotions. Kübler-Ross's work helped me identify these emotions and some of their sources, for which I am grateful. Like Freud, Kübler-Ross insists that you must do the "work of grieving," which she does not identify. The stages make you aware of the grief patterns, but they do not provide a cure. What exactly do you do during those stages, other than suffer and cry? After reading her book several times, the only grief work I could identify was in the following passage:

> "Telling your story often and in detail helps dissipate the pain. It is primal to the grieving process. You are the detective, searching out things to help you understand how to put the puzzle together."

The story Kübler-Ross refers to is "recalling the scene of the crime against your heart," meaning the last few days. It turned out to be a very good piece of advice. However, it was not enough for a cure. Once again, we're left with the good old *laissez faire* approach to grieving, which means that we heal with the passage of time. And, that can take a very long time. Even with "normal" grievers, the study reveals that about one-third of all participants were still depressed 24

---

[19] Meghan O'Rourke, "Good Grief," *The New Yorker* (February, 2010).

months after the death. For me, this long period of pain was unacceptable. So Kübler-Ross did not have all the answers. My search was still on.

The Dual-Process Model

In 1999, Margaret Stroebe and Henk Schut introduced the idea of a *Dual Process Model (DPM)* for coping with bereavement.[20] This innovative model cleverly integrates existing ideas to provide a new way of coping with loss. The main idea here is that you recover by alternating between two processes: normal grieving and the restoration of your life. You oscillate between these two coping strategies. You can think of the restoration process as a distraction from grieving. It lets you deal with the practical aspects of your loss, such as adjusting to a new daily routine, learning household chores, dealing with finances, and adapting to new social situations. You focus on restructuring your life after the loss. These practical, everyday life activities may give you a much-needed reprieve from loss-related thoughts.

Through the concept of *oscillation*, DPM reconciles two aspects of the grieving process: the need to move on with life and the desire to remain connected to our loved one. DPM lets us confront our grief and also forget it—at least for a while. Early on in our grieving, we tend to be more *loss-oriented*; but with time, we become more *restoration-oriented*. Also, women tend to be more loss-oriented, while men are more restoration-oriented.

DPM is a bit like Christa's strategy of giving me a "mini vacation" from my grieving. Remember, she encouraged me to set aside a specific time for grieving. The idea, of course, is to fill up the rest of the time with constructive activities that would distract me from my pain. Grief tends to come in waves, so there may be some time in between to venture into the immediate world.

---

[20] Margaret Stroebe and Henk Schut, "The Dual Process Model of Coping With Bereavement," *Death Studies* (Vol. 23, 1999).

The problem is that there are very few activities that can provide distraction from grief. Some think they can escape by remarrying. Most of the time, this doesn't seem to work. More than half of all remarriages entered within the first two years of widowhood end in divorce.[21] Others think they can escape by totally immersing themselves in their work—the "keep busy" strategy. According to DPM, you need to oscillate between staying busy and your grieving. You can't stay busy all the time to put your loved one out of your mind; it takes too much mental effort to maintain this level of suppression. You also can't give up on life and live in the past. You need to find your happy medium by oscillating back and forth.

DPM is very helpful, but it still doesn't tell us what to do during the normal grieving part. In this sense, it's still *laissez faire*. The oscillation may give us a breather from the pain, during which we can start to reconstruct our lives. In my case, I had no control over the grief bursts. They appeared whenever and wherever they wanted. However, they were less frequent and less intense when I was being actively distracted. Sometimes, this just meant they would hit me harder later on. It takes some level of control to choose when to grieve and when to go on with daily life. Regardless, we will add DPM to our grieving arsenal.

Bonanno's Resilience Model

In 2009, Dr. George Bonanno, of Columbia University, jolted the grieving profession with his new book, *The Other Side of Sadness*.[22] The book claims to be the foundation for "the new science of bereavement." Some of this new science seems to be built on a study called CLOC, which tracked the pre-loss and post-loss behaviors of 276 very elderly couples in the Detroit area.[23] The study began in

---

[21] Alan D. Wolfet, *Understanding Your Grief* (Companion Press, 2003).

[22] George A. Bonanno, *The Other Side of Sadness* (Basic Books, 2009).

[23] The CLOC study was initiated by Dr. Camille Wortman (see www.cloc.isr.umich.edu).

1987. Even though the data is skewed to this particular demographic group, I still found Bonanno's book to be very useful. My only regret is that I discovered it so late in my grieving.

According to Bonanno, the death of a spouse can be a painful and sometimes debilitating experience. However, bereaved individuals differ markedly in how much and how long they grieve. From the CLOC data, Bonanno postulates that surviving spouses exhibit one of three grieving outcomes: 1) relative absence of depression and other disruptions in functioning; 2) time-limited disruptions in functioning—such as elevated depression, cognitive disorganization, or health problems—lasting from several months to one to two years; or 3) chronic disruptions in functioning lasting several years or longer.[24]

The Resilient Type

Bonanno has quite a bit to say about each of the groups. Together, his observations provide a contrarian view—the new science of grieving. I found some of his insights to be very useful. Let's start with the first group. Why do some people get through grief so easily? In his book, Bonanno describes this first group as belonging to a *resilient* type:

"Many people who suffer difficult losses exhibit a natural resilience. They hurt deeply, but the hurt passes, and relatively soon after the loss they can resume functioning and enjoying life.... Then can we say there is actually a resilient type, a kind of person who by disposition is especially good at dealing with extreme stress? Although the CLOC study did not reveal such a type, other studies I've conducted have confirmed, at least in part, the existence of a resilient type.... We can safely say that some people are, in fact, more resilient than others, and a growing body of evidence even suggests a genetic underpinning to a resilient type."

Given my level of pain, I was clearly not of the "resilient type." However, you may remember from the last chapter that I grieved a

---

[24] G. Bonanno et al., "Prospective Patterns of Resilience and Maladjustment During Widowhood," *Psychology and Aging* (Vol. 19, 2009).

total of only two weeks for my beloved father when he died at age 55. This should have put me in the resilient category. At this point, I'm quite certain that relying on resilience alone was not enough to get me through the loss of my soulmate, Jeri.

Sadness and Oscillations Can Be Healing

Bonanno has a lot more to offer, especially for people in the second group. Here are some of his insights:

"The empirical fact is that most bereaved people will get better on their own, without any kind of professional help. They may be deeply saddened, they may feel adrift for some time, but their life eventually finds its way again, often more easily than they thought possible. This is the nature of grief. This is human nature."

For Bonanno, sadness (as long as it's not excessive) has some healing qualities:

"Everybody seems to agree that grief is dominated by sadness, but why? Why would nature have given us these reactions? What good do they do? Sadness dampens our biological systems so that we can pull back.... It's an essential tool that helps us accept and accommodate to the loss. There seems to be less need to pay attention to the world around us, so we are able to put aside normal, every day concerns and turn our attention inward."

Like DPM, Bonanno supports the idea of oscillation between grief and restoration. Here is his very clear explanation:

"Relentless grief would be overwhelming. Grief is tolerable, actually, only because it comes and goes in a kind of oscillation. We move back and forth emotionally. We focus on the pain of the loss, its implications, its meanings, and then our minds swing back toward the immediate world, other people, and what is going on in the present. We temporarily lighten up and reconnect with those around us. Then we dive back and continue the process of mourning.... These brief swings provide a temporary respite from the pain and keep us connected to the people around us, and by doing so, they help us gradually adapt to the loss.... Probably the most striking implication of the oscillation of mourning is that it bears so little resemblance to the conventional idea that grief unfolds in a predictable sequence of stages."

This is all good stuff, but I disagree with his last sentence. I don't see any reason why we couldn't experience DPM-like oscillations while still going through stages of grief. But let's not get hung up. I'm not a grief theorist; I don't have a dog in this race. I desperately want them all to succeed and help me alleviate my pain.

Memories Can Live Forever

Here are Bonanno's excellent observations on the function of memories:

"We grieve only what we remember of the relationship. And the accuracy of our memories does not determine how we grieve; that is determined by what we do with our memories, how we experience them, and what we take from them during bereavement.... Resilient people are generally better able to gain a feeling of comfort from remembering the relationship during bereavement.... They know their loved one is gone, but when they think and talk about the deceased, they find that they haven't lost everything. The relationship is not completely gone. They can still call to mind and find joy in the positive shared experiences. It is as if some part of the relationship is still alive."

Obviously, this is not Freud speaking. The new science of bereavement is on my side when it comes to preserving the memories of Jeri. Memories are not some kind of fancy substitution to mask her death. Of course, you must be "resilient" to enjoy the memories, which means that the pain must first go away.

Dependencies Can Complicate Grief

Bonanno has one of the best chapters anywhere on complicated grief. So he has quite a bit to say about the third group, those whose grief does not subside:

"I've emphasized resilience throughout this book, but we should not lose sight of the fact that not everybody copes so well. For some people, the death of a loved one is nothing short of devastating, and recovery from grief is a genuine struggle. Approximately 10 to 15 percent of bereaved people are likely to struggle with enduring grief reactions.... When we recognize that almost everyone must confront the pain of loss at some time, 10 to 15 percent represents a lot of people, and makes it clear that prolonged grief is indeed a serious matter."

He is describing the *complicated grief* that I covered in the previous chapter. Bonanno makes some interesting observations that complement what I covered. Here's what he has to say about memories in this situation:

"When grief persists over months and then years, the image of the deceased becomes elusive, fragmentary, and increasingly disturbing. Relentless suffering and yearning color everything. What was once a feeling of safety or happiness becomes mixed up with worry and fear and dread. Memories fester and sour. They become, literally, haunting."

For Bonanno, *dependency* in a relationship may be the primary cause of complicated grief: "The co-occurrence of the symptoms of prolonged grief with dependency is one of the most consistent patterns we have been able to identify." Oops! This does not bode well for us soulmates—we are intertwined with all types of dependencies, especially emotional ones. Bonanno suggests that we should get help if our grief symptoms don't improve after six months.

There Is No Grief Work

Why did I spend so much time on Bonanno? First, he's probably the most prolific grief theorist of our generation. Second, many of his ideas reinforced what I had already discovered, and that made me feel better. Finally, he was the first theorist who openly disagreed with the need for "grief work," at least for the majority of grievers. Bonanno thinks the idea of grief work is a major problem in current grief theory. Here's what he has to say:

> "Until recently, most theories about grief and bereavement viewed grief as a kind of progressive work that takes a long time to complete. Bereavement experts have, in fact, used the phrase 'grief work' to describe the extensive process that they assume all bereaved people must go through before they can successfully resolve a loss. They have fleshed out this idea in elaborate detail. Books and journals on bereavement often include charts and lists showing the various tasks and stages that comprise the normal mourning process.... Remarkably, though, after many years of studying bereavement, I've found no evidence to support any of these ideas."

To me, this argument is a bit of a red herring. Bonanno may be onto something, but it seems he picked the wrong culprit. Let me explain. As you know by now, these "tasks and stages" do not really tell us how to perform our grief work. Except for Freud's impossible prescription, the real problem is that no one is spelling out the details of this "grief work."

As you read earlier, even Worden's four basic "tasks of mourning" are long-term processes instead of step-by-step tasks. For example, his task "accept the reality of your loss" is certainly not a detailed prescription for grief work. How are we to to accomplish this? So, in reality, *there is no grief work*. Instead, we have a *laissez faire* approach to grief and therein lies the problem. Bonanno simply formalizes this approach, which he explicitly espouses for most grievers. Very soon I will tell you how I dealt with this gaping hole.

The Latest Research: Reconstructing Our Worlds

For those living in the Victorian period, grief was the lasting sign of a "broken heart" resulting from the loss of a loved one. Freud's emphasis on "letting go and moving on" became the foundation of modern grief theory.[25] It was progress; we were not condemned to die from a broken heart. After Freud, grief theorists gave us some more workable models for moving on. We've come a long way, and there's still more to come.

Reconstruction Is a Multi-Disciplinary Approach

In addition to dealing with broken attachment bonds, grief theory's newest frontier also focuses on reconstructing the world of the bereaved. It recognizes that our world was shattered into pieces and is now in shambles; it needs to be reconstructed. In the past, this task was left as an exercise for the bereaved. Reconstruction is just too personal and open-ended. Psychology alone cannot provide the answers. It requires an inter-disciplinary approach with help from theology, religion, multi-cultural studies, and philosophy.

Luckily, some avant-garde grief theorists are beginning to address these complex issues. As Thomas Attig puts it, "Grieving is the process of relearning the world." In Margaret Stroebe's words, "It's a matter of slowly and painfully exploring and discovering what has been lost and what remains: what must be relinquished versus what can be retained, created, and built on."[26]

Each of us experiences the world from our own personal vantage points. Our lives are different. The death of a soulmate uniquely disrupts our life and the once-shared daily patterns. This means that we all face different challenges in reconstructing our lives after the death. However, there are some common patterns which grief theory is starting to identify. Here are some of the still-fuzzy areas that are being worked on:

• *Repairing our outer disruption.* We don't have our loved one to help us validate our experience of the world. We feel alienated from our

---

[25] M. Stroebe et al., "Broken Hearts or Broken Bonds," *American Psychologist* (Vol. 47, 1992).

[26] M. Stroebe et al., "Attachment and Coping in Bereavement," *Review of General Psychology* (Vol. 9, 2005).

surroundings. We need to deal with the loss of the world as we had previously experienced it. In attachment terms, we are experiencing *separation distress*—we just lost our primary safe haven and secure base. We must relearn our physical and social surroundings. We must repair and revive what still works and then find our way back home among familiar things. We must recreate the rhythms of life without our mate.

• ***Repairing our inner disruption.*** The death of our loved one disrupts our sense of meaning and identity. We feel estranged within. We must relearn our very selves. We must recover our self-confidence and self-esteem. We must conserve as much meaning as possible from before our loss while reconstructing new meanings. We must reconcile the old meaning with the new. In the process, we gradually revise our identity.

• ***Relearning the meaning of life.*** Our loss has disrupted our taken-for-granted understandings of reality. We need to find meaning in a life without our loved one. As part of our grieving, we must reconstruct our sense of meaning to integrate the death of our soulmate. We must find a new wholeness. We must assign meaning to our loss. Intellectually, we seek fresh new answers and existential meanings. We must restore coherence to the narratives of our life.[27]

• ***Relearning how to love our soulmate in absentia.*** The question of whether we can continue our ongoing attachment—the *continuing bonds* theory—remains a source of raging debate in the field. However, the theory is now starting to recognize the potentially healthy roles of continued symbolic bonds with our lost lover. As Nigel Field writes: "The endpoint of grief work from an attachment perspective does not involve detachment per se; rather the goal involves a reconstruction of the relationship with the deceased that accommodates the reality of the ending of the physical

---

[27] Robert Neimeyer, *Meaning Reconstruction & the Experience of Loss* (Sheridon, 2000).

relationship."[28]   So, in grieving we can relearn how to love our soulmate in absentia. As Thomas Attig writes: "We move toward a *lasting love*. We begin to open places in our hearts where we hold their legacies. We make ourselves receptive to what their lives still offer us. Memories become the basis for deeper lasting love."[29]

- *Reconstructing the narrative.* A promising new approach focuses on having us develop the *narrative* of our lost soulmate. Then, we are to *deconstruct* the narrative to analyze the loss and its impact. Finally, we must *reconstruct* the narrative to put the pieces back together— we must make sense of their life and death. In her new book, Linda Machin combines the narrative approach with Bowlby's attachment theory to develop an innovative model for practitioners of grief therapy.[30] I will use some of her ideas in the next chapters.

The research seems to be heading in the right direction. It's all good stuff which I was able to use. However, as you know by now, I am not willing to wait until resilience, time, oscillations, reconstruction of meaning, sadness, and tears cure me. I need a cure, and I need it now. It's time to provide the missing pieces and apply them to my grieving.

Providing the Cure's Missing Pieces

What did I learn from grief theory? From Freud, I learned that some form of grief work is needed, but I didn't like his prescription. From Bowlby, Freud, and Kübler-Ross, I learned that I had to come to terms with my loss; I needed to find a new equilibrium within myself. Maybe, I had to "relearn the world." From C.S. Lewis, Joyce Brothers, and George Bonanno, I learned that my memories of Jeri could be very supportive, if only I could get them to stop hurting. From Kübler-Ross and Bonanno, I learned to recognize a whole slew of emotions—

---

[28] M. Stroebe et al. (editors), *Handbook of Bereavement Research and Practice* (American Psychological Association, 2008).

[29] Thomas Attig, *The Heart of Grief* (Oxford University Press, 2000).

[30] Linda Machin, *Working with Loss and Grief* (SAGE Publications, 2009).

sadness, anger, self-pity, and so on. From Becker, I learned that I had to deal with the mortality issue, hopefully in a non-adversarial mode. From Christa, DPM, and Bonanno, I learned that oscillations between grief and restoration can help me cope better. From Bowlby, Kübler-Ross, and Bonanno, I learned how grief ideally progresses over time.

All this was very good, but I still needed a method for getting rid of my grief bursts. *Laissez faire* was not going to do it for me. In this section, I will tell you about my method, which consists of three parts: 1) capturing and measuring the daily grief-burst activity, 2) identifying each grief burst and assigning it to a *bucket*, and 3) dealing with the grief in each bucket type. It's really pretty simple. I call this *grief work*. Let me give you a few more details before we move on to the next chapters where I will deal with each type of grief burst.

Personal note: *I had to follow each grief burst to its source—the emotions, feelings, memories, and events that were the triggers. Once I found the source, I could then "zap" the grief burst out of existence. It's an old trick from my computer software days—just trace the bugs. Once you find the root cause, you fix it and get rid of the bug. I also had to classify and count the bugs. It's the same with grief bursts.*

Capturing a Grief Burst

How do you capture a grief burst? It's a two-step process. First, you must note each grief burst attack. Then, try to identify the source. Typically, the trigger is an emotion or feeling such as anger, sadness, self-pity, yearning, fear, or guilt. Sometimes, it's an activity, such as preparing a meal or watching a sunset. Often, it's a special date or event such as a birthday, anniversary, or holiday. Or, it could be a painful memory, such as your partner's pain, the disease, the end-of-life, or the body at the morgue. Before you go grief-burst hunting, I would encourage you to reread the parts in this chapter that describe emotions.

Chapter 6: The Grief Burst Cure

My Grief Meter

At the end of each day, tally up your grief bursts. Then record the daily score in your log. I came up with my own "grief meter" based on daily scores. It helped me keep track of my grieving progress. My goal was to get my numbers down fast. But first, let me introduce you to my grief scale.

I measured my daily grief on a scale of 0 through 4:

0   *Ecstatic day*—like a good day with Jeri alive.
1   *No pain*—0 grief bursts (normal everyday life).
2   *Light grieving pain*—less than 4 grief bursts per day (light pain).
3   *Heavy grieving pain*—4 to 15 grief bursts per day (heavy-hearted).
4   *Acute grieving pain*—over 15 grief bursts per day (like I can't go on).

Our tolerance for pain tends to be very individual—we all have different pain thresholds. Consequently, you'll need to develop your own grief scale. You can use mine as an example. It's important that you measure your pain on a daily basis using the same scale. If the numbers go down, you're on the right track—just keep going. However, rising numbers may be a sign of complicated grief. You may need professional help, especially if the numbers remain high or continue to rise six months after the death.

My Grief Burst Buckets

We will each experience our grief in our own individual ways. No two grief relationships are the same. If you're reading this, then you are grieving for your own soulmate, not my Jeri. We're not both longing for the return of the same person. The specifics of your grief will be different from mine. You will need to follow each of your grief bursts to its source and come up with your own buckets. You can think of these buckets as categories into which you dump, sort, analyze, and then eradicate your bursts. They give you a better handle on your grief and make it less overwhelming. It's simply divide and conquer. I was able to trace and capture five types of grief bursts, which I assigned to the following buckets:

- *The last days*—imagery and feelings aroused by the death process: Jeri's transformation from a surfer girl to a dying cancer patient; the last moments and the dead body; revisiting the painful memories; going through the various "what if" and "if only" scenarios caused by Jeri's end-of-life process; and so on.

- *Survivor's guilt*—she's not here to enjoy what life has to offer: she died so young; I'm alive, but she isn't; it's not fair that she died; I'm a witness to a crime against Jeri; and so on.

- *She's gone forever*—I miss her physical presence on this earth: I can't believe she's gone; she was just erased from every scene; I won't be able to hug her, kiss her, hear her voice, watch her surf, make love to her; and so on.

- *Self-pity*—I have to face life without Jeri: she left a big hole in my life; she left me with so many roles to fill; and how can I ever recover?

- *Deep existential issues*—the meaning of Jeri's life and death: facing my own mortality; revisiting the religious and philosophical beliefs Jeri and I held; and so on. Additionally, there's a slew of open questions: Why did she die? Where did she go? Does anything still make sense? How did she view her imminent death?

In each of the next five chapters, I'll go over my techniques for eradicating a grief burst type. I'll show you how I zapped them into oblivion. These techniques will serve as templates for dealing with your own grief bursts. So you'll learn by example.

Note: Again, I borrowed some of these techniques from computer software design. There, we use templates and patterns to capture the better software practices and techniques, so that other programmers can reuse them. Good software design is more art than science. The same can be said about grieving techniques. It's a way of applying some method to the grieving madness—even though death shatters our lives in different ways.

Conclusion

This concludes a long but necessary chapter. I believe that all this theory will help you in your grieving. Now that you better understand what you're up against, you'll be able to sort through the chaos that is grief. You'll be able to recognize the various emotions and feelings and understand their underlying causes. Grief hits us from many directions all at once; we need a multi-faceted approach to deal with it. You now have one or more frameworks in your arsenal to help you deal with your grief. Of course, your loss—and the subsequent disruption it caused in your world—is very personal. Consequently, you will need to adapt the frameworks to meet your needs. In the next five chapters, you'll see how I used this enhanced theory to get rid of my own grief bursts.

Chapter 7

My Grief Cure for The Last Days

*"It is a fearful thing
to love what death can touch."*

— *Anonymous*

Jeri's last days on this earth were the source of some incredibly painful grief bursts. And why wouldn't it be so? I had just witnessed the total destruction of my soulmate's body—including the mind that came with it. If there is a body we intimately know, it's that of our soulmate's. It's the body we made love to all those years. It kept us warm during winter nights. And we lovingly hugged it and squeezed it, every single day and night. This is the same body that was obliterated in front of my eyes, ravaged by the disease and then destroyed by death. What remained was incinerated. I saw it all happen—every detail.

Yes, the end-of-life is the stuff of nightmares. The scenes we witnessed are etched in our brains. We are now tormented by flashbacks of these painful memories. We constantly replay them in our minds. We are traumatized and we ruminate over these traumatic scenes in a seemingly endless loop. We don't need grief theorists to tell us that we are prime candidates for complicated grief. We know it.

My grief burst bucket from the last days was constantly being replenished. New grief bursts just kept appearing, every day. At least, they were easy to identify. Typically, these bursts tend to be associated with a flashback of a painful memory from the last days. The sobbing that results from these grief bursts is primal. I must have sounded like a wounded animal. In this chapter, I will tell you how I eradicated these grief bursts from hell.

This is the first of a five-chapter series on how I zapped my grief bursts out of existence using the cure described in the previous chapter. Here, I'm going to be zapping away at grief bursts of *the last days*. I'll first review what grief theory has to say about this type of grief. Then I'll tell you about the specific eradication technique I used. Finally, I'll give you some examples of grief bursts that I encountered and how I got rid of them. I was lucky to be able to draw from a trail of e-mails to refresh my memory of these painful events.

What Does Grief Theory Tell Us?

Grief theorists have a name for these flashbacks from the last days. They call them intrusive thoughts or *ruminations*. According to Archer, "It involves going over the same themes, and often the same material, again and again without much goal-directed progress."[1]

How do we make it stop? They tell us that we can't really suppress the thoughts—they'll just reappear. We could try to distract ourselves from them—for example, by doing the DPM oscillation stuff described in the last chapter. However, it's hard to distract ourselves from these flashbacks. They seem to hit us whenever and wherever they want. So, distraction alone won't work.

This leaves us with Kübler-Ross's idea of focusing on the painful memories and then tackling them directly. It's called "telling the story." Remember, she said, "Recalling the scene of the crime against your heart...often and in detail helps dissipate the pain."

Unfortunately, she does not tell us how to tackle these intrusive memories. I found that just recalling a scene won't make it go away—it just keeps returning. And the grief bursts don't go away on their own; they must be popped first. So grief theory gives us some ideas, but no effective solutions.

---

[1] John Archer, *The Nature of Grief* (Routledge, 1999).

The *New York Times* Had the Answer

The solution was in the *New York Times*. I stumbled upon it completely by chance; it was pure serendipity. Let me explain. About two months after Jeri's death, the paper ran a long article that covered, in great detail, the death of cancer patient Deborah Migliorea.[2] Strangely, I felt better after reading this article even though it had absolutely nothing to do with grieving. It was all about dying. Why would an article on dying help me grieve better? The answer is that, like most people, I was a death virgin. I was not familiar with death. Unfortunately, the first death I had witnessed up close was that of my soulmate, Jeri. The article helped me better understand Jeri's end-of-life process, which had been tormenting me. It was an eye opener.

You may remember from Chapter 3 that death is typically a messy organic process. It's the body shutting down slowly. It's not the Hollywood version of instant death. It takes time and effort for the engine to shut down. The scenes of the death we have witnessed can leave us with deep feelings of guilt and remorse that haunt us in the form of grief bursts. We expected a sanitized death. Instead, we experienced a natural process, and we tend to blame ourselves for the messy outcome. We wish we could have done more for our dying lover. We go through endless "what ifs" and "if onlys," revisiting every aspect of the death.

The only way to break out of this endless loop of ruminations is to better understand death, which is why the *Times* article was so helpful. It was my first in-depth article on that subject. After this, I read everything I could find on death. The result is Chapter 3. To deal with grief bursts from the last days, you must learn about death.

How It Comes Together

Once you understand the death connection, the cure for grief bursts from *the last days* is quite simple. Here's what may work for you:

---

[2] Anemona Hartocollis, "At the End, Offering Not a Cure but Comfort," *New York Times*, August 20, 2009.

- *Learn about death and the end-of-life process.* Start by re-reading Chapter 3, which contains almost everything you'll need to know about dying. This is the chapter I wish I had read both before and after Jeri's death. Reading it before would have helped me better navigate Jeri's death. Reading it after would have spared me some of the grief bursts from the last days. At least, I could have popped them faster. If reading Chapter 3 is not enough for you, then check some of the references in that chapter.

- *Revisit the scene of the crime, over and over again.* Once you understand death better, you can follow Kübler-Ross's prescription of "recalling the scene of the crime." Go over the story of the last days, as often as it takes. Try to reconstitute the events that led to the death. Replay the death scene in your mind. Revisit the body at the morgue; look at pictures, if you have them. Try to surface anything you may find disturbing. Eventually, you'll have a very clear picture of what really happened during these days. You may want to use my account of Jeri's death as an example. It's the level of detail you'll need.

- *Capture the grief bursts and then deal with them one at a time.* Typically, the grief bursts from the last days are associated with a tangle of emotions—anger, guilt, sadness, fear, and despair. Instead of untangling these emotions, try to focus on the flashback itself. It usually pinpoints the source of your grief burst. You must also deal with all the "if only" and "what if" thoughts that are linked to a grief burst. Remember, you did the best you could at the time with the information you had. Your newly-acquired knowledge of death will help defuse most of your ruminations. If you still have lingering questions, then try to research the answer. If you can't find the answer, then don't hesitate to call your soulmate's doctors to get some form of resolution. After all, your mental well-being is at stake. Each issue you resolve will pop the corresponding grief burst. In my experience, a grief burst does not return after it is popped.

That's all there is to it. In the rest of this chapter, I'll go over some grief bursts from Jeri's last days and tell you how I popped them.

The Death and Dying Grief Bursts

Most of the grief bursts in this bucket were associated with flashbacks of Jeri during her last days. Here are some of the scenes I got hit with: the incontinence on Sunday night; the painful breathing and terminal restlessness on Monday night; Jeri, on a stretcher, being transported out of the apartment for the last time; the ambulance ride to the hospice; Jeri, saying, "I want to go home;" the death rattle on Thursday night; Jeri's dead body; and so on. I was easily able to defuse these grief bursts after I brushed up on the death literature. I also discovered that most of these issues were beyond my control. They were part of Jeri's natural process of dying, which I covered in Chapter Three.

That Miserable "Shower" Grief Burst

I was repeatedly hit by two grief bursts that were death-related, but hard to defuse. Both were difficult to identify because they were not associated with any imagery. The first grief burst happened every evening in the shower. It came like clockwork. Here's an excerpt from an e-mail I sent on August 1, 2009, about six weeks after Jeri's death, which describes how I dealt with it:

Hello Debs and Kathys,

The shower bout was a mystery. Today, I finally had my eureka moment. The showering has an association with the last few months (hospices and hospitals). It was something I did in a hurry after my swims because I wanted to get back to her as soon as possible—she needed me very much then. And in the shower, all I could think of was that I wanted to be back with her at the hospital. So why the sobbing? Because, it reminded me of a very vulnerable Jeri—the one who desperately needed me at the end. Even with the worst of chemos, there never had been such desperate need or urgency. So, the association takes me to a different Jeri—the one in a wheelchair during her last two months. I cry because I feel very protective towards that Jeri.

Let me try to explain this better. Just imagine for a second that Jeri did not die the way she did. Assume for this exercise that she died instantly in a surf or car accident. In that case, the image we would all have of Jeri would be of the "surfer chick" (with chemo down days) who then had a tragic death. If this had happened, we would always remember Jeri as Jeri and I would not have the shower crying bouts (just the morning ones). So what's different? The difference is that in these last months we saw Jeri go from a strong, robust woman to a disabled person. Overnight, she became frail (and needy) like our parents in their eighties. So, there was a need to help her and assist her. Unlike chemo days, this was not a temporary problem. We saw someone from our cohort, our age group, grow feeble like our parents and then die in our arms. Typically, people in our cohort either don't die or if they die it's from an accident. This death was different. Jeri went from a surfer to a dying cancer patient very quickly.

Every day in the shower I keep crying out "I'm so sorry, Baby." First, I thought I must have done something wrong: Why was I sorry? However, after replaying this thing hundreds of times— thank you all for your memories and patience with me—I am now sure that I did nothing wrong in the last two months. I also think— again, thank you all—that we gave her a "good death" as defined in the article I sent you. So, "I'm sorry" means "I'm sorry, Jeri, that you had to go through the ordeal of the last two months." It probably would have been better if she had died instantly in her sleep (or in an accident) in early May. Of course she didn't, and this horrible disease took its course. We did a stellar job navigating her through it. It was a good death for a cancer patient.

From my perspective, the last two months were precious and created an even deeper bond with Jeri (I could help her in a time of extreme need). You also shared this experience, so you know what

I mean. I do miss those precious moments, but I wouldn't want Jeri to be in this predicament today. So I have to let go of this feeling. Now that I understand this feeling better, maybe I'll stop crying in the shower. I hope this helps you, too.

Aloha, Robert

The "I Couldn't Fix It" Grief Burst

The second persistent grief burst was associated with a guilt feeling. I felt like I had let Jeri down: I couldn't fix it, this time. I couldn't prevent Jeri's death. Of course, it was irrational, but this is the nature of most grief bursts. If you surface them, then you can deal with the irrationality, which in turn pops the grief burst. Here's an excerpt from an e-mail I sent on August 15, 2009. It describes how I dealt with this grief burst:

Hello Spinner,

Yesterday, I kept getting more "last few days" grief bursts, but with a new twist. I felt like I had also lost a child. Of course, Jeri was a strong and tough woman, but she always called me whenever anything went wrong and I'd fix it (many times it meant getting the right help). This happened during her operations, chemos, surf accidents, lymphedema treatments, pain management, and even during the last few weeks. By then, you were part of the "fix it" team, so you understand. However, when they took her back to the hospice the last time I felt that I had let her down—I just couldn't fix it this time. I even told her, "Sorry, Babe, they're going to take you away." Later at the hospice, she kept saying, "I want to go home."

So, her death means I couldn't protect her at the end. Of course, I don't have divine powers. And, I understand that she wanted a "good death" and they gave her just that at the hospice. They had the right equipment; it would have been more painful at home—so we absolutely did the right thing. Still, I feel like I have lost a child, in addition to all the other losses I described elsewhere.

Sorry to give you another earful, but that's one of the problems I'm currently working on.

Aloha, Robert

The "If Only" Grief Bursts

The next set of grief bursts were of the "what if" and "if only" variety: What if we had done more chemo? If only we had done Chemo X. If only we had not done radiation. If only I had hired an RN earlier. I had to defuse these ruminations by doing the necessary research. In Chapter 3, I went over the RN issue. Here's how I dealt with the radiation and chemo issues. (Note: Chemo X is a fictitious name for the real chemo.) This excerpt is from an e-mail I sent on July 16, 2009:

Dear Kathy,

I want to touch on the February chemo decision. In my opinion, none of the safe chemos were an option—they had all stopped working. The one we hadn't tried, Chemo X, was very dangerous for someone who had taken as many chemos as Jeri—there was probably a 50% chance it could have killed her by perforating her colon. And, would Chemo X have worked? The odds were less than 20%. The risk benefit ratio wasn't too good. I still think not doing Chemo X was the right decision.

Also, at that time, the cancer was progressing very rapidly (judging by the CA-125 counts). One of the older chemos could have given her perhaps another month of life (and maybe a bit less leg pain), but it wouldn't have stopped the progression of the cancer. In 20/20 hindsight, perhaps we should have done one of the older chemos in February.

Finally, was the radiation a waste of time? The sad answer is, yes. This was one procedure she could have skipped and it would have made her life a little bit easier. So, perhaps the right track should have been: Do an older chemo just to slow the growth a bit, and forget radiation. She might have then lived to mid-July with a not-so-good quality of life. Of course, this is all post-mortem knowledge. We did the best with the knowledge we had at the time. I hope to have put this one to bed. Again, thanks for your insights and incredible patience.

Aloha, Robert

This should give you a feel for the level of research that may be required to defuse some of the "what if" and "if then" hypothetical situations. Typically, you will discover that you (and your doctors) did your best given what you knew at the time. You'll also discover that there's not very much, if anything, you could have done to change the final outcome. At the end of life, we have much less control than we ever imagined. Death can be a humbling experience.

Note: There are cases where it's difficult to resolve these "what if" thoughts. You may then end up blaming yourself for the event. An example would be a death from a car crash where you were the driver. You may then find yourself constantly ruminating trying to "undo" the event. If this is your situation, you may need professional help.

"The Non-Event" Grief Burst

I'll describe one more grief burst before closing this chapter. I call it "The Non-Event." Initially, I thought it was a grief burst from the last days. Later, I discovered it was an existential grief burst. I'll tell you how I finally popped this burst in the existential chapter. However, I'll first introduce it here to give you a feeling for the confusion I experienced. This is an excerpt from an e-mail that I sent, on August 20, 2009, describing "The Non-Event" grief burst:

Dear Debs and Kathys,

You definitely know by now that of the five triggers of my "grief bursts" the one that causes me the most sorrow is: *a) Jeri's last days.* Every time I put an issue to rest, another seems to pop up. This last one is about Jeri's death being a complete non-event—the subject of this e-mail.

What do I mean by non-event? Jeri left us without a formal goodbye. Think Hollywood: We didn't get the "goodbye, I'm dying" scene. She never told us she was dying. She didn't even discuss the funeral. She just left. Yes, there was a warm scene the next morning at the hospice, but that was more like "good morning everyone. I'm glad to see you all here. Let's have some fun." We were the ones crying, not Jeri! She was serene that morning. So, what happened? Where was the dramatic final exit?

There wasn't one. It was quite an anti-climactic event, which is very unlike the Jeri I know. Death is a huge event in a person's life. I never expected Jeri to leave so quietly into the night. This is why at the time I did not think she was about to die, regardless of what they said. In any case, I am perplexed and puzzled by all this. It's also a trigger for grief bursts. So let's see if we can put it to rest. Here are some possible scenarios of what could have happened:

a) Jeri was too sedated to realize she was dying. Death caught her off-guard like the rest of us.

b) She was totally at peace with her death. She was serene to the point of not even bothering with it. She was going to live to the end, in her life-asserting way.

c) She knew she was dying, but didn't want to make us sad. She continued to be uplifting in her stoic manner.

So which one is it? We'll probably never know. Hopefully, it's not c). I hope it's either a) or b). From a philosophical viewpoint, b) would be almost perfect—an incredibly dignified and courageous final exit. Let me elaborate...

Aloha, Robert

I eventually came to the conclusion that b) was the right answer. So I will deal with this grief burst in the existential chapter. Here, I just wanted to make you aware of the confusion. Sometimes, the choice of bucket is not black and white. Was it a non-event because I didn't see it coming? Or, was it because she chose to go that way? I could have dealt with the former by familiarizing myself with the death process—

the pre-active and active phases of dying. Instead, I decided the latter made more sense. I never said goodbye because of my confusion about how she chose to make her final exit—in this case, with courage and without drama. It appeared to be an existential statement. Now, I had to understand Jeri's state of mind during those last moments: How did she view her imminent death? I'll answer this question (and others) in the existential chapter.

Note: The lesson I learned is that some grief bursts can be fuzzy. If you encounter such a grief burst—meaning one that falls into more than one category—just throw it into the bucket where it can most easily be popped.

Conclusion: Lessons Learned

This concludes the first chapter in my battle against grief bursts. There are four more to come. I found the grief bursts from *the last days* to be the most painful. On the other hand, they are the easiest ones to pop. The trick here is that you must first understand the death process. Then, it becomes a matter of surfacing the grief bursts. You pop them by rationalizing them away. In this case, the rationale comes from understanding death and your limitations in the face of it.

Most deaths today are from chronic diseases that have their own trajectories. At the end, there is very little we can do to control this trajectory or deflect it from its path. The best we can do for ourselves, and our loved ones who are dying, is to understand the process. In this case, knowledge of death is power. We can use this power in two ways: first, to help give our soulmate a good death; and second, to help us pop the grief bursts triggered by these last days.

Chapter 8

My Grief Cure for Survivor's Guilt

"The most I ever did for you was to outlive you,
But that is much."

— *Edna St. Vincent Millay* [1]

My *survivor's guilt* grief bursts would hit me every morning, shortly after I woke up. I felt guilty to be alive another day without Jeri. I felt guilty that Jeri was not here to enjoy another beautiful Hawaiian morning. I would look at the ocean and the deep sobbing would start— she would not be surfing today. I felt guilty to have survived my lover. Why hadn't I gone first? I almost went first last year, but she kept me alive. Why couldn't I have done the same for her? As her caregiver, I felt guilty for having let her die—I failed her. Her death was a horrible crime. I was the witness and I had no place to report it. Why did she have to die so young? It didn't seem fair. It also didn't seem fair that I would live, when she had died.

Of course, all this stuff is irrational, but try to tell that to a grief burst. Most of them are irrational by nature. They stem from unresolved emotions. In this case, all the guilt was self-directed anger. I was angry that my soulmate had been eliminated. I was angry that my life was spared and hers wasn't. It seemed like nature was arbitrary and capricious. I was a bit older than Jeri, so I should have gone first. To sum it up: I was the survivor. I felt guilty to be alive. The grief bursts would remind me of that, every single morning. In this chapter, I will tell you how I eliminated these grief bursts so that I could continue to live for both of us.

---

[1] Norma Millay (editor), *Collected Poems Edna St. Vincent Millay* (Harper, 1956).

This is the second of a five-chapter series on how I zapped my grief bursts out of existence using the cure described in Chapter 6. Here, I'm going to be zapping away at grief bursts of the *survivor's guilt* variety. Grief theory just notes the existence of this emotion but does not offer us a solution. So I'll start this chapter with the technique I used to get rid of these bursts. Then I will give you examples of some of the more difficult grief bursts that I encountered. Finally, I'll tell you how I got rid of them, too. Again, these examples are from my e-mails.

The Problem

How did I recognize these *survivor's guilt* grief bursts? Actually, it was quite easy. They happened first thing every morning. Before they started I would always say, "I'm so sorry you're not here, Babe." They became part of my before-coffee morning routine. Here's an excerpt from an e-mail I sent on August 29, 2009, about ten weeks after Jeri's death, identifying the problem:

> The good news is that the images of Jeri in my mind are back to the normal surfer chick. The replay scenes of the "last few days" are receding. The bad news is that I now feel guilty that the "surfer chick" is not enjoying her Waikiki playground—the morning coffee with truffles, surfing, dining, her world-view commentary, etc. Instead, I'm the one enjoying, in solo, that lifestyle she loved so much. I get grief bursts because I know how much she loved all this. I also remember that I'm alive today because she helped pull me through last year, when I was sick and almost died. She was a great caregiver. The survivor's guilt in me says, "she's the one who should be here today enjoying this, not me." Or, "I shouldn't be alive if she can't also be here." A gentler variation of this theme is, "I wish she were here, too—this is her world in which I live." Jeri's imprints are everywhere; I'm alive in her beloved world without her. Of course, I'd love to give her my place, if I could.

My First-Pass Solution

I thought I had a solution. Here's what I wrote in that same e-mail:

So, how am I dealing with this one? What a surprise—I've worked out an elaborate mental program! First, I accept that I could not have controlled the progression of Jeri's cancer and subsequent death or changed the outcome in any way. I'm not omnipotent. Second, I accept that my death would not bring her back. (I'm very sorry she had to go first.) Third, I accept that I'm here today because she kept me alive last year. So, I owe her the gift of life that I enjoy on a good day. Fourth, I'm now trying to live for both of us. Finally, by being alive I'm celebrating her life. When people see me, they also remember Jeri. Unfortunately, when they see me today they probably see the face of grief. I need to put a smile back on my face so that people can remember the radiant Jeri they once knew. Living in Waikiki—a place Jeri loved so much—helps me continue the life we had and keeps her alive in my heart. Our love continues every day and gives me a lot of inner strength. *Note:* I'm not idolizing Jeri or putting her on a pedestal. I'm just in love with her, period.

I was off to a good start. I used the above like a mantra. When a grief burst was about to hit me, I would say: "I'm so sorry you're not here. I'm so sorry you had to go first. I would love nothing more than to have you back, but I'm not omnipotent. There's nothing I can do to bring you back." I would repeat these sentences, over and over again. It seemed to attenuate the grief bursts. During the day, I kept repeating another mantra. I would say: "I'm trying to live for both of us."

For those of you who are not grieving, all this may sound very strange. Just remember that I was bordering on insanity. I was desperately trying to regain control over my mind. So I had to improvise and do whatever it took. If it meant I had to go around muttering a bunch of inane mantras, so be it. The alternative was much worse.

The Grief Bursts Were Celebrating Jeri's Birthday

My first big test came about a week later. It was Jeri's birthday. She would have been 57. In their sadistic way, grief bursts also seemed to celebrate birthdays, and worse, their celebrations started about a week before the actual day. They ramped up and became more intense as the birthday approached. Most of these grief bursts were of the *survivor's guilt* variety. Why? I think it's because she died so young. Her birthday seemed to drive that point home. My response was to tackle, head on, the issue of her early death. I had to resolve it in my mind. Here's an excerpt from an e-mail I sent on September 5, 2009:

Hello Friends,

Had she lived, Jeri would have been 57 today. Was her life cut down too short? From my perspective, it's a definite yes—I could never get enough time with Jeri. By today's average lifespan-at-birth numbers, Jeri did not fare well either—the average for a U.S. female is about 80 years. (The current world average for both sexes is 67 years.) However, if you step back and take a more historic view, Jeri had a longer lifespan than 99% of the people who lived on this planet from the beginning of all time. For example, on average, Jeri lived twice as long as the people in Classic Rome, Classic Greece, and Medieval Britain—their lifespan was 20-30 years. She lived much longer than people in the early 20th century whose average lifespan was 30-40 years. So Jeri did more than OK by historic standards. In geologic time, we all occupy this earth for a few microseconds, so these numbers are just noise.

Jeri liked to say, "It's not how long you live but how well you live." This is so true. I keep getting reminded of this every day, watching my mother suffer in her old age. I once told Jeri, "Hey, at least you won't get old, Babe. You'll be young forever like Marilyn and Janice." Indeed, she still looked very beautiful in her last days. On the day she died, I held her hand for hours. I couldn't help thinking how wonderful she looked—her skin was velvet soft, her hair was shiny, and her face, though a little gaunt, was beautiful. As you know, Jeri lived a very full life during her 57 years. Even with the cancer, her last ten years were wonderful. Her quality-of-life was incredibly good because she lived in Hawaii. When I looked at Jayne's surfing video (the one I sent you in the last message), I couldn't help but think that Jeri may have caught at least 25,000 waves in the last five years. Every one of these waves put a big smile on her face (like the smile Jayne had after her surfing session).

What would Jeri have done more of had she lived longer? I'd say more of the same—she was very content. Perhaps, she would surf more off the North Shore in the winter. Ever since we met, we always made sure to live each day to the max, so there are no regrets or things left undone. Of course, I'm greedy and would love to have had more time with Jeri, but this option is not on the table. I'm very grateful for the 30 years we had together and all the sweet memories I now have. In her time on this earth, Jeri lived a very full, happy, and productive life. She also had a "good death." May we all be that lucky.

From a grieving perspective, this birthday without her is a milestone I   must face. I used this note to reflect on Jeri's past birthdays and add some perspective to her life and death. That I miss her greatly goes without saying (and sadly, doesn't make a difference). It's my grief to bear—hopefully, it won't go beyond the pain level 2. Happy birthday, Jeri. You will be with us today and every day that I live.

Aloha, Robert

A New Mutant Variant Shows Up: "The Witness"

This meditation on Jeri's birthday was quite helpful. I was able to celebrate her birthday in peace—the early-morning grief bursts took the day off. Unfortunately, they were back the next morning with a vengeance. They had morphed into a new mutant, "The Witness," which I described in Chapter 5. Remember, this was a movie-like grief burst that kept replaying the scene of a crime—Jeri's death—to which I was a witness. I stood by helplessly, watching the crime as it played in slow motion. As I said before, "Jeri just disappeared from this earth.

She was erased from each scene in my life. I had witnessed a crime against humanity."

"The Witness" kept playing in my mind every single morning, just before coffee. It generated some terrific sobs. It was so bad that I had to shut all the windows. It felt like an old movie rerun, except that there were no pause or delete buttons. And I couldn't fast-forward—it always played in slow motion. This was one nasty grief burst. So how did I pop it?

Popping "The Witness"

Typically, you have to assign a grief burst to a bucket before you pop it. "The Witness" seemed to straddle across multiple buckets. Clearly, it had something to do with the last days. There was also an existential element: Jeri's life and death. Further, there was a strong dose of *survivor's guilt*—the surviving soulmate as the witness to the crime. I decided to put "The Witness" in the *survivor's guilt* bucket. Here's an excerpt from an e-mail I sent on September 12, 2009, that describes how I dealt with this new mutant variant:

Dear Debs and Kathys,

Here's what happens. It's the witness (or observer) who experiences the full impact of death—not the person that dies. The witness is left to make sense out of the capriciousness of death. This is where the deep grieving comes in. Most of us will want to forget and go back to living our lives. If you're not a full-impact witness, our death-denying culture can help you move on quickly. Our minds (and culture) have plenty of ways to abstract, mitigate, deny, gloss over, downplay, and rationalize death. I could do this with my own death. I also did it with my father's death because I was not living at home at the time. So, I didn't feel its full impact (the before, during, and after). I was not a full witness. However, my sister was a full witness and she was traumatized by the loss. This reminds me of a line from Woody Allen, "I'm not afraid of death. I just don't want to be there when it happens."

Now that this "witness thing" has surfaced, I can deal with it. So, in addition to my normal grieving—*I miss Jeri, she left a big hole,* and *the last days*—I must now deal with survivor's guilt and the existential meaning of Jeri's death. In other words, as "the witness" I must make sense out of Jeri's life and death. Even though I'm comfortable with my own mortality, I must now give meaning to Jeri's. If I had died first—for example, during my illness last year—I would never have had this full experience of death. So here's how I'm dealing with this conundrum:

- First, I now spend a good deal of time meditating on the meaning of Jeri's life—something I never did when she was alive. She definitely had a "good life." She made many contributions and also had a lot of fun. Some of her contributions made ripples in the world of technology. So she did leave something behind. She also touched people on a daily basis. I was a witness to this. In any case, she did everything she wanted to do on this earth and at the end, all she wanted was more of the same. Did she have unrealized potential? Yes, as a surfer. Had she lived, her next steps would have been to surf Waimea and Pipeline on big-wave days. With Jeri, nothing was impossible.

- Next, I meditate on the meaning of death in general. I just keep staring into the face of death and the finiteness of the human condition. We are all transients on this earth. I had to make new sense out of the "transiency" of life—i.e., death's finality. Religious people do not have this problem, as most religions simply deny death by offering an afterlife. In my pantheistic view, there is no afterlife—death is just a form of recycling back to nature. The Greek philosopher Epicurus says it best in his *symmetry* argument: "after death we're in the same state of non-being as before birth." And he concludes: "Where death is, I am not." The circle is complete. With enough meditation, death just becomes Nirvana—a state of blissful nothingness.

- Next, I revisit Jeri's death. In her case, death was ultimately the relief from the final phase of cancer. The crime I witnessed was the cancer attacking her body—the disease at the end. So how does this mind twister make it better? It's better because I've come to the realization that death is not ugly; only the cancer is. As far as deaths go, Jeri had a "good death." We will all die some day. We can argue over whether Jeri's life was too short (the subject of the last message). But as I previously wrote, it's the quality of life that counts not the quantity. For example, I'd currently gladly swap my entire remaining time on this earth for one more day with Jeri. (I enjoyed a full 30 years of those good days.) Jeri was able to savor the preciousness of each moment of her life. She lived life to the fullest in the here and now.

Now, a final meditation. I think I may have popped this grief burst. As a close witness of death, I lost my innocence—I am no longer a death virgin. With my defense mechanisms stripped down, I felt a tragic anguish: Jeri was the victim of a crime that I had helplessly witnessed and survived. In reality, death is part of the human condition.

The final phase of the disease made it appear ugly. With enough meditation, I came to accept death for what it is—the closing circle of life. It's the inevitable destiny of all humans: we are all mortals living on borrowed time. Like Jeri, I'm learning how to live with this terminal condition. Her trick was to enjoy the moment and make the best out of whatever time she had on this earth. Others may prefer strategies that seek immortality—however they choose to do that (monuments, religious faith, great works of art, wars-and-conquest, or whatever else works for them).

In the final analysis, for secularists (and pantheists), death is our collective destiny. We must learn to live with that reality—especially since there's nothing we can do about it. So now that I've put this one to rest, I can go back to my other grieving. I'm back to the more familiar issues like: "I miss her" and "How can I live the rest of my life without her?"

Aloha, Robert

As you can see, "The Witness" took me into new territory; I now had to deal with the larger issues of life and death. Luckily, it worked. I was able to pop it. Once it was gone, my early-morning grief bursts disappeared. I could now wake up with a smile. My day would start with pleasant memories of mornings with Jeri on the lanai. I could look forward to drinking my morning coffee again. Of course, there were still other grief bursts to be popped, but they were not of the *survivor's guilt* type.

Attention: Survivor's Guilt Is Real

Even though survivor's guilt is a real problem, most grief theorists just gloss over it. They do not seem to associate survivor's guilt with normal grieving. Instead, they associate it with traumatic situations like surviving the Holocaust, war, natural disasters, or a deadly accident. They don't normally associate it with the death of a soulmate and, therefore, do not provide tools for dealing with it. I had to improvise a cure. I had to invent mantras on the fly. I had to meditate on the meaning of life and death. To put it mildly, I had to fight hard to maintain my sanity.

I'm not a grief theorist, but I can tell you that the death of my soulmate was very traumatic. Like other trauma victims, I felt very guilty to have survived. Why shouldn't it be so? We lived as one. Death obliterated "my other half." As the surviving half, I was traumatized. Nothing made sense any more: Why was I spared? Why was I occupying a space that was once for two? Why was I still living on this earth when my loved one was gone? Why did she have to go so young? There were so many such questions. I was also the witness to an unresolved crime—the murder of my soulmate. This is all very traumatic stuff.

Conclusion: Lessons Learned

This concludes the second installment in the grief-burst zapping series. We learned that *survivor's guilt* is a trigger for a nasty breed of grief bursts. Let me quickly recapitulate how I dealt with them:

- *Learn to identify them.* Typically, these grief bursts are associated with an "I am sorry you're not here" statement. In my case, they also seemed to occur at the beginning of each day.

- *First mantra: "I'm not omnipotent."* You cannot bring your soulmate back to life. You are not responsible for death. You would love to have your soulmate back, but there's nothing you can do about it. Just keep repeating this over and over again. Eventually, you'll come to accept it. Your rational mind will regain control.

- *Second mantra: "I'm trying to live for both of us."* Carry the memories of your soulmate inside of you, as you go through your daily-life routines. As long as you live, they live within you. So enjoy your sunsets for two, and keep repeating the mantra until your rational mind kicks in.

- *Meditate on the meaning of life and death.* Yes, this is the beginning of a long meditation process on the finiteness of life. I started this process with Jeri's birthday and "The Witness." Your survivor's guilt will fade away when you fully come to grips with the inevitability of death—including the death of your soulmate. Yes, I know, it's a hard pill to swallow. I'll have a lot more to say in the existential chapter.

I think we may have put this one to bed. Hopefully, some of these techniques will work for you, too. Let's go on to the next set of grief bursts—*she's gone forever.*

Chapter 9

My Grief Cure for She's Gone Forever

I feel it when I sorrow most;
'Tis better to have loved and lost
Than never to have loved at all.

—Alfred Tennyson[1]

The death of a soulmate can abruptly shatter your world beyond comprehension. One moment I was enjoying the most complete relationship two people could have; the next moment I was alone on this earth. Death created absolute nothingness in one instant. It's no wonder that my "separation distress" alarms went haywire. I kept searching for Jeri; I wanted my soulmate back. Of course, I couldn't get Jeri back, so I started yearning for her. But her absence was everywhere, so I began to despair. Pretty soon, I was in grief burst hell.

This time, I was being attacked by the *she's gone forever* grief bursts. For some odd reason, they would strike around noon every day. They came like clockwork—they became my lunchtime grief buddies. They brought with them the deep sobs of despair. I just couldn't believe Jeri had left me forever. I missed her voice, her touch, her presence, her laughter, and the list goes on and on. There was no way to reach her—no phone, no e-mail, and no forwarding address. Where did she go? She left a gaping hole in her wake. My world was a scene of pure devastation. Was there a way out of this despair? Could I continue to live without her? The answers are in this chapter.

---

[1] Alfred Tennyson, *In Memoriam*, 1849.

This chapter is the third of the five-chapter series on how I zapped my grief bursts out of existence. Here, I'm going to be zapping away at *she's gone forever* grief bursts. I'll first review what grief theory has to say about these type of grief bursts. Then I'll tell you about the specific technique I used from the grief burst cure developed in Chapter 6. Again, I was lucky to be able to draw from a trail of e-mails to refresh my memory of these painful events.

What Do Grief Theorists Tell Us?

This time we're right up their alley. This is what grief theory is all about—the breaking of our attachment bonds. (You got the full story in Chapter 6.) Remember, classical grief theorists believe that we must break all ties with our dead soulmates to be whole again, which is the end-goal of the grieving process. This is where stages, phases, states and oscillations come into the picture. At the end of the day, you must *forget and detach*. You must fully accept that your loved one is gone, forever.

Of course, I did not want to break my attachment bonds with Jeri. Luckily, there's a new avant-garde of grief theorists who agree with me. They believe we can continue our ongoing attachment with our dead soulmates. They call it the *continuing bonds* theory. The idea here is that we can love our soulmates in absentia. We can benefit from their comforting presence in our hearts. Our memories then become a source of strength. The problem is that most of this continuing bonds work is still invisible. I had to dig really hard to find it. Occasionally, I found some little nuggets here and there, but there was no coherent coverage. I tried to remedy this in Chapter 6 by pulling it all together in one place.

As you will soon find out, this continuing bonds stuff was absolutely critical for my recovery. Without it, I probably never would have recovered from my *she's gone forever* despair. Initially, I read only the classical grief literature, which is the bulk of what's out there. It seemed to amplify my despair. I couldn't stand the thought of letting go of Jeri forever. The *forever* part felt like a stab in my heart. That reading almost put me in a state of *complicated grief.* You may remember from Chapter 5, that the chief symptom of complicated grief is "a persistent and intense yearning for the loved one."[2] I was certainly headed that way. And, classical grief theory was making it worse.

In my view—and I'm not a grief theorist—the loss of a soulmate requires the *continuing bonds* theory of grief. The classical *forget and detach* alternative can be quite destructive for people in our situation. So reader beware. In any case, I presented both views in Chapter 6. You can be the final judge.

My Eureka Moment

My Eureka moment for dealing with the *she's gone forever* grief bursts came about eight weeks after Jeri's death. It was not a moment too soon. Let me explain. The week before, I had experienced my first category 4 level pain—"it feels like I can't go on." I had two days of unbearable grief pain with more than 15 grief bursts per day. The cause of all this pain was a cycle of yearning and despair. I couldn't stand the thought that Jeri was gone forever. Here's an excerpt from an e-mail I sent on August 14, 2009, about eight weeks after Jeri's death:

Hello Debs and Kathys,

I missed Jeri so much that I started to feel that there was no way to continue to live without her. My loss of Jeri was just too much to accept. I missed her too much, needed her too much, and felt guilty that she was not alive to enjoy whatever I was doing that was pleasurable and that I knew she would like. So, how did I resolve some of these issues?

- First, I took a full inventory of my losses. Needless to say, it was a devastating scene. It was as if I were hit directly by a hurricane, Cat 5 or greater. Jeri had played hundreds of roles in my life and there was no way to reassign them all (i.e., put back together the

---

[2] Fran Schumer, "After a Death, The Pain That Doesn't Go Away," *New York Times*, September 28, 2009.

pieces that were ripped away). In the case of grieving, healing means trying to be "whole" again within a new identity. Obviously, there was no way I could do this without Jeri. This is when I hit pain level 4.

- Next, I took a closer look at my loss inventory and came to an important realization (a *eureka* moment)—all was not really lost. I did not lose 100% of Jeri, even though she was 100% gone. I had only lost the physical presence of Jeri in my life. Jeri still lives within me. Our relationship is still there, inside of me: Where else would it go? I still have 30 years of great memories to draw from, which is a huge reservoir of good feelings. I can never lose the love that is within me. So Jeri will be part of me as long as I live. Consequently, I'm starting to realize that I cannot be alone (or lonely) as long as she's part of me.

- Next, I resurveyed the loss inventory this time with the realization that Jeri was not 100% gone. How many roles could I salvage with our relationship still alive inside of me? The answer is that it greatly helps with the loneliness issue (a biggie) and I don't have to look for another relationship to fill her shoes (mission impossible). Also, I can enjoy her presence in many non-physical ways (remember, the website story). Of course, gone is the hugging and touching. And, I can't hear her voice or laugh. However, she is still my companion, sounding board, and life partner. I can still share everything with her. And, she can help me make decisions—she can even complete my thoughts, like I can hers. I could continue living life for both of us, albeit solo.

- My survey indicates that I lost approximately 30% of the roles Jeri played in my life, which is still a big loss that I need to fill. The good news is that I still have 70% of Jeri to help me through, which is incredibly good. Now, I must figure out how to subsume some of the roles (or find new sources of support) as I re-anchor myself and find a new equilibrium.

Chapter 9: My Grief Cure for She's Gone Forever

Note: Most of the grief literature does not touch on this salvaging process, although my counselor did say, "Carry the gift of the relationship. She's going to be part of your life as long as you live." In the literature, you must accept a 100% loss. They insist that you must recreate or rebuild yourself with a new identity. I would never be able to recover under these circumstances—life would just be a wilderness for me. I think (and hope) that there is a hole in the literature and that my analysis is correct—at least, for me. Time will tell.

In conclusion, the last eight weeks were incredibly painful and nothing had prepared me for this level of pain. When Jeri was first diagnosed with cancer, I was in pain but she was next to me. Last year, when her cancer progressed, I felt extreme pain, but she was next to me. She was even next to me during the last week of her life—so the pain was intense, but still under control. The pain I felt in the last eight weeks is unique, frightening, and I must face it alone.

Luckily, the realization that my loss was not 100% is what gave me three consecutive days of Pain level 2, which is relatively a very good thing. At least, I'm improving. I still have to work on: survivor's guilt, the 30% unfilled roles, the flashbacks from the last days, and the existential issues. This is my grieving project for the next month. I hope to report some more progress.

Aloha, Robert

I can't tell you what a big breakthrough this was—I still had 70% of Jeri to draw on! It changed the course of my grieving and put me on the path to recovery. I felt such a sense of relief to still have Jeri by my side. She would continue to be my safe harbor in this world. This realization helped me regain my strength and courage. I had Jeri inside of me.

If you think there's something delusional about all this, here's some food for thought. Imagine that you're on a scientific expedition on the Amazon for six months. During this time, you are parted from your soulmate. Then assume that you can't be reached by phone, e-mail, or even mail. Does this mean your relationship has ended? Of course not. It's the same with death. The relationship just continues in absentia, but without the physical element. Now try to explain all this to a classical grief theorist.

Yearning for the "Full Jeri"

Of course, Jeri is still physically gone forever, but it's wonderful to have her inside of me. It's much better than the *forget and detach* alternative. However, it's not better than having Jeri in her entirety here. I was still yearning for the "full Jeri." Here's an excerpt from an e-mail I sent two weeks later, on August 29, 2009:

> I'm still working on *she's gone forever*. It's not easy. I live in a place that's crawling with memories of Jeri—both good and bad. I still can't get over the shock that she's not in this world any longer: "that the dead stay dead is a constant surprise." I yearn to have her here physically. But, the best I can do now is to carry on with her within me. I talk to her often. She's within me from the moment I wake up.

This e-mail shows some progress. I was on the right path but not quite there yet. A month later, the *she's gone forever* grief bursts were slightly diminished but by no means gone. Here's an excerpt from an e-mail I sent on September 28, 2009:

> I'm still working on this one. Most of my current grief bursts are coming from this source. I yearn to have Jeri back here, physically. My most persistent grief bursts occur every morning as I prepare lunch. I also cry when I read her most recent life-philosophy book, *The Surfer Spirit* (more on this later). I cry when I see pictures of the surfer girl. I cry when I see traces she left behind (hallway and apartment remodels, automatic reminders via e-mail, contents of drawers, etc.) So, what am I doing about this? I'm drawing strength from the fact that Jeri still lives in my heart. I talk to her all the time. Our relationship is alive and well. Living in Waikiki is

very comforting and soothing. Surrounded by memories, I live every day for both of us. As long as I have her within me, I don't feel lonely. Her physical absence is still a huge blow, which is why the grief bursts are still coming. I can't stand the thought that she is erased from the scenes of life all around me. I'll have to keep working on this one.

It's not that easy to stop yearning for your lover's physical presence. By focusing on my continuing bonds with Jeri, I was finally able to break the yearning and despair cycle. Two weeks later, the *she's gone forever* grief bursts had almost completely dissipated. The sharp pains were gone. I still missed Jeri's physical presence, but only in a tender, melancholic way. Without the sharp pains, my memories of Jeri became gardenia-sweet. I could enjoy her company even more. Of course, I still had to resolve the self-pity and existential issues that we encountered in this chapter. So, there's still more work to be done.

Conclusion: Lessons Learned

It was a long healing process, which required a good deal of grief work based on the *continuing bonds* theory. It finally did work. My *she's gone forever* grief bursts are now forever gone. Unfortunately, this is the most common type of grief. It's the one that will hit us all. We will all search, yearn and despair when our loved one dies—even the most resilient among us. In my opinion, there's a serious flaw in the grief theory that makes it hard to deal with this type of grief. It started with Freud, but it's still being propagated by almost everyone in the field. I am grateful to Dr. Joyce Brothers for changing the course of my grieving when she pointed out: "Milt was part of me, and if he was part of me, how could I be lonely?" As you can see from this chapter, this is the prescription I used to get rid of my *she's gone forever* grief bursts. It finally worked for me.

Chapter 10

My Grief Cure for Self-Pity

"A soulmate is somebody with whom one has a feeling of deep and natural affinity, love, intimacy, sexuality, spirituality, and/ or compatibility."

— *Wikipedia*

My *self-pity* grief bursts were accompanied by howling sobs of pain— I had just lost my entire support system. It was gone—flushed away. I was feeling really sorry for myself. I had surveyed my loss and it was huge. I had lost my partner in life. In this chapter—the fourth in the grief-burst popping series—I'll show you how I dealt with these grief bursts. But first I'd like to take a closer look at the nature of the soulmate support system.

Soulmates: Life Partners in a Chaotic World

We live in a complex, fast-changing, random, and increasingly uncertain world. The modern soulmate relationship is an entirely new kind of life partnership with no historic precedent. It's designed to tackle *all* of modern-life's challenges, including the need for companionship, raising children, dual careers, gratifying sex, owning a home, building a nest egg, shopping, constant repairs, paying the monthly bills, taking care of elderly parents, mutual caregiving, finding meaning in life, and the list goes on.

This tightly-knit unit made up of two people is adaptive, agile, and nimble. In addition, it is incredibly mobile and self-contained. For example, the pair can be relocated anywhere, at a moment's notice, should the conditions require it. They're wired to resume their life in the new destination without missing a beat. It's a truly amazing, modern concoction. It can take on almost any challenge our tumultuous world throws at it. There's never been anything like it before. You may be asking: What makes this incredible unit work?

A Village in a Soulmate Capsule

First and foremost, the soulmate relationship is held together by romantic love. Love fuels the relationship: it provides the binding glue, and maintains the functional equilibrium. It allows the couple to unconditionally give to each other. They do not maintain balance sheets of who does what for whom. A soulmate relationship is an exquisitely fine-tuned division of labor between two people who are in love. In the old days, it took an entire village to fulfill the roles that are now assigned to this unit. You may remember Hillary Clinton's telling us "it takes a village to raise a child." Well, the same can be said of the myriad of other tasks that soulmates routinely provide—including mutual caregiving, working multiple jobs, and taking care of elderly parents in the age of chronic disease.

Soulmate Attachment Bonds

In Bowlby's terms, a soulmate relationship consists of multiple attachment bonds between two adults. Unlike dysfunctional marriages, the bonds in a soulmate relationship are fully functional; they're all in good working condition. It's a healthy relationship. So the bonds that would once glue together an entire village are now binding just two individuals. As you would expect, the bonding is tightly-coupled and highly-concentrated. These tightly-knit bonds replace the entire network of distributed village-style bonding. This is another way of saying that soulmates put all their eggs in one basket. In my case, the basket had just broken, and there were grief bursts of the *self-pity* variety.

Note: Is the modern soulmate relationship really without historic precedent? The short answer is yes. I know it sounds controversial, and I did get some flak from early reviewers, so let me elaborate. Of course, the world has always had soulmates. In pre-modern societies, classical soulmates typically had a deep romantic, intellectual, and existential affinity. Often, they were spouses and economic partners. However, the classical relationship almost always took place within the context of a tribe, clan, village, small town, or extended family. So the couple had a lot of support when it came to economics, caregiving, parenting, and similar functions. In contrast, the modern soulmate team is a self-contained unit that subsumes the functions that were once provided by a village or extended family. This dramatic shift has deep implications when it comes to grieving. In the new relationship, there is no village to share the grief load. We must learn to grieve alone, which is very modern. Most importantly, we have many more roles to fill when a soulmate dies—the roles are no longer distributed among a village, clan, or extended family.

What Does Grief Theory Tell Us?

Bowlby was the first to focus on the different types of attachment bonds. In the soulmate case, the bonding is between two adult *attachment figures*. Each soulmate provides the other with comfort and a safe harbor. According to Bowlby, we need to relocate the lost attachment figure within a new hierarchy of attachment figures. In simpler terms, we need to inventory the damage and fill the missing roles.

Having said this, we all have different relationships, so the roles we need to fill are very individual. This is where I found the self-help grieving literature to be the most useful. It focuses on the practical aspects of filling the missing roles. You get from them a ton of advice on how to carry on with your everyday life routines. I will give you a brief summary of this advice later in this chapter. I also found the *Dual Process Model (DPM)* to be very applicable. Remember, they want us to oscillate between grieving and the reconstruction of our lives. We must make time for both.

So How Did I Deal With Self-Pity?

I had an incredibly complete relationship with Jeri. We did everything together for thirty years. We were life partners in every sense of the word—we traveled around the world together, wrote books together, worked in the same computer software field, and took care of each other. We had a very fine-tuned division of labor. The love and physical attraction were always there, from the day we met till the very last moment of her life. So we had the glue that kept it all together.

As a team, we could face almost anything life might throw at us. With Jeri by my side, nothing was impossible; I could take on any challenge. Our team was more than just a survival unit; it was also a unit of pleasure—we enjoyed everything life had to offer, together.

In the previous chapter, I used the idea of *continuing bonds* to fill the emotional void Jeri left behind. She would continue to live within me. My love was intact. I had 70% of Jeri to sustain me. In this chapter, I deal with the remaining 30%. How would I fill the physical void Jeri left behind? I had to relearn everyday life, solo. I had to take on all the roles Jeri had performed and either fulfill them myself or find some way of outsourcing them.

Some of these roles would be harder to fill than others. For example, Jeri was my first responder. She was the person lying next to me in bed who would dial 911 if I had a heart attack in the middle of the night. How would I ever fill this role?

Yes, I was feeling sorry for myself. All it took was a slight cold for the grief bursts to come knocking. The emotions and feelings that trigger these *self-pity* bursts are a combination of fear, helplessness, and panic. The root cause was the fear of being alone. The antidote for these grief bursts is *reconstruction*. I had to reconstruct my life, one step at a time. I started with the easier tasks and progressively took on the harder ones. I had to baby-step my way slowly back into the world. Let me share some e-mails from that period.

The Reconstruction Process

My first taking of inventory revealed a scene of utter destruction. You may remember this passage from the e-mail I sent on August 14, 2009:

> Needless to say, it was a devastating scene. It was as if I was hit directly by a hurricane, Cat 5 or greater. Jeri played hundreds of roles in my life and there was no way to reassign them all (i.e., put back together the pieces that were ripped away).

Two weeks later, I had a better understanding of what was happening to me. Here's a segment from an e-mail I sent on August 29, explaining my reconstruction efforts:

> Hello Debs and Kathys,
>
> In our society, we turn to our spouse for the protection and emotional connections that in the past were provided by a multitude of social networks. We now have a complete dependence on one person—our spouse. As a result, deep fear is one of the key emotions that accompanies the death of a spouse. As C.S. Lewis put it, "no one told me that grief felt like fear." I was hit hard with this feeling during a recent cold. I suddenly felt very vulnerable.
>
> Of course, this triggered some red-hot grief bursts. It's much easier to face "aloneness" if you're healthy. Deborah #3 wrote, "The two of you never needed anyone but each other." This was true until the end, when I couldn't do it alone (so, thank you all). Now, I also lost my caregiver. So I need to put together a support system for when I'm sick. Luckily, there's a home-care agency that provides this type of help.
>
> Like Jeri, I'm not afraid of death itself. I'm very comfortable with my mortality and I would certainly not feel cheated if I died tomorrow. However, I'm terrified of a prolonged disease and pain. And, surprise, I'm not looking forward to getting old alone. In the meantime, I'm making the best out of every good day life hands me. The ocean is being good to me. And, as you probably know,

Hawaii spoils me with its natural gifts on a daily basis. These gifts helped sustain Jeri and they are now sustaining me.

Aloha, Robert

The e-mail seemed to have hit the nail right on the head: In modern society our soulmate provides the "protection and emotional connections that in the past were provided by a multitude of social networks." I had to reconstruct these networks from a solo position. Like most of us, I do not live in a traditional village or small town. I had to reconstruct this support system in a modern urban setting. And, as I described earlier, in our modern world a soulmate partnership is much more efficient and viable than doing it solo.

Everywhere I looked, there were everyday life roles to reconstruct. For example, Jeri was the technician responsible for programming the TiVo, iPhone, our computer network, the Kindles, and every gadget in the house. She had highly automated our lives around these gadgets. Jeri was technically-savvy and she had time on her hands after her chemo sessions—so she was endlessly reprogramming these gadgets. To keep my life together, I had to quickly master what she had done. As you can imagine, she left me with some interesting challenges.

Eventually, I was able to piece most of my life back together. I would keep to-do lists on my iPhone and then try to accomplish something every day. I baby-stepped my way through the tasks. I started with the most urgent tasks and kept moving down the list. It was a long trek, but I felt some sense of accomplishment every day as I kept checking off items on my various to-do lists. Whenever I could, I would simplify my life so as not to become overwhelmed. Gradually, I became more independent and my fears started to subside. The *self-pity* grief bursts disappeared when the fear was gone.

Tips from Self-Help Literature

In this section, I provide a quick summary of reconstruction tips from the self-help grief literature. It's a very small selection. I just want to give you a taste of what's out there.

Chapter 10: My Grief Cure for Self-Pity

From Dr. Joyce Brothers, in *Widowed,* we learn that we must stay in charge of our lives: "do not let your children try to run your life for you. Do not let them manage your money or your affairs...get advice from professionals as well as your family." She cautions us to avoid making hasty decisions: "Put every major decision on hold for a year." She advises the elderly widow to "take stock of her physical condition and come to a tentative decision about how long she can continue to live on her own."

Dr. Brothers urges us to initially "stick to the old routine." But, "plan ahead for anniversaries, holidays and weekends." She wants us to get together with old friends, but also make new friends: "Try to talk with one new person a week." She cautions us that "old friends, especially those who are married, tend to drop away. One reason is that they are couple-oriented and do not know how to deal with an unattached woman."

Dr. Brothers wants us to pamper ourselves: "When there is no one at home to give you a hug or rub your back, I believe in finding a substitute. Make an appointment for a facial, for a massage." She also has advice on how widows can handle their sex drive, if it revives: "There is an easy and natural answer—masturbate. It takes care of that part of your life. Think of it as a crutch that allows you not to feel like a needy, sexually deprived person. It is a very natural thing, and it leaves you better off." Finally, she wants us to get out of the house: "Find something to do that will get you out of the house at least a couple of days a week."

In *Waking Up Alone*, Julie Cicero tells us: "Now that you have remained to pick up the pieces, it is imperative that you remember to eat, sleep and breathe." It will take "an inordinate amount of time to adjust to your new reality, your new normal.... So many of the everyday activities become so very difficult. Now you often stand paralyzed, unable to complete even the basic tasks of daily living." She cautions: "Initially, it is wise to minimize your expectations of what you can accomplish. So always have a backup plan or escape route."

Cicero has some deep insights on the grieving process: "For the first year I wore my widowhood in front of me. I viewed myself as a widow first and everything else was secondary." She later reversed her victim role: "Then somewhere I heard that it is better if you allow your experience to refine you and not define you." With that, she went from victim to survivor. She tells us that the ultimate goal of grieving is to say to your late spouse: "It was my privilege to have known you, having no regrets for the relationship, just that it ended."

In *The Widow's Journey*, Janet Wright has quite a bit to say about finances: "My struggle with finances kept me in a state of anxiety—high anxiety. Because of this the bank became my closest friend." She had to learn everything about finances, but she was lucky to have survived with some money to manage. In her words, "Not every widow has the luxury of having finances available to her. Many widows, like my mother, had no finances. They have to worry constantly about keeping food on the table and roofs over their family's heads."

In *I Wasn't Ready To Say Goodbye,* Brooke Noel and Pamela Blair write, "Grief is a journey. The goal is reconciliation with life. To learn to live in the present, to reap the gifts of the moment, is the best tribute we can give." You must "take it one step at a time, and as you're ready add another *piece* to yourself." You must learn "how to do things alone" but do this "at your own pace—no one else's." They tell us that "the first year will be a first time for everything." They have tips for how to handle these different firsts. For example, New Year's could be, "Celebrate! You are moving in your recovery." Or, "you may simply want to acknowledge this is a new year and leave it at that."

Widow to Widow by Genevieve Ginsburg is the ultimate self-help guide for widows. It tells a widow how to empty her partner's closets and drawers, handle dinners for one, take care of finances, date again, travel alone, go from wife to mechanic, and so on. She tells widows,

"You can sit on your duff and feel safer or get off your duff and feel scared." She wants you to "just do it." You must overcome "that feeling of unending desolation." When you come home just say, "Hello, who is home?" Then answer, "Hello, I am home." She wants us to: "build, fall down, and rebuild." At the end, "we grow stronger for having coped."

Conclusion: Lessons Learned

This concludes the fourth chapter in the grief-burst popping series. We learned that the soulmate relationship is a modern innovation designed to handle the requirements of our increasingly complex world. It's a unit of survival glued together by love. When one partner dies, this finely-tuned division of labor is totally shattered. A completely balanced support system has been destroyed. The survivor must reconstruct alone what was once a very efficient support network.

Remember, the soulmate relationship is a modern substitute for a village—in fact, for some, it replaces a village. Luckily, the most important element is still salvageable—the continuing love bond, which I described in the last chapter. I could still have 70% of Jeri. The good news is that we do not have to rebuild from scratch. We're not completely solo, at least emotionally. The bad news is that our physical support system is totally shattered; it must be rebuilt from scratch. My *self-pity* grief bursts were telling me that the job ahead was enormous.

In this chapter, I went over my technique for getting rid of the *self-pity* grief bursts. I had to overcome the fear of being alone by reconstructing my physical world. I spent some time on the nature of the soulmate bond because it requires a new form of grieving. Before death, the soulmate bonds were all in mint condition. There were literally thousands of these bonds—enough to sustain an entire village. The soulmate relationship is very different from the arranged marriages of the past or dysfunctional modern marriages that end in divorce. Unlike soulmate relationships, these bonds are more distributed and dysfunctional so that when a partner dies, the survivor has less to rebuild.

Soulmates will need to rebuild their extensively-damaged physical support network. It's a long trek and we will each do it our way. I shared with you the techniques I used. Maybe they can help you, too. You may also want to check the self-help literature. Eventually, you'll have to rebuild your own support system one piece at a time. The final outcome will never be as efficient as the soulmate unit you once belonged to. Fortunately, with some effort, you can cobble together a working system. You'll need that system for two reasons: 1) to conquer your fears and consequently zap away these *self-pity* grief bursts; and 2) to rejoin the world. Always remember that you can build on your love, even "in absentia." All is not lost.

Chapter 11

My Grief Cure for
Deep Existential Issues

"Under normal circumstances, most of us cruise through our busy days without the slightest thought of life and death and those other annoying existential questions, like where we came from and where we stand in the grand scheme of the universe. The death of a loved one tends to peel back the curtain on those existential questions, at least temporarily, and begs us to take a larger view of the world and our place in it."

— Dr. George Bonanno[1]

This is the last of the five-chapter series on how I zapped my grief bursts. Jeri's death shook the very foundation of my belief system. I had to re-examine my entire sense of meaning. I began to ponder the big issues of life, death, and human mortality. Most importantly, I had to ascribe meaning to Jeri's life and her death—she was the one who had just disappeared from this earth. What was her life all about? Why did she die? How did she face her upcoming death? Was she afraid? What were her thoughts during those last moments? For some reason, all these questions were very disturbing. Of course that means they were triggers for grief bursts. This chapter deals with these *deep existential* grief bursts.

Typically, this is the time when you'll need to see a priest or some member of the clergy. From the beginning of time, the world's great religions have been grappling with these big issues. Death is their

---

[1] George Bonanno, *The Other Side of Sadness* (Basic Books, 2009).

thing and they provide full coverage. Their antidote for death is an afterlife. The major religions compete with different visions of an afterlife. You can have your choice. If you belong to a religion with an after-life plan, then you can definitely skip over this chapter. Your religion is all you need. It has the answers that can help you get through this.

If you are secular with a veneer of spirituality, this chapter is definitely for you. It provides that missing framework some of us may need to grapple with these big issues from a secular perspective. I was alone and in the midst of grief bursts while dealing with these questions. I faced a massive existential crisis with nowhere to go for quick answers. It took quite a bit of time and grappling to find the answers, but when I did, *all* of my remaining grief bursts just melted away. They disappeared into oblivion, never to come back again. I was pain-free for the first time since Jeri's death. The *existential* grief bursts were the last to go. This chapter, the last of the series, is about how I got rid of them.

How Do Seculars Deal with Death?

From Bonanno's quotation, you can tell that grief theorists are aware of "those annoying existential questions." However, their solution is to leave it to your religious support system. So, besides a psychologist, you'll also need a priest. But what happens to those of us who are secular? Well, we're completely on our own. We're the uninsured with no after-life coverage. Consequently, we need to become our own philosophers. I had to reconstruct my belief system to absorb the shock of Jeri's death. How did I do that? I'll walk you step-by-step through the process using my e-mails. But before we start, let me give you a quick preview of where we're going.

Post-War Existentialism with a Spiritual Touch

I was born after World War II and came to intellectual age during the late 1960s—a time of great intellectual ferment. The reigning philosophy of that time was *Secular Existentialism*. It was based on the individual's attempt to find meaning in the post-war period. It was about the affirmation of life after a period of destructive madness that tore the world apart. Existentialism is a philosophy of life that asserts that our individual essence is defined by our existence. We are simply the sum of our actions. There is no other essence. The courage to be is the courage to become—through our actions—what we want to be.[2]

Many, in my generation, took existentialism for granted. In fact, the ideas were so ingrained and pervasive that many of us were existentialists without even knowing it. It was how we lived our lives: "We are what we make of ourselves." Many of us felt comfortable with our existentialist base, but we needed to add a little bit of spirituality to it without going to an organized religion. Our search took us in many directions—including Eastern mysticism, Goddess religions, and psychedelic drugs. Eventually, we settled for existentialism with a spiritual veneer. Typically, it meant being in harmony with nature. It was a good life philosophy, but could it handle the end of life and death?

As a rule, death is the real acid test for a philosophy. After Jeri's death, I revisited my philosophical belief system with the following questions in mind: Could it help me withstand the shock of my soulmate's death? Could it provide answers to my deep existential questions? Could it help me ascribe meaning to Jeri's death? To my surprise, the answers were a resounding yes. The philosophy passed muster with flying colors. Of course, this is all good news for us seculars. It means we have an off-the-shelf philosophy combo—Existentialism with a touch of spirituality—that can help us deal with death. To do this, we need to brush up on our old philosophical roots. Let me take you through the process that got me there.

How widespread are these ideas today? *Without being too scientific, I think these ideas continue to be popular with anyone who was born after 1945, not just my cohort from the 60's generation. Today, young*

---

[2] Paul Tillich, *The Courage To Be* (Yale University Press, 1952).

people seem to be more than ever in tune with the natural world. Columnist Ross Douthat tells us that they were weaned on "Star Wars" and the "Jedi," whose "mystical Force surrounds us, penetrates us, and binds the galaxy together." The trend continues, he states, with "Avatar" where the Na'Vi are saved by their faith in Eywa, the "All Mother," described variously as a network of energy and the sum total of every living thing.[3] If you ask me, this is the natural spiritual veneer that we added to our existentialism. So these ideas are still alive and growing stronger.

"The Non-Event" Revisited

Let's return to Jeri's death and my *existential* grief bursts. In Chapter Seven, I introduced "The Non-Event" grief burst and told you that I would resolve it in the existential chapter. Here we are. Just to refresh your memory, this grief burst was about Jeri's not saying goodbye. I was trying to understand her state of mind during those last moments: How had she viewed her imminent death? I took a stab at the answer in an e-mail I sent on August 20, 2009. We concluded that she had been at peace with herself, the "b) answer." Here's a long excerpt from the same e-mail that explains the elaborate thinking that led me to that conclusion:

Dear Debs and Kathys,

.... From a philosophical viewpoint, b) would be almost perfect—an incredibly dignified and courageous final exit. Let me elaborate. When I met Jeri over 30 years ago, our relationship started with long discussions covering sex, death, and life philosophies—in that order. Why death? It was something she was really interested in then, perhaps because of the death of her father. She kept talking about Kübler-Ross's work, *Death and Dying,* and the stages of death. I was not familiar with the work of Kübler-Ross then. Luckily, I did know quite a bit about death—mostly, from an

---

[3] Ross Douthat, "Heaven and Nature," *New York Times,* December 20, 2009.

178

Existential and Post-Freudian viewpoint with a touch of Woody Allen.

Jeri and I quickly agreed that because death was inevitable, life was a precious gift and we'd better live every day to the maximum. So our relationship was very life-affirming and pleasurable (more Zorba and less Woody). We made sure that there was nothing on our bucket list. In philosophical terms, we did not dwell on the body/mind dichotomy. We agreed they were both necessary, transient, and part of the natural universe. There was no need to worry about eternity, immortality, or the soul—so let's have fun now. We revisited this many times and always came to the same conclusion.

When we found out about Jeri's cancer, we again revisited all these issues. I told her, "We're all terminal—no one is coming out of this alive. You just happen to know what you're going to die from." So we decided to live by the Jeri rules. In the last ten years, we had many philosophical talks on death and the human condition. I kept it abstract, but I was trying to get a feel for where she really stood on the topic. Of course, she wanted to live but she claimed that she was not afraid to die. Her exact words were, "I'm not afraid to die. I just don't want to be in pain." I promised her that as long as I was alive, I'd make sure she was not in pain.

At the end, all I could focus on was doing everything I could to keep the pain under control. I had to figure out where she would be the most comfortable—at home, in the hospital, or in the hospice. We did not have time to revisit her thoughts on death and dying. At the very end, the topic made us cry a lot, so we avoided it. One night, six days before she died, I told her, "Thank you for this beautiful relationship. I wish it could go on for another 30 years." She answered, "And another 30 more years after that." This was the last time we discussed the topic.

So, was she afraid to die? What were her thoughts on death and dying? Why didn't she talk to us about it? Where was she getting comfort from? I don't have answers. I know she brushed away the priests and did not revert back to religion. She was very brave to go at it alone, or maybe she was just too drugged. I was expecting something more dramatic, but she left very peacefully and quietly. Last week, I finally got to read Kübler-Ross's *On Death and Dying*. She mostly covered how the terminally ill view death. I felt that Jeri must have known quite a bit from just reading this work— more than your average person. But, there was still nothing to help me answer the questions I'm raising here.

Two days later:

I've been meditating on this question quite a bit. I now think I have the answer: "It's the ocean, Stupid." Yes, the ocean and surfing is where Jeri was finding her peace with nature. I think she understood that she was part of the natural world. She loved the movie *Big Fish*. It made her cry—she said it was her. Jeri was not afraid of the ocean (i.e., nature). She felt very comfortable there. Last December, we ran into a huge Tiger shark in the ocean off the Big Island. I was absolutely terrified, but she was totally fearless. I think she accepted the shark as being where he belonged—in nature's world, her home as well. I think her view of death was that she would simply be returning to nature's womb. At the end, she was not narcissistic at all, which is why it was a non-event. She was one with nature and the universe.

Before closing, I have one more insight to share. When Jeri's body started to shut down on Sunday (the active dying phase) she said "like a baby." I guess it could mean that she was returning to the womb—nature's womb. Maybe, "I want to go home" was also an expression of this feeling. Of course, this last paragraph is pure speculation. I'm on much firmer ground with my ocean hypothesis.

The Next Morning:

Actually, I had totally forgotten the philosophical (and religious) discussions Jeri had with the chaplain at Queen's Hospital and later with different priests at the hospice. Mostly, she told them outright that she didn't believe in an afterlife and that they were wasting their time with her. In some cases, she would engage in theological debates with a priest and use quotations from the Bible to support her stance as a non-believer. One day, I was wheeling her in the parking lot outside the hospice, when a priest we hadn't met before parked next to us and engaged us in the following conversation:

Priest: It's a beautiful day. Which of you two is the patient?

Robert: Actually, we're both terminal but Jeri is the one staying at the hospice.

Priest: OK, so I'm here to visit you, Jeri.

Jeri: Father, you're wasting your time. I already told Father George and others that I don't believe in that stuff. There's nothing you can really do for me.

Priest: We can hold your hand.

Jeri: OK, but that's what Robert is here for.

Priest: But surely you must be spiritual. Look at all the beauty around you. How can anyone live in Hawaii and not be spiritual?

Jeri: Of course I am spiritual, but what does it have to do with religion?

Priest: Religion is just organized spirituality.

Jeri: I am spiritual and don't need to have it organized or interpreted for me. I can feel nature myself without intermediaries.

Priest: Yes, yes. I understand. I am really here to give solace to people who are about to die.

Conclusion:

OK, so that was a lot of rambling thoughts on the subject. Still, I think it's quite important for two reasons: 1) To try to fathom what Jeri was thinking during these last few days when she faced death squarely. (It was no longer just an intellectual exercise.) 2) To deal with our own mortality triggered by being so close to Jeri when she died.

Generally, human beings tend to avoid thinking too much about their own death. We know of death intellectually, but deep inside we don't think it's really going to happen to us—only to others. Our mind deludes us into thinking we're immortal. It's a survival mechanism. It's the sublimation upon which civilization is built. If we were to dwell on our mortality, we wouldn't be able to function. So we put it aside until we're confronted with it—either when we're almost ready to die or when someone very close to us dies. In any case, this type of close encounter with death shatters our veneer and exposes us to the reality of being mere mortals. In other words, the deep existential questions arise. It also makes us feel very vulnerable. Jeri was incredibly courageous to the very end. She died with dignity (again, thank you all). May we all be so lucky.

Aloha, Robert

As you can see, I was going back to my philosophical roots looking for a direction. I even tried to see it all from Jeri's perspective. For the first time since my college years, I was in a deep philosophical quest looking for the meaning of life and death. It was exhilarating, but the grief bursts just kept coming and I had to keep on searching.

Religion and Pantheism

Next, I received an e-mail from Steve, my deeply-religious friend. He challenged some of the ideas in my last e-mail from a Christian perspective. All this discussion was starting to stimulate my dormant philosophical mind. I was revisiting my old haunts. Here's an e-mail, sent on August 25, 2009, that responds to the issues Steve raises:

Hello Steve,

You should have had this religious discussion with Jeri, when she was still here. She was a born-again Christian in her early days, who then rejected religion based on discrepancies in the Bible and many other things (which I don't claim to understand). In my "Non-Event" e-mail, I described what I perceived to be Jeri's state-of-mind when she confronted death. She was brave and stuck to her views to the very end. Like you say, it would have been comforting to accept a God and the afterlife at the very end, but she didn't.

My views are a bit different. I am religious in the sense that god is the universe. The ancient Greeks called it *pantheism*. When I die, I will be part of the universe—just like I am now, but without my current body or self. I just believe one line about pantheism: "we're all part of the universe." I don't know what the rest of pantheism is about, nor do I care.

I respect other people's religious choices. Accepting death and the human condition is very hard, so whatever works for them (and keeps them sane) is fine with me. To be honest, everyone needs "a crutch" when it comes to dealing with their mortality; it's not easy. You ask, "I mean who wouldn't want to believe in life after death?" I guess the problem is that there are too many competing views of this "life-after-death"—every religion seems to have one. Pantheism probably has the most simplistic view—it's just recycling.

I think Jeri was leaning towards the pantheistic view (one with the universe) when she answered the priest. Like I said, the ocean made her at peace with this belief, which is very spiritual in a natural sense. It seems to have worked. At the end, she was pretty much at peace with the whole death thing, which is why I referred to it as a "non-event." We were dealing with priests because it was their hospice. In Hawaii, there are no pantheistic hospices, yet.

In summary, pantheism does the job for me. If I had to choose a more organized religion, I'd lean towards the Goddess or Buddhist faiths—i.e., a more naturalist view of God. Even though I was born Christian, I wouldn't pick the monotheistic religions that originated in the Near-East. Why? They were much too influenced by the desert cultures—it's God and man against nature, and vice versa. Again, this is my personal choice and taste. I respect other people's choices. There are no right or wrong answers when it comes to faith. That's why it's faith. So, we should agree to disagree on our choices of faith.

Aloha, Robert

I felt like I was a freshman in college. For the second time in my life, I had embarked on a full-blown search for meaning. I was reexamining all of my beliefs. I tried to brush up on my old philosophical ideas. Pantheism? I hadn't used that term in years. It was starting to come back to me. I was desperately looking for meaning. My grief bursts grew more existential with each passing day.

It's Not Easy to Die in Paradise

Here's an excerpt from an e-mail I wrote on August 29, 2009, explaining my new search for meaning:

Dear Friends,

I'm in the middle of a philosophical and intellectual crisis. I feel like a freshman in college, exploring the big questions of life and death. Reading Becker gave me a huge jolt. For the first time in years, I'm discussing religion with people. I've just had a lively exchange with Steve on religion. I was trying to deal with the issue of how Jeri faced her forthcoming death—from a philosophical and religious viewpoint. In the process, I found myself revisiting my own beliefs (or the lack of them). I found myself reverting to my old pantheistic outlook on life, which I shared with Jeri. I even tried to remember why I gave up on the Christianity of my youth. It all feels very strange. I'm having an intellectual rebirth.

.... I want to conclude with a final observation on dying in Hawaii. The beauty of Hawaii is a powerful and life-asserting force. As a result, it's very hard to depart from this place. Tourists feel it when they leave the islands. For Jeri, it must have been hard to leave this place she loved so much. All she wanted was to repeat every day— more of the same. She would have loved to put her life on a repeat loop, but without the chemo. She didn't even feel it necessary to cross the Ala Wai Canal to get out of Waikiki. She was exactly where she wanted to be.

Aloha, Robert

My search was still on. I was still trying to assign meaning to Jeri's life and death. It wasn't easy. The grief bursts were letting me know that I still did not have all the answers.

The Search Continues

One month later I was still searching. While trying to unravel Jeri's spiritual framework, I noticed that the *existential* grief bursts would hit me hard when I read Jeri's bed-side book *The Surfer Spirit*. Here's an excerpt from an e-mail I sent on September 28th, 2009, explaining how I was still grappling with these *existential* grief bursts:

Dear Friends,

This one is still a work-in-progress. It's still a source of grief bursts. You can tell it's bad from my e-mail on "The Witness." I still can't ascribe meaning to Jeri's death, and that is very painful. Here's how I'm working on it now. Last Christmas, Sonny and Fred gave Jeri a copy of *The Surfer Spirit*. It's a beautiful picture book with poetic words that capture the life-philosophy of surfing in Hawaii. Jeri loved that book. She just kept reading and rereading it; she cried every time. She said, "This is what I am, a surfer." A few days ago, a long-time beach boy (Kaleo) told me, "You know, Robert, Jeri in the last five years became one of us. She really understood the ocean." Here are a few quotations (without the beautiful shots) from *The Surfer Spirit*:

- "I am a surfer. It's what I do. It's what I am. It's my spirit."

- "I leave my troubles onshore as I paddle into Bliss. I am free."

- "I know that life has its own rhythms. I dance to nature's heartbeat."

- "I go with the flow and surrender to life. I accept that sometimes you just have to eat it."

- "I live in the moment. I must surf every day. I need to return to my element—My Source."

- "Some days bring special gifts. I am honored that I'm not alone."

- "My health club is the ocean. It's priceless."

As you can see, this is all pantheistic stuff. Jeri is now where she eventually wanted to be—where she belongs.

Aloha, Robert

Completing the Narrative: "The Surfer Spirit"

I spent the next few weeks in a long archeological dig that took me deep inside Jeri's mind. I was methodically trying to piece together Jeri's inner narrative. At the end, it all came together. The result is in my e-mail titled "The Surfer Spirit" (not to be confused with the book by the same title). As you will see, I was able to complete Jeri's story. And my grief bursts were suddenly *all* gone. I felt a complete sense of inner peace when I hit the "send" button. I know this e-mail is long, but I strongly urge you to read it in its entirety. Why? Because it will give you a feel for the level of detail you're going to need to get closure. You must unravel the inner meaning of your partner's life and death. You must complete their narrative. Here's the complete e-mail I sent on October 12, 2009:

Hello Friends,

Grieving provides a big intellectual luxury—it forces you to look at the existential issues of life-and-death, squarely in the face. In my case, I must make sense out of Jeri's life and death, as well as what remains of my own. As the survivor, I must understand what it meant for Jeri to go from the state of being to that of non-being. And, where did she find her existential courage *to be* in the face of death for all these years?

For those who belong to an organized religion, this would be the time to seek help from the clergy. Almost all religions have perfected the arts of mourning and dealing with death. The management of the soul is their primary business and they've been at it for a long time.

I do not belong to an organized religion. Like many of my cohorts who came to their philosophical age in the late sixties and early seventies, I have chosen to follow my own spiritual path, which has guided me throughout my life. As a result, I'm now completely on my own, left to deal with the greatest philosophical issue of all time: the meaninglessness of death. The last time I checked, there was no *Church of Pantheism* in the local phonebook. So I have become my own pastor, psychologist, and philosopher. I can't outsource any of it, although I'm grateful for some of the guidance I get from my grief counselor. Consequently, I must use every shred of intellect I've accumulated to come to grips with this situation. If you're ever in the same predicament, hopefully you'll find some of this writing helpful.

In Search of the Inner Jeri

As part of my grieving, I've been meditating for some time, trying to answer the following questions: What made Jeri so strong and radiant, particularly during her last years? Where did she get her inner strength? What was the enigma behind that beautiful radiant smile we all so loved? Where did she get her incredible zest for life? What made her so serene in the face of death? I've tried to answer these questions before: It's the ocean. I still think that answer holds true. It's certainly a good first-level explanation. In this note, I'll delve deeper. I'll try to unravel exactly how Jeri got to her destination in her intellectual journey. Think of it as a more rigorous explanation of her philosophy of life. It's her intellectual narrative.

Why is this exercise necessary, now? First, it will give me a better understanding of Jeri's life and death, which is an important part of grieving. Second, discovering the source of Jeri's inner strength may help me find my own courage to be. Lastly, it may give me some form of closure, which may help me with my healing process.

Having just said that, I now realize that Jeri's inner strength did feed me the courage I needed to help her fight her cancer over the years. It was a classical positive feedback loop. Like Deborah #3 said, "The two of you only needed each other." So I'm looking for the Holy Grail of grieving: The source of Jeri's existential courage when she faced terminal cancer and death.

Jeri's Philosophical Evolution: The Christian Years

As a devout, born-again Christian, Jeri first attended Baptist College in Los Angeles. I think it was a university for Christian missionaries. After two years, she and three of her girlfriends decided that they should transfer to San Jose State University (SJSU) to directly confront the heathens. I guess they grew bored with the Christian echo chamber and needed some stimulation. At SJSU, Jeri enrolled in Sociology, thinking it was a training ground for social work. Instead, the department was a hotbed of critical thinking. It was the home of some star professors who were at the top of their game, with many books under their belts. So our Christian girl found herself surrounded by intellectual sharpies who challenged her core beliefs. And being a very young woman, the raging hormones were not on her side. In no time, Jeri dropped her faith in Christianity. Someone must have done a heck of an intellectual job on her. She also started dating one of her star professors. He was at least ten years older than she was and had a very keen intellect. Jeri graduated at the top of her class in Sociology with a minor in Psychology (Marriage and Family Counseling).

The Intellectual-Sponge Years

At the time I met Jeri, she was a graduate student at SJSU's Cybernetic Systems department—another avant-garde program, where you could study almost anything you wanted as long as it had something to do with General Systems Theory (i.e., the study of the dynamics of complex systems—like corporations, computer networks, economies, and ecosystems). I loved the inter-disciplinary approach it provided. I encouraged her to write her master's thesis on computer networks, an almost non-existent field then. You can read more about the outcome of this work in *My Jeri*. (It became the basis for both of our careers in the computer industry.) Here, I want to focus on Jeri's philosophical evolution and how it gave her so much inner strength.

I was surprised that, aside from Sociology, Jeri had almost no foundation in the Social Sciences. She was not aware of the great intellectual upheavals of the sixties or even the classic works of philosophy, literature, and psychology. Of course, this was always my passion. So, I had the great pleasure of introducing Jeri to Eastern philosophy and many of its sixties variants. I also introduced her to Western philosophy, Neo-Freudianism, the Great Russian novels, modern Feminist literature, and other related areas. She had a razor-sharp intellect. Like a sponge, she quickly absorbed this fire hose of new knowledge. So as not to be overwhelmed, she used her General Systems Theory to develop a framework to organize this incoming knowledge. I can't tell you how much pleasure it gave me to see her develop so rapidly. In record time, she became an outstanding critical thinker. She was absolutely brilliant.

The Existentialist Years (with a Touch of Goddess)

Like many of our generation, Jeri was attracted by Existentialism: mostly of the Sartre and Simone de Beauvoir variety, with a slight touch of Nietzsche and Hiedegger. So what does this really mean in terms of philosophical practice? It's a philosophy of life that asserts that our essence is defined by our existence. We are what we make of ourselves. We are the sum of our actions. There is no other essence. The courage to be is the courage to become—via our actions—what we want to be. If you think about it, this is Western philosophy's most courageous response *ever* to humanity's despair over the finiteness of life (i.e., the death problem). This variant of Existentialism affirms life without being delusional about an afterlife. You face the inevitability of death with the courage to be in the here and now. In practical terms, it means that you'd better live every day of your life to the maximum. At the end of the day, it's all that you'll have.

In the seventies, many of us tried to add a mystical element to Existentialism: Could we transcend the self and be part of some bigger whole? What if death were a return to something bigger than ourselves? Could we be one with the universe? Many of us went searching for this communion in the worlds of psychedelic drugs, Eastern philosophy, and Goddess religions. We liked our existentialism but also wanted to be part of a bigger whole—typically, in some form of mystical union.

Goddess and Mother Nature

As you would expect, Jeri explored some of these options. She eventually gravitated towards the Goddess stuff. Unlike many New Agers, she did not believe in mystical unions and all the ritualistic nonsense they involved. She simply liked the mythological aspects of "God is a woman"—it agreed with her new feminist worldview. Goddess and Mother Nature seemed to be one and the same in her mind. However, it never evolved into a religious belief. She was a secular existentialist with a deep respect for Mother Nature and the universe. Existentially speaking, she was able to actualize herself through work and also experience the deep joy of being. She was a real *bon vivant*. She liked the life-asserting force of the Greek Islands—they gave her a deep *joie de vivre* in a naturalistic setting. Those of us who saw her belly dancing, also knew she was a creative artist and talented dancer. She did her own choreography and made her own costumes. To sum up, Jeri's philosophy of life gave her a nice balanced existence for the next twenty years. She was very happy and fulfilled.

Around 1998, Jeri started to feel that Silicon Valley was becoming too materialistic, and that there was just too much greed in our industry. It also seemed that every open space was being paved with new construction. Things started to feel out of balance. So we decided to move to Hawaii, a place of incredible beauty which we had grown to love over the years. We packed our stuff and moved to Kailua on Oahu. We could work and write from there. Eighteen months later, Jeri was diagnosed with ovarian cancer. From then on, our combined energies went into fighting the disease. In addition, something subtle seemed to be happening on the philosophical front. Jeri was becoming a Hawaiian at heart. What does this really mean?

The Hawaii Years: Natural Existentialism

Jeri became very aware of the natural beauty that surrounded her in Hawaii. The mountains, waterfalls, and rainbows gave her strength. I would drive her through the rain forest before and after chemo which had an incredibly calming effect. The ocean became very dear to her.

I noticed that Jeri also became immersed in Hawaiian culture and history. She closely studied the natural relationship the old Hawaiians had with their land and ocean. She had a tremendous respect for the symbiotic balance they had achieved with nature. She was in awe of the economic systems they had created to achieve total harmony with their environment. Their fish ponds and taro farms were perfect examples.

She studied the Hawaiian legends and how they related to the natural environment that surrounded her—for example, the tales of Pele the goddess of fire. She even knew a lot about the geological formation of the islands.

In addition, Jeri spent a good amount of time exploring the parallel world of under-water Hawaii. She became an expert on Hawaiian fish and had a very good understanding of the coral reef ecosystems. I have to say that Jeri was also very well versed in modern Hawaiian history. Yes, she was a busy girl!

The Hawaii Years: The Surfer Spirit

As you all know, Jeri became a surfer in her last five years (seven years, if you include body boarding). With surfing, she acquired an even deeper understanding of the ocean—she could now read the waves and tap into the ocean's energy. Philosophically, I can now explain what this means by quoting from her bed-side book, *The Surfer Spirit* (see previous e-mail):

She saw herself as a surfer: *"It's what I am; it's my spirit."* For Jeri, the ocean became a healing force: *"My health club is the ocean; it's priceless."* It was liberating: *"I leave my troubles onshore as I paddle into bliss—I am free."* It made her feel a deep harmony with nature: *"I know that life has its own rhythms; I dance to nature's heartbeat."* And, she may have even made a mystical connection with Mother Nature: *"I live in the moment. I must surf every day. I need to return to my element—My Source."* Eventually, she becomes one with Mother Nature (or the universe): *"I go with the flow and surrender to life. I accept that sometimes you just have to eat it."* Finally, she breaks out of her existential loneliness when she connects with the sea life in the ocean: *"I am honored that I'm not alone."*

I think that Jeri, via surfing, had a mystical experience with a bigger whole—what Tillich would call the "God above God." In Jeri's case, the God above God was Mother Nature—that is, pantheism. The ocean was her conduit. Every surfing session was a communion with nature—she connected with the power of the universe. Jeri knew she was part of a bigger system, which she came to understand at many levels. Remember, she was a General Systems Theorist by training.

The Grand Finale: Existentialism, Surfer Style

So how does this all play together? Twentieth century Existentialism offers us the most radical form of courage "to be as oneself." As a modern existentialist, Jeri accepted that life (or being) is a finite process with a beginning and an end. At birth, you go from non-being to being. Death is the reverse. Life lets you invent yourself—or self-actualize. Clearly, Jeri had a great life that oozed with creativity. She felt very self-actualized. As she wrote, "I've had an amazing, fulfilling life of which I would like more."

In her last years, Jeri understood this process to be part of a larger system: Nature. Through her connection with the ocean she gained a deeper understanding of the system. When she surfed, she connected with the power of the universe. The ocean became her friend and healer. It made her comfortable with her life and upcoming death. She did not despair at the finiteness of life though she wanted more, of course. She conquered her fears—including the fear of death. For example, many years ago she backed off in terror when she ran into a reef shark at Lanikai. Later, she was able to surf with a reef shark in Waikiki. Last year, she was fearless when she swam eye-to-eye with a huge Tiger shark off the Big Island. This woman was not afraid of death or the natural world.

Jeri was at peace with herself and the natural world that surrounded her. She saw herself as an integral part of the universe. She could participate in something that transcended her own death, while at the same time rejecting the supernatural. This is similar to the Stoic courage to be. In my mind, she achieved the highest form of self-actualization possible. As I wrote in a previous e-mail, "At the end, she really felt she was part of nature (and the universe) and death was just Nirvana (deep peace)." With death, she just returned to nature's womb. She was totally at peace with this final outcome. As her survivor, I hope some of this insight rubs off on me. It may help me find the inner strength I need to face my grief.

Aloha, Robert

"The Surfer Spirit" e-mail is Jeri's inner narrative. Her external narrative is "My Jeri" (see Chapter 4). Between the two narratives, I had pieced together Jeri's entire story: Her life, her philosophical evolution, and her death. I had closed the circle. It was the complete story of a person who had lived on this earth. The story had a beginning and an end. My own life narrative is still unfinished—a work in progress. However, my soulmate's narrative is now complete. The story gave meaning to both Jeri's life and her death, and it helped me find meaning for what remains of my life. I can now accept my death as the natural ending of my life. So, I learned quite a bit from this existential search.

In Jeri's Own Words: Excerpt from *High Surf*

Before closing this chapter, I'd like to share one more e-mail that I sent on October 22, 2009, about ten days after "The Surfer Spirit." I include it here because it supports the main theme in "The Surfer Spirit" in Jeri's own words.

Hello Friends,

I found another real gem! This morning I was going through Jeri's surfing books to give them to Kathy, when I ran across a book called *High Surf* by Tim Baker.[4] It's a compilation of articles and interviews "profiling the surfing world's most inspiring characters encountered over two decades of surf writing. From salty old surf legends to modern pro-surf stars, to surfers from all walks of life, the common theme in all these surfers' lives is how their personal journeys have been shaped and informed by their experiences in the ocean."

What did I find in very bold print on page 312 of the book? Drum roll, please, a piece written by Jeri. Here's our girl, again, in her own words:

I'm 54, and just started surfing three years ago, but I surf almost every day. I was diagnosed with cancer seven years ago, and I believe surfing heals me and makes me strong (physically and spiritually) so I can bounce back from all the constant chemo. I believe in the "mana" of the ocean. As many

---

[4] Tim Baker, *High Surf* (Harper, 2007).

of the beach boys will tell you, it heals. Blue Makua, the well-known Waikiki beach boy, often tells me that this is what is keeping me alive: I believe it. Less than 20% of women with my particular cancer live after five years. I'm still kicking after seven. Many days after chemo, I go surfing weak and with a terrible headache, but I come in clear-headed, refreshed, and stronger. I don't know why it works, but I know it works. Physically, surfing keeps my muscles strong so I can bounce back after treatments. I will never lose my fight with cancer. No matter what happens in the end, every day I go out surfing is a day I have beaten cancer—I have already won.

Jeri

Again, her words support the philosophical narrative I drew in my last e-mail: "The Surfer Spirit." Jeri wrote those words about three years before she died. Notice that she already talks about the "mana of the ocean." Later, her thinking evolved along the lines of her bed-side book, *The Surfer Spirit.*

Aloha, Robert

Conclusion: Lessons Learned

This completes the five-chapter series on grief-burst zapping. Knock on wood, I am now pain free. The *existential* grief bursts were the last to go. Why? At its heart, grieving is a crisis of meaning—it's an ontological crisis. You have to come to terms with the meaning of death, which is a deep existential issue with a spiritual angle.

The death of a soulmate disrupts our sense of continuity. It shatters our sense of permanence. Nothing is forever again—everything becomes transient. Life itself is transient. Death can instigate a crisis of belief in even the most deeply religious among us. Look at what happened to C.S. Lewis after the death of his soulmate. He called God "a cosmic sadist." Conversely, death can prompt even the hardiest of atheists to explore the big spiritual issues: "There are no atheists in foxholes," the old saw goes. If the death of your soulmate does not instigate a crisis of meaning, then probably nothing will.

My grieving pains ceased only after I was able to resolve the deeper spiritual and existential issues surrounding Jeri's death. I found meaning by meditating on Jeri's inner life. It was like an archeological dig into her mind—I just kept unveiling the layers. The crescendo was my e-mail "The Surfer Spirit."

This begs the question: Why did I not get all this information from Jeri, herself, before she died? The answer is that I tried to avoid the topic of death while we were fighting her cancer. Every day had to be life-affirming. This is a conversation we should have had *before* her cancer. From the e-mails you can tell that we had pieces of this conversation over the years. As you can tell from the Hawaii years of the narrative, she became much more spiritual *after* her cancer. So I had to piece together the story after she died.

There is a silver lining in this cloud. I discovered that our philosophy, Existentialism with a touch of spirituality, allowed us both to go through the death thing. It helped Jeri face her death and it helped me deal with my grief. Neither of us had to resort to an organized religion. This is all good news for those in my age group (and younger) who do not belong to an organized religion with an after-life plan. We may have all the necessary philosophical gear—as described in "The Surfer Spirit" e-mail—to get us through life till the very end. Of course, we may have to replace Jeri's ocean with our own source of spirituality. Most likely it will have something to do with nature. Like Jeri, I was able to resolve my crisis of meaning by finding this harmony. Death is just part of the natural process. We don't need an afterlife; we really need more of this life.

Personal Note: *Buddhists have a lot to teach us about death and the impermanence of life. They overcome their fear of death by trying to familiarize themselves with it. Their religion focuses on the transient nature of life. They try to find harmony with nature by transcending* *the self, which they consider to be illusory. Also, their practice of meditation can help us grieve. It's all good stuff. So, why am I not a Buddhist? The short answer is that I can't accept their fundamental premise that "life is suffering." We do have our good days, and hopefully life is more good than bad. And, more importantly, they do not accept the finality of death. They use reincarnation as a hedge. As you know by now, the afterlife is not my thing.*

The bottom line is that Existentialism is extremely well-suited for dealing with the needs of modern life; it encourages us to self-actualize as individuals. Existentialism—when augmented with a touch of spirituality—can deal with the death thing as well as any religion, Eastern or Western. This combination is incredibly powerful. It provides us with a philosophy that can help us live better and then later let us peacefully face death. It also helps the survivors grieve and deal with their crisis of meaning. Needless to say, I was pleasantly surprised by this unexpected outcome. I hope there is enough in this chapter to get you through your existential grief pains without the help of an afterlife.

Note: If you need more help to guide you through this philosophical maze, I recommend that you view Shelly Kagan's lectures at Yale on the topic of death. The link is: http://www.academicearth.org/speakers/shelly-kagan-1. You get 24 hours of video-taped lectures at no cost. I found that Kagan's lectures resonated with what I had written in "The Surfer Spirit." Unfortunately, he does not go into either Existentialism or the spiritual stuff. But it helps to just listen to him talk about death. Personally, I found it to be very therapeutic—almost like a meditation on the meaning of death.

Chapter 12

Till Death Do Us Part

"There is no cure for birth or death save to enjoy the interval."

— *George Santayana*[1]

The year was 1983. The Beatles' song, *When I'm Sixty-Four*, was blaring on the car radio. Jeri was singing along as we raced down Highway 101 on our way to Los Angeles. We were young and in love. Age 64 seemed like an eternity away. I was listening to the song's fading words, when Jeri asked: "Will you still love me when I'm 64?" At the time, I couldn't even imagine age 64. What was the song about? What were the Beatles smoking? But without any hesitation, I told Jeri: "Yes, I'll love you forever." As you know, Jeri never made it to 64. I hope to get there someday and make good on my vow. For you, my readers, the song should be a powerful reminder that soulmates—if they're lucky—will grow old together. At the end, death will "do us part." The love story, however, will sustain us through the end-of-life and the grieving that follows.

As the surviving soulmate, I tried to capture this powerful "final love" experience and put it into words. There's more death and grieving in this book than you'll find anywhere else in print, but it's still a love story. I tried to convey, in intimate detail, that there is love during the dying and after the death. The soulmate bond is about sustenance; yes, you can draw from it at the end. This is the all-important lesson in this book, which we're about to close.

We've come a long way together. By now, you know quite a bit about my Jeri in her final days. I even shared her deathbed with you. I also

---

[1] George Santayana, *Soliloquies in England* (Scribners, 1922).

shared my grieving pains and the remedies I concocted. Hopefully, all this will help you with your "death do us part" experience. In this last chapter, I'll first give you the final report on my grieving status. Then, I have a few parting thoughts for what I imagine to be three groups of readers: 1) you who have loved and lost; 2) you who are both alive and in love; and 3) you who are about to embark on a soulmate relationship.

My Grieving Status: One Year Later

I experienced my last grief burst on October 21, about four months after Jeri's death. The grief bursts stopped shortly after I sent the "The Surfer Spirit" e-mail. Of course, I still feel sad every now and then. I get teary-eyed sometimes. For example, it happened during the holidays when I went to visit Dr. Terada and Jeri's chemo nurses. I was teary-eyed when I wrote parts of this book. But teary-eyed is just fine. It's a sweet tender feeling, which I can enjoy. Unlike a grief burst, there is no pain associated with an occasional teary-eyed emotion.

Do I get lonely? Not really. If I feel a bout of loneliness coming, I quickly deflect it by starting an inner conversation with Jeri. Do I miss Jeri? Of course, I miss her. But when that happens, I just remember she was here and I celebrate her life. Do I want her back? Of course, I do. But I console myself by talking to her and feeling her presence. Was I able to reconstruct my life? Yes, I'm becoming more independent with each passing day, and it does help to have good friends. Do I still have a crisis of meaning? Not any longer. I can now accept both my life and my forthcoming death. I also live for the moment. At the end of the day, I celebrate that I had 30 wonderful years on this earth with my soulmate, Jeri. And there's enough of Jeri left in me to help me enjoy the rest of my life.

Am I looking for another soulmate relationship? Absolutely not. At this point, there are no emotional barriers that would preclude me from having such a relationship. However, I choose not to. Why? The answer consists of two parts. First, it's not easy to develop a soulmate relationship—all the stars must line up. Second, I have enough of Jeri to sustain me for the rest of my life. I'm really quite happy the way things are. I have to tell you that I really enjoy my sweet memories of Jeri. Again, it's all a matter of personal taste. This is how I want to live my life. You, however, can do whatever works for you—including starting a new relationship.

You Have Loved and Lost

For my readers who have "loved and lost." I *really* feel your pain, and that is why I wrote this book. I wish I could give you a big hug right now. Don't give up. The pain of losing your soulmate is really beyond understanding. I tried to gather the best grieving theory has to offer and put it all in one place for you. Hopefully, something you read in Chapter 6 can help you. The next best thing I could do was to dissect my own pain. I tried to break it down into grief buckets and show you how I was able to handle each type of grief. Again, I hope there's something there that can help you. My relationship with Jeri was incredibly tight, but I was able to get over the grief pains in quite a short time. So, I can tell you that there is light at the end of the tunnel. Just hang in there. Hopefully, you'll get to the other side very quickly.

You're Both Alive and in Love

You're part of an active soulmate team. You've found the time to read this book and are now on the last chapter. If so, congratulations. This book will help you later when you need it. You already own a copy, so have your soulmate read it, too. This way your partner will know what to do in case you go first. After your soulmate reads the book, I recommend that you both go out for a nice, romantic dinner. The conversation at dinner should revolve around this book. Use Jeri's example to simulate your own end-of-life days. Go over the lessons learned at the end of Chapter 3. Are you both prepared? If not, this is a good time to prepare yourself. Get everything in order.

When you come home that night, turn on your video camera. Then take turns asking the following questions: What kind of treatment do you want at the end of your life? How aggressive do you want it to be?

What kind of funeral do you want? Describe your funeral in detail. What is your life narrative—your "My Jeri"? What is your inner narrative—your "Surfer Spirit"? How do you want me to remember you after your death? How do you want me to live my life after your death?

After you're finished recording the answers, put the video in a safe location and forget about it. Later, one of you may need it. You'll then find in the video answers to many of the questions I spent a long time grappling with in this book. Your dead soulmate's pre-recorded answers will help cut down your grieving time substantially. I wish I had recorded that video with Jeri.

You're About to Become Soulmates

Congratulations. A soulmate relationship is the most precious thing you can have in this life. I don't know how you found this book. Maybe it was a pre-wedding gift from a thoughtful friend. In any case, you're lucky to have read it *before* you embark on your journey. I appreciate that you took time from your busy schedule to read this book. I know you have a wedding and honeymoon to plan. I'm sure you've discussed some of life's important issues with your lover: Where are you going to live? How will you divide the household chores? How will you manage your dual careers? Will you have children? How will you raise those children? How will you handle parents and in-laws? Where will you have your Thanksgiving dinners?

There's still one important discussion you must have: The "death do us part" one. It's a discussion that you can't afford to ignore. So, add two more questions to your list: Will you be there for me at the end? Do you know what that involves? The chances are that your soulmate does not know what the answers entail. It's a bit like Jeri's asking me: "Will you still love me when I'm 64?"

If I were you, here's what I would do. First, mark the pages in the book that you want your partner to read—I'd certainly include Chapter 3.

Then, ask your partner to read the pages you have marked. Next, book a table at a restaurant for a romantic dinner. The dinner conversation that night should revolve around the reading material. I call it the *end-of-life quiz*. Use Jeri's example to simulate your own end-of-life days. Are you both prepared to do this for each other? If so, you're a very lucky couple. You've found your soulmate. What if the answer is no? Cancel the wedding. This is a good time to move on.

Conclusion

It's now time to say goodbye. It was a long and intimate journey. Hopefully, it will help you deal with the "death do us part" stuff, which is an inevitable part of our life cycle. Our Buddhist friends tell us that the best way to overcome our fears is to familiarize ourselves with death. Hopefully, they're right and this book is of some benefit. The death of a soulmate is a truly earth-shattering experience. However, this very special love relationship will continue to sustain us till the very end. In this book, I tried to convey the message that the love affair continues during the last days and the grieving that follows. The important lesson I learned is that *continuing love* is what helped me heal. I'm very glad to report: "There is love after death." My love for Jeri is alive and well. The death of a soulmate is the final act in a beautiful love story. It's an incredibly profound experience.

Appendix: My E-mail Correspondence

In this appendix, I include the full text of my e-mails following Jeri's death. They were written in the latter half of 2009 and appear in chronological order. You've already encountered excerpts of these e-mails throughout this book. This presentation should give you a better idea of how my thinking about grief evolved over time. Initially, the e-mails were to the girlfriends who were with Jeri at the very end. Through these e-mails, we shared the pain of Jeri's last days. As time progressed, the e-mails focused entirely on my grieving. Consequently, I expanded the distribution list to include a larger circle of friends. I was lucky to have these e-mails when I wrote this book. They served as my memory bank for these painful experiences that I would gladly have forgotten.

Letter from Hal—"Life is Still Good" (July 6)

Dear Robert,

I just heard about Jeri's passing and want to offer my condolences. She was a very special, wonderful person! You two were the closest to soulmates that I have ever met so I know this is really hard on you. I saw Jeri's fantastic website and the video of the funeral. It was a perfect tribute. I feel she was the fantastic woman everyone saw in large part because of your love, support, and the wonderful person that you are. I have never met such a selfless husband as you. Unfortunately I will never be half the husband, but your care and loving of her often remind me what I should aspire to.

I know Jeri would want, and probably told you many times, for you to go on with a full and happy life remembering her, but living every day to the fullest. Anyway, I think the best thing you can do now is be a little selfish. Life is still good, special, the greatest gift we have and I hope you will do your best to live it to your fullest! That, I think, can be the best legacy you can leave Jeri.

My condolences,
Hal

My Response—I Don't Know What I'm Doing (July 7)

Dear Hal,

Thank you for your thoughtful advice. After Jeri was diagnosed, I made the decision to dedicate every second I had to her. As a consequence, the last ten years of our relationship brought us even closer than the previous twenty years, which were incredibly good. So I had a very full and fulfilling relationship with this very special woman. It was mutual unconditional love. She took care of me last year when I nearly died, so I could be here for her during her last days.

Of course, the challenge is now: How to live with this incredible void she has left in my life? You touched on this very well in your note. Jeri's life philosophy is a good start if I can apply it to my current condition. I figured that I've been dealing with two different pains: 1) the pain of the last days of her life (i.e., the process of dying), and 2) the pain of missing her.

The first pain is also shared by three of Jeri's girlfriends who were constantly by her side at the end. It's a bit like post-traumatic stress combined with facing the existential reality of death. We constantly call each other and are dealing with this by crying and talking.

The second type of pain—filling the void—will take much longer to heal but it's less intense. Swimming in the ocean every day helps with all these pains and makes me feel close to Jeri—I swim to the spot where her ashes are. Maybe the ocean will also be my healer (it has before). In conclusion, I really don't know how this is going to work itself out for me.

Aloha,
Robert

I'm in Pain (July 15)

Dear Friends,

I'm a walking blob of pain—a scary sight. Here's what my typical day is like:

- I cry when I wake up every morning and do not find her in bed or in the apartment (about 10 minutes of deep sobbing).
- I have my coffee, logged on to her website. I watch the same slideshows every morning. Then, I call poor Jayne (the webmaster) and have her add a picture or modify something, almost daily.
- I cry when I fix brunch because I know she's not going to be eating with me.
- I'm mostly OK when I perform tasks throughout the day.
- I cry when I visit hospitals or drive by the hospice. I cry when I go grocery shopping. Sometimes, I cry spontaneously when I'm driving.
- I cry after my swim when I'm in the shower (about 5 minutes of sobbing).
- I cry before I go to sleep and until the sleeping pill takes effect (about 5 minutes).
- I dream of her every night. I wake up two or three times a night, but go back to sleep crying when I realize she's not next to me.

Mostly, I miss her and can't believe she's gone. I feel guilty that she's not with me enjoying her morning coffee, the ocean, and the joy of being alive. I feel a lack of purpose in life without her. I'd be ready in a second to take care of her in a wheelchair, under chemo, or whatever. I go over and over the events of the last two months of her life trying to figure out if I missed something or could have done anything differently.

I have examined in extreme detail all of the events leading to her death (the last five days). Did I do something wrong? I fret over whether she should had done more chemo and less radiation at the end. Did I let her down? The answer is no, based on the best info I had then (but, not now).

Yes, I understand that I must now find a new identity without her presence (but while keeping the memories). The problem is that I don't know if I want to do this. My identity with her "as is" may be just fine. I want to be like her: Live one day at a time and then see what the next day brings—no big identity quests.

I need to better understand this grieving process: When do I know I've reached the peak of my suffering and pain? When will I start to be less raw? Will the pain ever go away? Also, all this crying gives me sinus problems, headaches, and neck pains. I want it to stop, but it only seems to get worse every day.

I have fond memories of our life together. The website puts a smile on my face and reminds me of all the good times we've had together. We had a wonderful life. With these happy memories, there will always be love. But there's just too much pain now. My memories of Jeri's last days are just too raw and painful.

Aloha, Robert

Should She Have Done More Chemo? (July 16)

Hello Kathy #2,

Thanks for your patience while I continue to work through this. Yes, I will see the counselor. Yes, I will live one day a time and see what it brings. Thanks for your good advice. Now, I just want to touch on the February chemo decision. In my opinion, none of the safe chemos were an option—they had all stopped working. The one we hadn't tried, Chemo X, was very dangerous for someone who had taken as many chemos as Jeri—there was probably a 50% chance it could have killed her by perforating her colon. And, would Chemo X have worked? The odds were less than 20%. The risk benefit ratio wasn't too good. I still think not doing Chemo X was the right decision.

Also, at that time, the cancer was progressing very rapidly (judging by the CA-125 counts). One of the older chemos could have given her perhaps another month of life (and maybe a bit less leg pain), but it wouldn't have stopped the progression of the cancer. In 20/20 hindsight, perhaps we should have done one of the older chemos in February.

Finally, was the radiation a waste of time? The sad answer is, yes. This was one procedure she could have skipped and it would have made her life a little bit easier. So perhaps the right track should have been: Do an older chemo just to slow the growth a bit, and forget radiation. She might have then lived to mid-July with a not-so-good quality of life. Of course, this is all post-mortem knowledge. We did the best with the knowledge we had at the time.

To end on a positive note: We were very lucky that this rapid progression of the disease did not occur eight years earlier, as is the norm. So we got eight extra years with a good quality of life. I hope to have put this one to bed. Again, thanks for your insights and incredible patience having to listen to my ramblings.

Aloha, Robert

Desperately Reading Everything (July 20)

Hello Deborah,

I'm still here mostly working on my grief. I'm seeing a counselor on Friday to work on the issues. In the meantime, I'm devouring everything I can find on the topic. I'm still swimming every day, which helps a lot. At this point, I've dealt with some of the issues surrounding Jeri's death, but I miss her very much, which is another source of big-time grief.

I spend a lot of time reading books on grieving and that is helping me develop a model. In other words, I'm trying to create a mental framework that will help me deal with the waves of pain and absorb (or redirect) the shocks. By the time I see the counselor on Friday, I think I'll become one myself. It's amazing how much I'm discovering. It's a fascinating intellectual topic in its own right. Of course, it's also a very taboo topic, which scares the living daylights out of most people.

In a funny way, Jeri has directed me to some of my current research. When I first met her she had done a lot of work on grieving and dying as part of her degree in Psychology. I'm starting to revisit some of that work—mostly by the psychologist Elizabeth Kübler-Ross, who was her favorite then. Mine was Woody Allen. Anyway, it's a long story. I'll give you a call tomorrow.

Aloha, Robert

From Surfer Girl to Dying Cancer Patient (August 1)

Hello Debs and Kathys,

I want to share with you some new insights. I am now down to two crying bouts per day: one in the mornings (and through lunch) and the other one happens in the shower. (Note: a bout consists of multiple waves of grief—or "grief bursts"). In a sense, this is progress because I am down to two instead of three (the evening bout is gone). On the other hand, there is something deeply primal going on. These are not your normal tears, the crying is much more primal and deep—it's like that of a wounded animal. So what's going on?

Crying is just the surfacing (and release) of some deep emotion. I think I've identified some of the emotions. Actually, there are different sets of emotions at play—for example, the one in the morning is different from the one in the shower.

I'll start with the morning bout. I think that this one is your vanilla "I miss Jeri and how will I live without her." It's very strong because we had such a deep relationship. In fact, the only time I heard such sobbing was from Jeri when she thought I was dying last year. It was her mirror reflection of the loss I'm feeling today. She told me then that it was the worst pain she had experienced in her life. I now understand exactly what she went through. I think I'm working my way through this pain with my research, counseling, and other things I'm doing. So I won't dwell on it.

The shower bout was a mystery. Today, I finally had my eureka moment. The showering has an association with the last few months (hospices and hospitals). It was something I did in a hurry after my swims because I wanted to get back to her as soon as possible—she needed me very much then. And in the shower, all I could think of was that I wanted to be back with her at the hospital. So why the sobbing? Because, it reminded me of a very vulnerable Jeri—the one who desperately needed me at the end. Even with the worst of chemos, there never had been such desperate need or urgency. So, the association takes me to a different Jeri—the one in a wheelchair during her last two months. I cry because I feel very protective towards that Jeri.

Let me try to explain this better. Just imagine for a second that Jeri did not die the way she did. Assume for this exercise that she died instantly in a surf or car accident. In that case, the image we would all have of Jeri would be of the "surfer chick" (with chemo down days) who then had a tragic death. If this had happened, we would always remember Jeri as Jeri and I would not have the shower crying bouts (just the morning ones). So what's different? The difference is that in these last months we saw Jeri go from a strong, robust woman to a disabled person. Overnight, she became frail (and needy) like our parents in their eighties. So there was a need to help her and assist her. Unlike chemo days, this was not a temporary problem. We saw someone from our cohort, our age group, grow feeble like our parents and then die in our arms. Typically, people in our cohort either don't die or if they die it's from an accident. This death was different. Jeri went from a surfer to a dying cancer patient very quickly.

Every day in the shower I keep crying out "I'm so sorry, Baby." First, I thought I must have done something wrong: Why was I sorry? However, after replaying this thing hundreds of times—thank you all for your memories and patience with me—I am now sure that I did nothing wrong in the last two months. I also think—again, thank you all—that we gave her a "good death" as defined in the article I sent you. So, "I'm sorry" means "I'm sorry, Jeri, that you had to go through the ordeal of the last two months." It probably would have been better if she had died instantly in her sleep (or in an accident) in early May.

Of course she didn't, and this horrible disease took its course. We did a stellar job navigating her through it. It was a good death for a cancer patient.

From my perspective, the last two months were precious and created an even deeper bond with Jeri (I could help her in a time of extreme need). You also shared this experience, so you know what I mean. I do miss those precious moments, but I wouldn't want Jeri to be in this predicament today. So I have to let go of this feeling. Now that I understand this feeling better, maybe I'll stop crying in the shower. I hope this helps you, too.

Aloha, Robert

Eight Weeks Later (August 14)

Hello Debs and Kathys,

Eight weeks have passed since we lost Jeri. The "presence of her absence" seems to be everywhere in my world. I feel a terrible void: How can she be so alive one moment (just play the surfing videos on www.JeriOrfali.com) and then be so dead the next? Yes, that the "dead stay dead" is a constant surprise. According to the literature, my primary task in grieving is to "fully recognize my own loss in its entirety to clear the deck for growth." So, I'm trying to comprehend and make some sense out of the incomprehensible. However, what's the alternative? To avoid the pain of loss, I would have had to avoid the life and love Jeri and I shared. In C.S. Lewis's words, "the pain now is part of the happiness then."

During most of the last eight weeks, I felt like a blob of pain wandering aimlessly in a mental wilderness, with no destination. It was a time of intense feelings—from terrifying to numbing—that I encountered for the first time. However, even as an aimless blob, I did manage to eat solo in some of our favorite restaurants, swim every day, read voraciously, and carry on with everyday life routines. In addition, I'm doing better in terms of pain (as you will read in this progress report). Incredibly, I survived these last eight weeks.

Pain Index

To borrow from Jeri, let me define my pain scale for this report. I measured my daily grief on a scale of 0 through 4:

0 *Ecstatic day*—like a good day with Jeri alive.
1 *No pain*—0 grief bursts (normal everyday life).
2 *Light grieving pain*—less than 4 grief bursts per day (light pain).
3 *Heavy grieving pain*—4 to 15 grief bursts per day (heavy-hearted).
4 *Acute grieving pain*—over 15 grief bursts per day (like I can't go on).

Most of my pain in the eight weeks following Jeri's death has been at level 3. I feel a heavy heart and get hit with waves of "grief bursts," mostly in the mornings. Paradoxically, last week I experienced my best and worst days. For the first time, I had two days of pain level 4 (really unbearable grief). They were followed by three days of pain level 2— my first light-hearted days since Jeri died. Now, I'm back to 3 with an occasional 2. I'll explain how I got to 2 later in this report. On a good note, "if you can see progress, then the healing process is on track."

What's a Grief Burst?

A grief burst is an unexpected wave of grief—a sharp stab of emotional pain and anxiety. Generally, it lasts about two minutes; it is relieved by deep sobbing (or just crying, if you're in a public place). Sobbing is like wailing—it comes from your inner core; it's a healing aid. The bursts come in waves, each wave brings a dose of pain.

I read somewhere that if it all came at once, the totality of the pain would probably kill you. Fortunately, it is doled out in small doses— amidst pain-free blocks of time—to let you absorb it. These bursts are an outward expression of some inner pain. In my case, they are associated with some deep emotion that falls into one or more of these categories:

a) The last days—imagery and feelings aroused by the death process: Jeri's transformation from a surfer to a dying cancer patient; the last moments; the dead body; revisiting the painful memories;

going through the various "what if" and "if only" scenarios caused by Jeri's end-of-life process; and so on.

b) Survivor's guilt—she's not here to enjoy what life has to offer: she died so young; I'm alive but she isn't; it's not fair; I'm witness to a crime; and so on.

c) She's gone forever—I miss her physical presence on this earth: I can't believe she's gone; she was just erased from every scene; and I won't be able to hug her, kiss her, hear her voice, watch her surf, make love to her and so on.

d) Self-pity—I have to face life without Jeri: she left a big hole in my life; she left me with so many roles to fill; and how can I ever recover?

e) Deep existential issues—the meaning of Jeri's life and death: facing my own mortality—I'm going to die next; revisiting the religious and philosophical beliefs Jeri and I held; and so on. Then there's a slew of open questions: Why did she die? Does anything still make sense? How did she view her forthcoming death?

The most painful grief bursts are produced by a) followed by b) and so on. Deep sadness accompanied by anguish and despair are the most hurtful feelings during these bursts. You want to find immediate relief from this very intense pain.

How I reduced my category a) grief bursts

First, I'm doing a lot of reading on the topics of grief and death. Second, I constantly play and replay the last days in my mind to deal with the "what ifs..." and "if only..." issues (with your help). I reach the same conclusion over and over again: we gave her a "good death" (thank you, girlfriends). However, the imagery from these days is still haunting me. This is an area I'm currently working on. I can't stand seeing Jeri weakened and crippled. I need to see her as "surfer girl." The good news is that most of my current grief bursts are not in category a). I have also stopped crying in the shower. So there is real progress in this area.

How I reduced my category b) through d) grief bursts

This was pretty tricky and not easy. I missed Jeri so much that I started to feel that there was no way to continue to live without her. My loss of Jeri was just too much to accept. I missed her too much, needed her too much, and felt guilty that she was not alive to enjoy whatever I was doing that was pleasurable and that I knew she would like. So, how did I resolve some of these issues?

- First, I took a full inventory of my losses. Needless to say, it was a devastating scene. It was as if I were hit directly by a Cat 5 hurricane. Jeri had played hundreds of roles in my life and there was no way to reassign them all (i.e., put back together the pieces that were ripped away). In the case of grieving, healing means trying to be "whole" again within a new identity. Obviously, there was no way I could do this without Jeri. This is when I hit pain level 4.

- Next, I took a closer look at my loss inventory and came to an important realization (a *eureka* moment)—all was not really lost. I did not lose 100% of Jeri, even though she was 100% gone. I had only lost the physical presence of Jeri in my life. Jeri still lives within me. Our relationship is still there, inside of me: Where else would it go? I still have 30 years of great memories to draw from, which is a huge reservoir of good feelings. I can never lose the love that is within me. So Jeri will be part of me as long as I live. Consequently, I'm starting to realize that I cannot be alone (or lonely) as long as she's part of me.

- Next, I resurveyed the loss inventory this time with the realization that Jeri was not 100% gone. How many roles could I salvage with our relationship still alive inside of me? The answer is that it greatly helps with the loneliness issue (a biggie) and I don't have to look for another relationship to fill her shoes (mission impossible). Also, I can enjoy her presence in many non-physical ways (remember, the website story). Of course, gone is the hugging and touching. And, I can't hear her voice or laugh. However, she is still my companion, sounding board, and life partner. I can still share everything with her. And, she can help me make decisions—she can even complete my thoughts, like I can hers. I could continue living life for both of us, albeit solo.

- My survey indicates that I lost approximately 30% of the roles Jeri played in my life, which is still a big loss that I need to fill. The good news is that I still have 70% of Jeri to help me through, which is incredibly good. Now, I must figure out how to subsume some of the roles (or find new sources of support) as I re-anchor myself and find a new equilibrium.

Note: Most of the grief literature does not touch on this salvaging process, although my counselor did say, "Carry the gift of the relationship. She's going to be part of your life as long as you live." In the literature, you must accept a 100% loss. They insist that you must recreate or rebuild yourself with a new identity. I would never be able to recover under these circumstances—life would just be a wilderness for me. I think (and hope) that there is a hole in the literature and that my analysis is correct—at least for me. Time will tell.

How I reduced my category e) grief bursts

I can't deal with those right now. The grief bursts are there. I need to do some more thinking. I don't have a plan, yet.

Conclusion

In conclusion, the last eight weeks were incredibly painful and nothing had prepared me for this level of pain. When Jeri was first diagnosed with cancer, I was in pain, but she was next to me. Last year, when her cancer progressed, I felt extreme pain but she was next to me. She was even next to me during the last week of her life—so the pain was intense, but still under control. The pain I felt in the last eight weeks is unique and frightening, and I must face it alone.

Luckily, the realization that my loss was not 100% is what gave me three consecutive days of Pain level 2, which is relatively a very good thing. At least, I'm improving. I still have to work on: survivor's guilt, the 30% unfilled roles, the flashbacks from the last days, and the existential issues. This is my grieving project for the next month. I hope to report some more progress.

Aloha, Robert

I Couldn't Fix It (August 15)

Hello Spinner,

I sent you a very long progress report ("Eight Weeks Later"). Yesterday, I kept getting more "last few days" grief bursts, but with a new twist. I felt like I had also lost a child. Of course, Jeri was a strong and tough woman, but she always called me whenever anything went wrong and I'd fix it (many times it meant getting the right help). This happened during her operations, chemos, surf accidents, lymphedema treatments, pain management, and even during the last few weeks. By then, you were part of the "fix it" team, so you understand. However, when they took her back to the hospice the last time I felt that I had let her down—I just couldn't fix it this time. I even told her, "Sorry, Babe, they're going to take you away." Later at the hospice, she kept saying, "I want to go home."

So, her death means I couldn't protect her at the end. Of course, I don't have divine powers. And, I understand that she wanted a "good death" and they gave her just that at the hospice. They had the right equipment; it would have been more painful at home—so we absolutely did the right thing. Still, I feel like I have lost a child, in addition to all the other losses I described elsewhere. Sorry to give you another earful, but that's one of the problems I'm currently working on. I think I may have popped it.

Aloha, Robert

A Non-Event? (August 20)

Dear Debs and Kathys,

You definitely know by now that of the five triggers of my "grief bursts" the one that causes me the most sorrow is: *a) Jeri's last days.* This one is turning out to be a miserable problem. Every time I put an issue to rest, another seems to pop up. The purpose of this note is to clarify this trigger point further in the hope of making it go away. So far, I've identified the following issues associated with the last days:

1) Jeri's transformation from surfer girl to dying cancer patient. We put this one to rest in a previous note.

2) Did we give her a good death? Yes, we covered this in detail.

3) Could we have done anything differently? No, we did the best with the knowledge we had. We covered this one.

4) "I want to go home." This is the one where I felt like I was not able to "fix it" this time. We covered this one.

5) Jeri's death was a complete non-event—the subject of this e-mail. Note that this one also has an existential element: it's more than Jeri's last days.

What do I mean by non-event? Jeri left us without a formal goodbye. Think Hollywood: We didn't get the "goodbye, I'm dying" scene. She never told us she was dying. She didn't even discuss the funeral. She just left. Yes, there was a warm scene the next morning at the hospice, but that was more like "good morning everyone. I'm glad to see you all here. Let's have some fun." We were the ones crying, not Jeri! She was serene that morning. So, what happened? Where was the dramatic final exit?

There wasn't one. It was quite an anti-climactic event, which is very unlike the Jeri I know. Death is a huge event in a person's life. I never expected Jeri to leave so quietly into the night. This is why at the time I did not think she was about to die, regardless of what they said. In any case, I am perplexed and puzzled by all this. It's also a trigger for grief bursts. So let's see if we can put it to rest. Here are some possible scenarios of what could have happened:

a) Jeri was too sedated to realize she was dying. Death caught her off-guard like the rest of us.

b) She was totally at peace with her death. She was serene to the point of not even bothering with it. She was going to live to the end, in her life-asserting way.

c) She knew she was dying, but didn't want to make us sad. She continued to be uplifting in her stoic manner.

So which one is it? We'll probably never know. Hopefully, it's not c). I hope it's either a) or b). From a philosophical viewpoint, b) would be almost perfect—an incredibly dignified and courageous final exit. Let me elaborate.

When I met Jeri over 30 years ago, our relationship started with long discussions covering sex, death, and life philosophies—in that order. Why death? It was something she was really interested in then, perhaps because of the death of her father. She kept talking about Kübler-Ross's work, *Death and Dying,* and the stages of death. I was not familiar with the work of Kübler-Ross then. Luckily, I did know quite a bit about death—mostly, from an Existential and Post-Freudian viewpoint with a touch of Woody Allen.

Jeri and I quickly agreed that because death was inevitable, life was a precious gift and we'd better live every day to the maximum. So our relationship was very life-affirming and pleasurable (more Zorba and less Woody). We made sure that there was nothing on our bucket list. In philosophical terms, we did not dwell on the body/mind dichotomy. We agreed they were both necessary, transient, and part of the natural universe. There was no need to worry about eternity, immortality, or the soul—so let's have fun now. We revisited this many times and always came to the same conclusion.

When we found out about Jeri's cancer, we again revisited all these issues. I told her, "We're all terminal—no one is coming out of this alive. You just happen to know what you're going to die from." So we decided to live by the Jeri rules. In the last ten years, we had many philosophical talks on death and the human condition. I kept it abstract, but I was trying to get a feel for where she really stood on the topic. Of course, she wanted to live but she claimed that she was not afraid to die. Her exact words were, "I'm not afraid to die. I just don't want to be in pain." I promised her that as long as I was alive, I'd make sure she was not in pain.

At the end, all I could focus on was doing everything I could to keep the pain under control. I had to figure out where she would be the most comfortable—at home, in the hospital, or in the hospice. We did not have time to revisit her thoughts on death and dying. At the very end, the topic made us cry a lot, so we avoided it. One night, six days before she died, I told her, "Thank you for this beautiful relationship. I wish it could go on for another 30 years." She answered, "And another 30 more years after that." This was the last time we discussed the topic.

So, was she afraid to die? What were her thoughts on death and dying? Why didn't she talk to us about it? Where was she getting comfort from? I don't have answers. I know she brushed away the priests and did not revert back to religion. She was very brave to go at it alone, or maybe she was just too drugged. I was expecting something more dramatic, but she left very peacefully and quietly. Last week, I finally got to read Kübler-Ross's *On Death and Dying*. She mostly covered how the terminally ill view death. I felt that Jeri must have known quite a bit from just reading this work—more than your average person. But, there was still nothing to help me answer the questions I'm raising here.

Two days later:

I've been meditating on this question quite a bit. I now think I have the answer: "It's the ocean, Stupid." Yes, the ocean and surfing is where Jeri was finding her peace with nature. I think she understood that she was part of the natural world. She loved the movie *Big Fish*. It made her cry—she said it was her. Jeri was not afraid of the ocean (i.e., nature). She felt very comfortable there. Last December, we ran into a huge Tiger shark in the ocean off the Big Island. I was absolutely terrified, but she was totally fearless. I think she accepted the shark as being where he belonged—in nature's world, her home as well. I think her view of death was that she would simply be returning to nature's womb. At the end, she was not narcissistic at all, which is why it was a non-event. She was one with nature and the universe.

Before closing, I have one more insight to share. When Jeri's body started to shut down on Sunday (the active dying phase) she said "like a baby." I guess it could mean that she was returning to the womb—nature's womb. Maybe, "I want to go home" was also an expression of this feeling. Of course, this last paragraph is pure speculation. I'm on much firmer ground with my ocean hypothesis.

The Next Morning:

Actually, I had totally forgotten the philosophical (and religious) discussions Jeri had with the chaplain at Queen's Hospital and later with different priests at the hospice. Mostly, she told them outright that she didn't believe in an afterlife and that they were wasting their time with her. In some cases, she would engage in theological debates with a priest and use quotations from the Bible to support her stance as a non-believer. One day, I was wheeling her in the parking lot outside the hospice when a priest we hadn't met before parked next to us, and engaged us in the following conversation:

Priest: It's a beautiful day. Which of you two is the patient?

Robert: Actually, we're both terminal but Jeri is the one staying at the hospice.

Priest: OK, so I'm here to visit you, Jeri.

Jeri: Father, you're wasting your time. I already told Father George and others that I don't believe in that stuff. There's nothing you can really do for me.

Priest: We can hold your hand.

Jeri: OK, but that's what Robert is here for.

Priest: But surely you must be spiritual. Look at all the beauty around you. How can anyone live in Hawaii and not be spiritual?

Jeri: Of course I am spiritual, but what does it have to do with religion?

Priest: Religion is just organized spirituality.

Jeri: I am spiritual and don't need to have it organized or interpreted for me. I can feel nature myself without intermediaries.

Priest: Yes, yes. I understand. I am really here to give solace to people who are about to die.

Conclusion:

OK, so that was a lot of rambling thoughts on the subject. Still, I think it's quite important for two reasons: 1) To try to fathom what Jeri was thinking during these last few days when she faced death squarely. (It was no longer just an intellectual exercise.) 2) To deal with our own mortality triggered by being so close to Jeri when she died.

Generally, human beings tend to avoid thinking too much about their own death. We know of death intellectually, but deep inside we don't think it's really going to happen to us (just to others). Our mind deludes us into thinking we're immortal. It's a survival mechanism. It's the sublimation upon which civilization is built. If we were to dwell on our mortality, we wouldn't be able to function. So we put it aside until we're confronted with it—either when we're almost ready to die or when someone very close to us dies. In any case, this type of close encounter with death shatters our veneer and exposes us to the reality of being mere mortals. In other words, the deep existential questions arise. It also makes us feel very vulnerable. Jeri was incredibly courageous to the very end. She died with dignity (again, thank you all). May we all be so lucky.

Aloha, Robert

Non-Event Correspondence (August 24)

From Deborah #3

Robert,

Again, so very thoughtful on your part. I certainly think it was (b), she knew the time was near and she was totally at peace with it, feeling loved by all those around her and feeling fortunate for the wonderful life she lived with you. I also believe that Jeri was not into "drama"—at least I never saw a single flash of that in the years I knew her. As a result, she would not be into the Hollywood Goodbye. Does the Hollywood Goodbye make the survivors feel better? I'm not sure. My friend Joan planned her entire funeral and then had her sisters with her at home (they were hospice nurses) for three weeks while she took no food or water. She slowly faded away. Everyone knew it was coming, as did she, and they all spent some time with her (as the girlfriends and you did with Jeri)...but there was no "final goodbye."

Seems to me like everyone wants to feel it will go on a few minutes, days, or weeks longer. You want to hold on as long as you possibly can —us and them. Do you wish you had those final, final words? Would you have said anything differently than you had all those years of your lives together? I have always felt that there was nothing unsaid between the two of you, but that is only a guess. She had the greatest gift any human can have—someone who loves you unconditionally and is your soulmate for life.

Love, Deborah #3

My Response To Deborah #3

Hello Deborah #3,

You are right, there was nothing unsaid between the two of us. Of course, no one can predict how humans will react when they finally come face-to-face with death. Like the old saying goes: "there are no atheists in the trenches." Would she have resorted to her earlier Christianity to get the afterlife part? She did not. It seems—thanks to the ocean—that she was really at peace with herself and the natural world. I think she really felt she was part of nature (and the universe) and death was just Nirvana (deep peace). We were very lucky that she did not starve slowly the way your friend Joan did.

Aloha, Robert

From Spinner

Hello Robert,

Jeri was absolutely not afraid of dying. I talked to her three times about this when we were alone. When I would ask her how she felt about dying she calmly told me she knew it was coming now, and that she was not afraid at all. Then I told her not to worry about you, that I promised I would help look after you. Instantly she went from calm to hysteric crying. She then said, "I am so worried about him, it is *all* I am worried about."

That said, my view is that her dying was *not* a non-event: I do not view dying as a single moment (unless of course you have an accident). I am sure you'll agree that Jeri began dying on Sunday night. So, all those last days were her dying. In my mind she handled everything exactly the way she had planned for the last few years. Her number one concern was that she would not be in pain. She got exactly what she wanted. So, of your options, I'd say Jeri lived exactly how she wanted, and then, strong and at peace, she died exactly as she wanted. She did not want or need any big production. That would have not been her.

Love, Spinner

Religion and Pantheism (August 25)

Hello Steve,

You should have had this religious discussion with Jeri, when she was still here. She was a born-again Christian in her early days, who then rejected religion based on discrepancies in the Bible and many other things (which I don't claim to understand).

In my "Non-Event" e-mail, I described what I perceived to be Jeri's state-of-mind when she confronted death. She was brave and stuck to her views to the very end. Like you say, it would have been comforting to accept a God and the afterlife at the very end, but she didn't.

My views are a bit different. I am religious in the sense that god is the universe. The ancient Greeks called it *pantheism*. When I die, I will be part of the universe—just like I am now, but without my current body or self. I just believe one line about pantheism: "we're all part of the universe." I don't know what the rest of pantheism is about, nor do I really care.

I respect other people's religious choices. Accepting death and the human condition is very hard, so whatever works for them (and keeps them sane) is fine with me. To be honest, everyone needs "a crutch" when it comes to dealing with their mortality; it's not easy. You ask, "I mean who wouldn't want to believe in life after death?" I guess the problem is that there are too many competing views of this "life-after-death"—every religion seems to have one. Pantheism probably has the most simplistic view—it's just recycling.

I think Jeri was leaning towards the pantheistic view (one with the universe) when she answered the priest. Like I said, the ocean made her at peace with this belief, which is very spiritual in a natural sense. It seems to have worked. At the end, she was pretty much at peace with the whole death thing, which is why I referred to it as a "non-event." We were dealing with priests because it was their hospice. In Hawaii, there are no pantheistic hospices, yet.

In summary, pantheism does the job for me. If I had to choose a more organized religion, I'd lean towards the Goddess or Buddhist faiths—i.e., a more naturalist view of God. Even though I was born Christian, I wouldn't pick the monotheistic religions that originated in the Near-East. Why? They were much too influenced by the desert cultures—it's God and man against nature, and vice versa.

Again, this is my personal choice and taste. I respect other people's choices. There are no right or wrong answers when it comes to faith. That's why it's faith. So, we should agree to disagree on our choices of faith.

Note: I am currently reading *The Denial of Death* by Ernest Becker. He won the Pulitzer Prize for this work in 1974, when it was first published. He died shortly after from cancer. The book despairs on the human condition, so I don't know if I want to recommend it to you. I also finished reading *A Grief Observed* by C.S. Lewis. In spite of the man's very intelligent (and deep) belief in Christianity, he suffered as much as I am today from the death of his spouse. It almost made him lose his "faith."

Aloha, Robert

Grieving in Hawaii: Week 10 (August 29)

Hello Debs and Kathys,

Thank you all for your patience and feedback. Please let me know when you get tired of my mad ramblings. I'm glad to report that the framework I described in the previous progress report still works. My pain level has been at a steady 2, except for three days of 3 when I had a cold (more on this later).

I spend about five hours each day working on my grieving (mostly reading and thinking). This is the level of intellectual energy it takes just to keep myself together. It has to be done. Some suggested I should find some big diversion (or project) to keep me occupied. That would be absolutely wrong. I need the time to go through this and do it right—it's my survival that's at stake, nothing less. If I weren't feeling such pain, I'd even say it's a splendid intellectual project. It's the most challenging one I've ever undertaken. Diversions, alcohol, and drugs don't work. They would only postpone the pain. I must keep facing my fears, emotions and the emptiness. I will continue to grieve until there are no more emotions to let out. If I do it right, the painful part won't last forever—like some say.

I'm already finding thoughts of Jeri to be a bit less painful. There's now more sweet sadness with wonderful memories in the mix. Some of her pictures (like the one with the orange glasses) even put a smile on my face—she's so cute. Of course, I still feel these waves of grief bursts, which is why I'm at pain level 2. The bursts are still coming from the same five sources I described in the last progress report. Here's what I've done over the last two weeks to further clarify and attenuate these sources of pain:

a) The last days

Still working on this one. We covered quite a bit of ground in the e-mail exchanges on "non-event" and "I couldn't fix it this time." From your responses, we learned: Jeri's death was a four-day process not a single event; that she was more worried about the pain she'd cause to those left behind than her own dying; and that there was no "final goodbye" because nothing was left unsaid between us. Thank you for your feedback. Also, the *New York Times* article explains the delirium and baby talk we experienced at the end. It also deals with some of the issues like "going home."

b) Survivor's guilt

The good news is that the images of Jeri in my mind are back to the normal surfer chick. The replay scenes of the "last few days" are receding. The bad news is that I now feel guilty that the "surfer chick" is not enjoying her Waikiki playground—the morning coffee with truffles, surfing, dining, her world-view commentary, etc. Instead, I'm the one enjoying, in solo, that lifestyle she loved so much. I get grief bursts because I know how much she loved all this. I also remember that I'm alive today because she helped pull me through last year, when I was sick and almost died. She was a great caregiver. The survivor's guilt in me says, "she's the one who should be here today enjoying this, not me." Or, "I shouldn't be alive if she can't also be here." A gentler variation of this theme is, "I wish she were here, too— this is her world in which I live." Jeri's imprints are everywhere; I'm alive in her beloved world without her. Of course, I'd love to give her my place, if I could.

So how am I dealing with this one? What a surprise—I've worked out an elaborate mental program! First, I accept that I could not have controlled the progression of Jeri's cancer and subsequent death or changed the outcome in any way. I'm not omnipotent. Second, I accept that my death would not bring her back. (I'm very sorry she had to go first.) Third, I accept that I'm here today because she kept me alive last year. So, I owe her the gift of life that I enjoy on a good day. Fourth, I'm now trying to live for both of us. Finally, by being alive I'm celebrating her life. When people see me, they also remember Jeri. Unfortunately, when they see me today they probably see the face of grief. I need to put a smile back on my face so that people can remember the radiant Jeri they once knew. Living in Waikiki—a place Jeri loved so much—helps me continue the life we had and keeps her alive in my heart. Our love continues every day and gives me a lot of inner strength. *Note:* I'm not idolizing Jeri or putting her on a pedestal. I'm just in love with her, period.

c) She's gone forever

I'm still working on this one. It's not easy. I live in a place that's crawling with memories of Jeri—both good and bad. I still can't get over the shock that she's not in this world any longer—"that the dead stay dead is a constant surprise." I yearn to have her here physically. But, the best I can do now is to carry on with her within me. I talk to her often. She's within me from the moment I wake up.

d) Self-pity

In our society, we turn to our spouse for the protection and emotional connections that, in the past, were provided by a multitude of social networks. We now have a complete dependence on one person—our spouse. As a result, deep fear is one of the key emotions that accompanies the death of a spouse. As C.S. Lewis put it, "no one told me that grief felt like fear." I was hit hard with this feeling during a recent cold. I suddenly felt very vulnerable.

Of course, this triggered some red-hot grief bursts. It's much easier to face "aloneness" if you're healthy. Deborah #3 wrote, "The two of you never needed anyone but each other." This was true until the end when I couldn't do it alone (so thank you all). Now, I also lost my caregiver. So I need to put together a support system for when I'm sick. Luckily, there's a home-care agency that provides this type of help.

Like Jeri, I'm not afraid of death itself. I'm very comfortable with my mortality and I would certainly not feel cheated if I died tomorrow. However, I'm terrified of a prolonged disease and pain. And, surprise, I'm not looking forward to getting old alone.

In the meantime, I'm making the best out of every good day life hands me. The ocean is being good to me. And, as you probably know, Hawaii spoils me with its natural gifts on a daily basis. These gifts helped sustain Jeri and they are now sustaining me.

e) Deep existential issues

I'm in the middle of a philosophical and intellectual crisis. I feel like a freshman in college, exploring the big questions of life and death. Reading Becker gave me a big jolt. For the first time in years, I'm discussing religion with people. I've just had a lively exchange with Steve on religion. I was trying to deal with the issue of how Jeri faced her forthcoming death—from a philosophical and religious viewpoint. In the process, I found myself revisiting my own beliefs (or the lack of them). I found myself reverting to my old pantheistic outlook on life, which I shared with Jeri. I even tried to remember why I gave up on the Christianity of my youth. It all feels very strange. I'm having an intellectual rebirth. I'm feeling intellectually young.

I want to conclude with a final observation on dying and grieving in Hawaii. The beauty of Hawaii is a powerful and life-asserting force. As a result, it's very hard to depart from this place. Tourists feel it when they leave the islands. For Jeri, it must have been hard to leave this place she loved so much. All she wanted was to repeat every day: more of the same. She would have loved to put her life on a repeat loop, but without the chemo. She didn't even feel it was necessary to cross the Ala Wai Canal. She was exactly where she wanted to be. Given that it's hard to leave paradise, it made it much harder for her to die and leave this beautiful place.

I also find Hawaii to be a double-sword when it comes to grieving. On one hand, it sustains me with its life-asserting beauty and helps me continue to celebrate the wonderful life Jeri and I shared here. On the other hand, it hurts me that Jeri is not here to enjoy this beautiful place she loved so much.

Aloha, Robert

Jeri Would Be 57 Today (Sept. 5)

Hello Friends,

Had she lived, Jeri would have been 57 today. Was her life cut down too short? From my perspective, it's a definite yes—I could never get enough time with Jeri. By today's average lifespan-at-birth numbers, Jeri did not fare well either—the average for a U.S. female is about 80 years. (The current world average for both sexes is 67 years.) However, if you step back and take a more historic view, Jeri had a longer lifespan than 99% of the people who lived on this planet from the beginning of all time. For example, on average, Jeri lived twice as long as the people in Classic Rome, Classic Greece, and Medieval Britain—their lifespan was 20-30 years. She lived much longer than people in the early 20th century whose average lifespan was 30-40 years. So Jeri did more than OK by historic standards. In geologic time, we all occupy this earth for a few microseconds, so these numbers are just noise.

Jeri liked to say, "It's not how long you live but how well you live." This is so true. I keep getting reminded of this every day, watching my mother suffer in her old age. I once told Jeri, "Hey, at least you won't get old, Babe. You'll be young forever like Marilyn and Janice." Indeed, she still looked very beautiful in her last days. On the day she died, I held her hand for hours. I couldn't help thinking how wonderful she looked—her skin was velvet soft, her hair was shiny, and her face, though a little gaunt, was beautiful. As you know, Jeri lived a very full life during her 57 years. Even with the cancer, her last ten years were wonderful. Her quality-of-life was incredibly good because she lived in Hawaii. When I looked at Jayne's surfing video (the one I sent you in the last message), I couldn't help but think that Jeri may have caught at least 25,000 waves in the last five years. Every one of these waves put a big smile on her face (like the smile Jayne had after her surfing session).

So what did we usually do on Jeri's birthdays? In the last few years, we tried to celebrate this event at the Mauna Lani on the Big Island. There we would snorkel to a beautiful coral wall, which we called, "the most beautiful spot on earth" and I would sing Happy Birthday to her in many languages. She loved this. Later, we would have dinner at Brown's Beach House overlooking the ocean at sunset with great music and hula. She loved her Big Island birthdays. It was one of the few times she'd leave Waikiki for some other destination.

In addition, Jeri and her girlfriends—Annette, Deborah, and Dee—had their bi-yearly birthday luncheons. These celebrations were marked by lots of laughter and leis.

What did we do before we moved to Hawaii? We celebrated her birthdays in the Wine Country north of San Francisco. We stayed in our favorite Bed-and-Breakfast outside the town of Sonoma. Dinner was usually at the Culinary Institute of America, Della Santina, or Auberge Du Soleil—overlooking the vineyards. It was all beautiful, but not as romantic as holding hands in the ocean at "the most beautiful spot on earth."

What would Jeri have done more of had she lived longer? I'd say more of the same—she was very content. Perhaps, she would surf more off the North Shore in the winter. Ever since we met, we always made sure to live each day to the max, so there are no regrets or things left undone.

Of course, I'm greedy and would love to have had more time with Jeri, but this option is not on the table. I'm very grateful for the 30 years we had together and all the sweet memories I now have. In her time on this earth, Jeri lived a very full, happy, and productive life. She also had a "good death." May we all be that lucky.

From a grieving perspective, this birthday without her is a milestone I must face. I used this note to reflect on Jeri's past birthdays and add some perspective to her life and death. That I miss her greatly goes without saying (and sadly, doesn't make a difference). It's my grief to bear—hopefully, it won't go beyond the pain level 2.

This year I will celebrate Jeri's birthday with my daily swim with her followed by dinner at a good restaurant with Deborah and Rich. So the good traditions live on. Happy birthday, Jeri. You will be with us today and every day that I live.

Aloha, Robert

The Witness (Sept. 12)

Dear Debs and Kathys,

Please let me know if these ramblings are getting to be a bit too much for you. In the last few weeks, I was able to identify a new source of grief bursts—meaning the surfacing of a new emotion within me. Unlike my other flashbacks that are bursty, this one is more movie-like. It's more like a reel than a snippet. It typically starts with Jeri appearing very vibrant in some previous phase of her life. It then moves to her sick bed and then her dead body at either the hospice or the morgue. And it ends with some deep void that represents Jeri's absence from her surroundings. Obviously, this new flashback represents a replay of Jeri's death. It feels like a knife going through me because I'm reliving her death each time. It's a big ouch! on the grief-burst meter. So what's going on? And, how am I handling it?

Some background on my experience with death

I've always accepted death as the normal outcome of life. The thought of my own death was never a problem. I had a chance to test this theory last year when I faced death. I was absolutely not afraid and fully accepted my own mortality. In addition, I've always been very philosophical about other people's death; it was just their time to go. I loved my father very much. Yet, when he died at age 55, I hardly cried. I grieved for a day or two and then decided I should be celebrating his life instead. He was a bon-vivant who had lived a great life and had a good death. (He died instantly from a heart-attack.) I really thought I had the "death thing" under control: I was comfortable with mine and I accepted other people's deaths as the natural outcome of things. I thought that grieving was something the people left behind do while they readjust to the loss. If they just accepted death as a natural outcome, it would be much easier. At least, I thought so then.

After Jeri was diagnosed with cancer, I knew it was really a death sentence. However, I also felt we were all living with a death sentence. Again, our strategy was to live life to the fullest and not worry too

232

much about the upcoming death. I was, however, worried about the pain that cancer might cause her at the end. I promised Jeri that I would do everything possible not to let her suffer. I told her, "just live your life and let me worry about the cancer." To be honest, I never really thought about life without Jeri. So I never imagined her death. Like all human beings, I find death to be something you want indefinitely postponed but I also accept it as a normal outcome of life on this planet. This puts me in the camp of those who are comfortable with the idea of death in the abstract.

The witness

Surprise, I was not able to handle Jeri's death well. Unlike my previous encounters, this time I faced death (unfortunately, Jeri's) in its full manifestation. I fully experienced what it means to die. I know exactly how vibrant and alive Jeri had been while on this earth. And now I can see exactly the void she left behind. She's gone—Pouf! I am her life-witness (and also her death-witness). It feels like I witnessed a crime in slow motion with both my hands tied behind my back, unable to do anything about it. A human being was annihilated in front of my eyes. I am a witness to this crime against humanity and I have nowhere to report it. I look around me and life just keeps going on, as if nothing happened. Yet, Jeri has just "disappeared" from this earth. She is erased from each scene in my daily life. I am left deeply traumatized.

What happens on the intellectual level?

Here's what happens. It's the witness (or observer) who experiences the full impact of death—not the person that dies. The witness is left to make sense out of the capriciousness of death. This is where the deep grieving comes in. Most of us will want to forget and go back to living our lives. If you're not a full-impact witness, our death-denying culture can help you move on quickly. Our minds (and culture) have plenty of ways to abstract, mitigate, deny, gloss over, downplay, and rationalize death. I could do this with my own death. I also did it with my father's death because I was not living at home at the time. So, I didn't feel its full impact (the before, during, and after). I was not a full witness.

However, my sister was a full witness and she was traumatized by the loss. This reminds me of a line from Woody Allen, "I'm not afraid of death. I just don't want to be there when it happens."

So how did I deal with this?

Now that this "witness thing" has surfaced, I can deal with it. So, in addition to my normal grieving—*I miss Jeri, she left a big hole*, and *the last days*—I must now deal with survivor's guilt and the existential meaning of Jeri's death. In other words, as "the witness" I must make sense out of Jeri's life and death. Even though I'm comfortable with my own mortality, I must now give meaning to Jeri's. If I had died first —for example, during my illness last year—I would never have had this full experience of death. So here's how I'm dealing with this conundrum:

- First, I now spend a good deal of time meditating on the meaning of Jeri's life—something I never did when she was alive. She definitely had a "good life." She made many contributions and also had a lot of fun. Some of her contributions made ripples in the world of technology. So she did leave something behind. She also touched people on a daily basis. I was a witness to this. In any case, she did everything she wanted to do on this earth and at the end, all she wanted was more of the same. Did she have unrealized potential? Yes, as a surfer. Had she lived, her next steps would have been to surf Waimea and Pipeline on big-wave days. With Jeri, nothing was impossible.

- Next, I meditate on the meaning of death in general. I just keep staring into the face of death and the finiteness of the human condition. We are all transients on this earth. I had to make new sense out of the "transiency" of life—i.e., death's finality. Religious people do not have this problem, as most religions simply deny death by offering an afterlife. In my pantheistic view, there is no afterlife— death is just a form of recycling back to nature. The Greek philosopher Epicurus says it best in his *symmetry* argument: "after death we're in the same state of non-being as before birth." And he concludes: "Where death is, I am not." The circle is complete. With enough meditation, death just becomes Nirvana—a state of blissful nothingness.

- Next, I revisit Jeri's death. In her case, death was ultimately the relief from the final phase of cancer. The crime I witnessed was the cancer attacking her body—the disease at the end. So how does this mind twister make it better? It's better because I've come to the realization that death is not ugly; only the cancer is. As far as deaths go, Jeri had a "good death." We will all die some day. We can argue over whether Jeri's life was too short (the subject of the last message). But as I previously wrote, it's the quality of life that counts not the quantity. For example, I'd currently gladly swap my entire remaining time on this earth for one more day with Jeri. (I enjoyed a full 30 years of those good days.) Jeri was able to savor the preciousness of each moment of her life. She lived life to the fullest in the here and now.

Now, a final meditation. I think I may have popped this grief burst. As a close witness of death, I lost my innocence—I am no longer a death virgin. With my defense mechanisms stripped down, I felt a tragic anguish: Jeri was the victim of a crime that I had helplessly witnessed and survived. In reality, death is part of the human condition. The final phase of the disease made it appear ugly. With enough meditation, I came to accept death for what it is—the closing circle of life. It's the inevitable destiny of all humans: we are all mortals living on borrowed time. Like Jeri, I'm learning how to live with this terminal condition. Her trick was to enjoy the moment and make the best out of whatever time she had on this earth. Others may prefer strategies that seek immortality—however they choose to do that (monuments, religious faith, great works of art, wars-and-conquest, or whatever else works for them).

In the final analysis, for secularists (and pantheists) death is our collective destiny. We must learn to live with that reality—especially since there's nothing we can do about it. So now that I've put this one to rest, I can go back to my other grieving. I'm back to the more familiar issues like: "I miss her" and "How can I live the rest of my life without her?"

Please, read this book:

I usually don't make it a point of recommending books. However, everyone should read Virginia Morris's *Talking About Death*. It's a very useful book on how we die in the U.S. with lots of practical information (it doesn't deal with the philosophical issues). Like I said earlier, death is really OK (or neutral). The issues are the process (the illness) that leads to it and the grieving that follows. Jeri did have a "good death," compared to the 90% who linger for 2-3 years before they die, usually in ICUs and nursing homes—in very uncomfortable situations. Only 15% die in hospices—most of those discover hospice in their last few days. Jeri died surrounded by friends. She was surfing two months before her death. She ate dinner at Roy's in Waikiki ten days before she died. And she was at the Moana dipping her feet in ocean water just five days before she died. The sad news is that death won't be that comfortable for most people. The Virginia Morris book describes, in detail, all the problems one can expect at the end and how to prepare for them. Given that we weren't prepared at all, we did very well for Jeri. Thank you, girlfriends.

Aloha, Robert

In Her Own Words (Sept. 15)

Hello Friends,

I just unearthed an e-mail Jeri wrote to Kathy #2 on April 19, 2008 (14 months before she died). It says very clearly, in her own words, what I've been trying to say about her life. This is an excerpt from a long message in which she goes over her treatment options after learning the cancer had spread to her lungs for the first time. I've been trying to put words in her mouth ever since she died, so I'm glad to have this confirmation that I was on the right track. It's a wonderful gift to finally read in her own words her views on the life and death issues that she faced back then. She's such a clear thinker; I miss her so much. It made me cry a lot, but it's so beautiful to read. Enjoy:

Dear Kathy,

Warning—gushy, philosophical paragraph ahead: If I do find something out there, I need to figure out how much quality time I will gain vs. how much I will lose. I've had an amazing, fulfilling life of which I would like more. The last 8 years have been absolutely wonderful—probably the best years of my life, even if I was sick. I'm so thankful for them. More quality time would be priceless to me. But, of course, I don't want to waste whatever quality time I have taking last-ditch treatments or chasing mirages. Forgive the analogy, but life is like surfing a wave: it's the quality of the ride, not the ending, that counts—but a nice kick-out would be good. I hope no one will ever say that I lost my battle with cancer: I know I already won it by beating the survival odds by far, no matter what the final outcome is. And I've tried very hard to adhere to my three rules: Live every day to the fullest, fight the disease, and after that, leave the rest to the universe. Making the trade-off between rules 1 and 2 is not easy. I hope I'm granted the wisdom to make the right choice now.

With much love,

Jeri

In Her Own Words: Correspondence (Sept. 16)

From Jayne

Aloha Robert,

This is amazing...Jeri is amazing! What a great choice of words she used to describe her thoughts. She truly managed to find her way. I always will admire her for that.

Big hug, Jayne

From Alexandra

Oh Robert,

This e-mail read has knocked me to my knees. How timely and wise was our Jeri. How perfect and full of love she still is in my heart.

Thank-you, Alexandra

From Spinner

Robert,

I am really touched so very much by what Jeri wrote. I couldn't agree with you more that all you have been thinking has been verified by her words. She obviously put so much thought into those feelings. What a special thing for us all to get to read that.

Love, Spinner

From Anita

Dear Robert,

Yes, this is beautiful to read. You did know that all along, but what a gift to have this in her own words. Thank you again. It is very uplifting for me to read all of this wisdom...hers and yours...and it's never too much for me.

Aloha, Anita

From Deborah #3

Robert,

She was amazing and you enabled those eight years to happen. They would not have happened without you. Do you mind if I share Jeri's wonderful words with my friends who knew her? Robert, they all ask about how you are doing.

Deborah

My Reply

Hello Deborah,

Of course, you can share her words. Note that her e-mail was written early last year. She survived the cancer for over 9.5 years in total. In that last year she also saved my life, which was good because I could then help navigate the end of her life. I am glad to have found these words by Jeri. It's helped me a lot. She wrote them when her mind was clear. It certainly reinforces the narrative I sketched of her. She gave me the feedback I needed.

You once said, "Nothing was left unsaid between the two of you." True. But we did not spend much time discussing death other than in abstract terms. Our focus was mainly on living the day. Oh yes, she really wanted me to make sure that she would not suffer at the end. She wanted the nice "kick out" at the end of the ride, and she got it.

Aloha, Robert

100 Days Later (Sept. 28)

Hello Debs and Kathys,

Thank you all for your patience and feedback. I can't believe that I have survived 100 days on this earth without Jeri. The pain of her loss has been with me every day. I'm glad to report that the framework I described in the previous progress reports still works. My pain level has been at a steady 2 for the past month. I still spend about five hours each day working on my grieving (mostly reading and thinking). It must be working because I'm experiencing much less of the red-hot pain—but there is a lot of sadness and yearning.

My remaining grief bursts are still coming from the same five sources I described in the last progress report. Most are now originating from c), which is a good thing. Here's what I've done over the last four weeks to attenuate these sources of pain:

a) Jeri's last days

I was lucky to unearth, "In Her Own Words." It's done marvels for me. I also revisited with my therapist the pictures of the last two weeks. She re-assured me that Jeri did have a good death. I may be able to finally get closure on this front. No new grief bursts to report since. I'll

239

keep my fingers crossed because this is the most painful source of grief bursts. Thank you for your feedback.

b) Survivor's Guilt

We recently covered this one in the e-mail exchange on "Jeri's 57th birthday." No new grief bursts to report from this source. After reading the Virginia Morris book, I came to the conclusion that the luckier ones go first. Last year, it looked like I was going to be the first to go. However, with Jeri's help, and that of others, I survived. I'm glad I was here for her during her final days. It was the best gift I could ever have given her (although the most painful for me). We were able to give her a good death.

Also, the program I described in a previous message ("Grieving in Hawaii: Week 10") works very well. Living in Waikiki—a place Jeri loved so much—helps me continue the life we had and keeps her alive in my heart. Our love continues every day and this gives me a lot of inner strength.

c) She's gone forever

I'm still working on this one. Most of my current grief bursts are coming from this source. I yearn to have Jeri back here, physically. My most persistent grief bursts occur every morning as I prepare lunch. I also cry when I read her most recent life-philosophy book, *The Surfer Spirit* (more on this later). I cry when I see pictures of the surfer girl. I cry when I see traces she left behind (hallway and apartment remodels, automatic reminders via e-mail, contents of drawers, etc.)

So, what am I doing about this? I'm drawing strength from the fact that Jeri still lives in my heart. I talk to her all the time. Our relationship is alive and well. Living in Waikiki is very comforting and soothing. Surrounded by memories, I live every day for both of us. As long as I have her within me, I don't feel lonely. Her physical absence is still a huge blow, which is why the grief bursts are still coming. I can't stand the thought that she is erased from the scenes of life all around me. I'll have to keep working on this one.

d) Self-pity

I still feel sorry for myself, but it's not a source of grief bursts. For a time, it felt like I was going to re-start my *entire* life again without Jeri —a very depressing thought. Then, it occurred to me that I had rolled the time machine too far back in my attempt to recreate Jeri's life on the website (and in my memories). The problem got fixed when I remembered that I am now 61 and had almost died last year. I already had 30 years with Jeri. I will only have to be without her for whatever time I have left. Finally, I am working on the practical aspects of living life solo at age 61. In the meantime, I'm making the best out of every good day life hands me. The ocean and Hawaii continue to spoil me.

e) Deep Existential issues

This one is still a work-in-progress. It's still a source of grief bursts. You can tell it's bad from my e-mail on "The Witness." I still can't ascribe meaning to Jeri's death, and that is very painful. Here's how I'm working on it now. Last Christmas, Sonny and Fred gave Jeri a copy of *The Surfer Spirit*. It's a beautiful picture book with poetic words that capture the life-philosophy of surfing in Hawaii. Jeri loved that book. She just kept reading and rereading it; she cried every time. She said, "This is what I am, a surfer." A few days ago, a long-time beach boy (Kaleo) told me, "You know, Robert, Jeri in the last five years became one of us. She really understood the ocean." Here are a few quotations (without the beautiful shots) from *The Surfer Spirit*:

- "I am a surfer. It's what I do. It's what I am. It's my spirit."
- "I leave my troubles onshore as I paddle into Bliss. I am free."
- "I know that life has its own rhythms. I dance to nature's heartbeat."
- "I go with the flow and surrender to life. I accept that sometimes you just have to eat it."
- "I live in the moment. I must surf every day. I need to return to my element—My Source."
- "Some days bring special gifts. I am honored that I'm not alone."
- "My health club is the ocean. It's priceless."

As you can see, this is all pantheistic stuff. Jeri is now where she eventually wanted to be—where she belongs.

Conclusion:

The bottom line: I wish Jeri could be here with me enjoying this beautiful place she loved so much. I had 30 years with Jeri (eleven of them in Hawaii), but I would love to have had more. She's in my heart but I do miss her physical energy and presence. The beauty of Hawaii remains a powerful and life-asserting force. Living in Waikiki helps me continue to celebrate the wonderful life Jeri and I shared here. I just wish my red-hot pain would go away. I could easily live with the sweeter tears.

Aloha, Robert

The Surfer Spirit (October 12)

Hello Friends,

Grieving provides a big intellectual luxury—it forces you to look at the existential issues of life-and-death, squarely in the face. In my case, I must make sense out of Jeri's life and death, as well as what remains of my own. As the survivor, I must understand what it meant for Jeri to go from the state of being to that of non-being. And, where did she find her existential courage *to be* in the face of death for all these years?

For those who belong to an organized religion, this would be the time to seek help from the clergy. Almost all religions have perfected the arts of mourning and dealing with death. The management of the soul is their primary business and they've been at it for a long time.

I do not belong to an organized religion. Like many of my cohorts who came to their philosophical age in the late sixties and early seventies, I have chosen to follow my own spiritual path, which has guided me throughout my life. As a result, I'm now completely on my own, left to deal with the greatest philosophical issue of all time: the meaninglessness of death. The last time I checked, there was no

Church of Pantheism in the local phonebook. So I have become my own pastor, psychologist, and philosopher. I can't outsource any of it, although I'm grateful for some of the guidance I get from my grief counselor. Consequently, I must use every shred of intellect I've accumulated to come to grips with this situation. If you're ever in the same predicament, hopefully you'll find some of this writing helpful.

In Search of the Inner Jeri

As part of my grieving, I've been meditating for some time, trying to answer the following questions: What made Jeri so strong and radiant, particularly during her last years? Where did she get her inner strength? What was the enigma behind that beautiful radiant smile we all so loved? Where did she get her incredible zest for life? What made her so serene in the face of death? I've tried to answer these questions before: It's the ocean. I still think that answer holds true. It's certainly a good first-level explanation. In this note, I'll delve deeper. I'll try to unravel exactly how Jeri got to her destination in her intellectual journey. Think of it as a more rigorous explanation of her philosophy of life. It's her intellectual narrative.

Why is this exercise necessary, now? First, it will give me a better understanding of Jeri's life and death, which is an important part of grieving. Second, discovering the source of Jeri's inner strength may help me find my own courage to be. Lastly, it may give me some form of closure, which may help me with my healing process.

Having just said that, I now realize that Jeri's inner strength did feed me the courage I needed to help her fight her cancer over the years. It was a classical positive feedback loop. Like Deborah #3 said, "The two of you only needed each other." So I'm looking for the Holy Grail of grieving: The source of Jeri's existential courage when she faced terminal cancer and death.

Jeri's Philosophical Evolution: The Christian Years

As a devout, born-again Christian, Jeri first attended Baptist College in Los Angeles. I think it was a university for Christian missionaries. After two years, she and three of her girlfriends decided that they should transfer to San Jose State University (SJSU) to directly confront the heathens. I guess they grew bored with the Christian echo chamber and needed some stimulation. At SJSU, Jeri enrolled in Sociology, thinking it was a training ground for social work. Instead, the department was a hotbed of critical thinking. It was the home of some star professors who were at the top of their game with many books under their belts. So our Christian girl found herself surrounded by intellectual sharpies who challenged her core beliefs. And being a very young woman, the raging hormones were not on her side. In no time, Jeri dropped her faith in Christianity. Someone must have done a heck of an intellectual job on her. She also started dating one of her star professors. He was at least ten years older than she was and had a very keen intellect. Jeri graduated at the top of her class in Sociology with a minor in Psychology (Marriage and Family Counseling).

The Intellectual-Sponge Years

At the time I met Jeri, she was a graduate student at SJSU's Cybernetic Systems department—another avant-garde program, where you could study almost anything you wanted as long as it had something to do with General Systems Theory (i.e., the study of the dynamics of complex systems—like corporations, computer networks, economies, and ecosystems). I loved the inter-disciplinary approach it provided. I encouraged her to write her master's thesis on computer networks, an almost non-existent field then. You can read more about the outcome of this work in *My Jeri*. (It became the basis for both of our careers in the computer industry.) Here, I want to focus on Jeri's philosophical evolution and how it gave her so much inner strength.

I was surprised that, aside from Sociology, Jeri had almost no foundation in the Social Sciences. She was not aware of the great intellectual upheavals of the sixties or even the classic works of philosophy, literature, and psychology. Of course, this was always my passion. So, I had the great pleasure of introducing Jeri to Eastern philosophy and many of its sixties variants. I also introduced her to Western philosophy, Neo-Freudianism, the Great Russian novels, modern Feminist literature, and other related areas. She had a razor-sharp intellect. Like a sponge, she quickly absorbed this fire-hose of new knowledge. So as not to be overwhelmed, she used her General Systems Theory to develop a framework to organize this incoming knowledge. I can't tell you how much pleasure it gave me to see her develop so rapidly. In record time, she became an outstanding critical thinker. She was absolutely brilliant.

The Existentialist Years (with a Touch of Goddess)

Like many of our generation, Jeri was attracted by Existentialism—mostly of the Sartre and Simone de Beauvoir variety, with a slight touch of Nietzsche and Hiedegger. So what does this really mean in terms of philosophical practice? It's a philosophy of life that asserts that our essence is defined by our existence. We are what we make of ourselves. We are the sum of our actions. There is no other essence. The courage to be is the courage to become—via our actions—what we want to be. If you think about it, this is Western philosophy's most courageous response *ever* to humanity's despair over the finiteness of life (i.e., the death problem). This variant of Existentialism affirms life without being delusional about an afterlife. You face the inevitability of death with the courage to be in the here and now. In practical terms, it means that you'd better live every day of your life to the maximum. At the end of the day, it's all that you'll have.

In the seventies, many of us tried to add a mystical element to Existentialism: Could we transcend the self and be part of some bigger whole? What if death were a return to something bigger than ourselves? Could we be one with the universe? Many of us went searching for this communion in the worlds of psychedelic drugs, Eastern philosophy, and Goddess religions. We liked our existentialism but also wanted to be part of a bigger whole—typically, in some form of mystical union.

Goddess and Mother Nature

As you would expect, Jeri explored some of these options. She eventually gravitated towards the Goddess stuff. Unlike many New

Agers, she did not believe in mystical unions and all the ritualistic nonsense they involved. She simply liked the mythological aspects of "God is a woman"—it agreed with her new feminist worldview. Goddess and Mother Nature seemed to be one and the same in her mind. However, it never evolved into a religious belief. She was a secular existentialist with a deep respect for Mother Nature and the universe. Existentially speaking, she was able to actualize herself through work and also experience the deep joy of being. She was a real *bon vivant*. She liked the life-asserting force of the Greek Islands —they gave her a deep *joie de vivre* in a naturalistic setting. Those of us who saw her belly dancing, also knew she was a creative artist and talented dancer. She did her own choreography and made her own costumes. To sum up, Jeri's philosophy of life gave her a nice balanced existence for the next twenty years. She was very happy and fulfilled.

Around 1998, Jeri started to feel that Silicon Valley was becoming too materialistic, and that there was just too much greed in our industry. It also seemed that every open space was being paved with new construction. Things started to feel out of balance. So we decided to move to Hawaii, a place of incredible beauty which we had grown to love over the years. We packed our stuff and moved to Kailua on Oahu. We could work and write from there. Eighteen months later, Jeri was diagnosed with ovarian cancer. From then on, our combined energies went into fighting the disease. In addition, something subtle seemed to be happening on the philosophical front. Jeri was becoming a Hawaiian at heart. What does this really mean?

The Hawaii Years: Natural Existentialism

Jeri became very aware of the natural beauty that surrounded her in Hawaii. The mountains, waterfalls, and rainbows gave her strength. I would drive her through the rain forest before and after chemo which had an incredibly calming effect. The ocean became very dear to her. I noticed that Jeri also became immersed in Hawaiian culture and history. She closely studied the natural relationship the old Hawaiians had with their land and ocean. She had a tremendous respect for the symbiotic balance they had achieved with nature. She was in awe of the economic systems they had created to achieve total harmony with their environment—like the fish ponds and Taro farming. She studied the Hawaiian legends and how they related to the natural environment that surrounded her—for example, the tales of Pele the goddess of fire. She even knew a lot about the geological formation of the islands. In addition, Jeri spent a good amount of time exploring the parallel world of under-water Hawaii. She became an expert on Hawaiian fish and had a very good understanding of the coral reef ecosystems. I have to say that Jeri was also very well versed in modern Hawaiian history. Yes, she was a busy girl!

The Hawaii Years: The Surfer Spirit

As you all know, Jeri became a surfer in her last five years (seven years, if you include body boarding). With surfing, she acquired an even deeper understanding of the ocean—she could now read the waves and tap into the ocean's energy. Philosophically, I can now explain what this means by quoting from her bed-side book, *The Surfer Spirit* (see previous e-mail):

She saw herself as a surfer: *"It's what I am; it's my spirit."* For Jeri, the ocean became a healing force: *"My health club is the ocean; it's priceless."* It was liberating: *"I leave my troubles onshore as I paddle into bliss—I am free."* It made her feel a deep harmony with nature: *"I know that life has its own rhythms; I dance to nature's heartbeat."* And, she may have even made a mystical connection with Mother Nature: *"I live in the moment. I must surf every day. I need to return to my element—My Source."* Eventually, she becomes one with Mother Nature (or the universe): *"I go with the flow and surrender to life. I accept that sometimes you just have to eat it."* Finally, she breaks out of her existential loneliness when she connects with the sea life in the ocean: *"I am honored that I'm not alone."*

I think that Jeri, via surfing, had a mystical experience with a bigger whole—what Tillich would call the "God above God." In Jeri's case, the God above God was Mother Nature—that is, pantheism. The ocean was her conduit. Every surfing session was a communion with nature

—she connected with the power of the universe. Jeri knew she was part of a bigger system, which she came to understand at many levels. Remember, she was a General Systems Theorist by training.

The Grand Finale: Existentialism, Surfer Style

So how does this all play together? Twentieth century Existentialism offers us the most radical form of courage "to be as oneself." As a modern existentialist, Jeri accepted that life (or being) is a finite process with a beginning and an end. At birth, you go from non-being to being. Death is the reverse. Life lets you invent yourself—or self-actualize. Clearly, Jeri had a great life that oozed with creativity. She felt very self-actualized. As she wrote, "I've had an amazing, fulfilling life of which I would like more."

In her last years, Jeri understood this process to be part of a larger system: Nature. Through her connection with the ocean, she gained a deeper understanding of the system. When she surfed, she connected with the power of the universe. The ocean became her friend and healer. It made her comfortable with her life and upcoming death. She did not despair at the finiteness of life though she wanted more, of course. She conquered her fears—including the fear of death. For example, many years ago she backed off in terror when she ran into a reef shark at Lanikai. Later, she was able to surf with a reef shark in Waikiki. Last year, she was fearless when she swam eye-to-eye with a huge Tiger shark off the Big Island. This woman was not afraid of death or the natural world.

Jeri was at peace with herself and the natural world that surrounded her. She saw herself as an integral part of the universe. She could participate in something that transcended her own death, while at the same time rejecting the supernatural. This is similar to the Stoic courage to be. In my mind, she achieved the highest form of self-actualization possible. As I wrote in a previous e-mail, "At the end, she really felt she was part of nature (and the universe) and death was just Nirvana (deep peace)." With death, she just returned to nature's womb. She was totally at peace with this final outcome. As her survivor, I hope some of this insight rubs off on me. It may help me find the inner strength I need to face my grief.

Aloha, Robert

Excerpt from *High Surf* (October 22)

Hello Friends,

I found another real gem! This morning I was going through Jeri's surfing books to give them to Kathy, when I ran across a book called *High Surf* by Tim Baker. It's a compilation of articles and interviews "profiling the surfing world's most inspiring characters encountered over two decades of surf writing. From salty old surf legends to modern pro-surf stars, to surfers from all walks of life, the common theme in all these surfers' lives is how their personal journeys have been shaped and informed by their experiences in the ocean."

What did I find in very bold print on page 312 of the book? Drum roll, please, a piece written by Jeri. Here's our girl, again, in her own words:

I'm 54, and just started surfing three years ago, but I surf almost every day. I was diagnosed with cancer seven years ago, and I believe surfing heals me and makes me strong (physically and spiritually) so I can bounce back from all the constant chemo. I believe in the "mana" of the ocean. As many of the beach boys will tell you, it heals. Blue Makua, the well-known Waikiki beach boy, often tells me that this is what is keeping me alive: I believe it. Less than 20% of women with my particular cancer live after five years. I'm still kicking after seven. Many days after chemo, I go surfing weak and with a terrible headache, but I come in clearheaded, refreshed, and stronger. I don't know why it works, but I know it works. Physically, surfing keeps my muscles strong so I can bounce back after treatments. I will never lose my fight with cancer. No matter what happens in the end, every day I go out surfing is a day I have beaten cancer—I have already won.

Jeri

Again, her words support the philosophical narrative I sketched in my last e-mail: "The Surfer Spirit." Jeri wrote those words about three years before she died. Notice that she already talks about the "mana of the ocean." Later, her thinking evolved along the lines of her bed-side book, *The Surfer Spirit.*

Aloha, Robert

150 Days Later (Nov. 20)

Hello Friends,

It's been 150 days since Jeri's death. And it's been 50 days since my last grieving report. In the last 50 days, I've had, on average, 1 grief burst per day—down from 3 per day. I haven't had a single grief burst in the last month. My grief score is now 1.5, down from 3. All of last month, I was down to a 1 (meaning, zero grief bursts). So I'm almost back to being human again. I'm probably a lot more melancholic than your average person, but without the horrible grief bursts that's OK. Jeri's presence (not absence) is now everywhere in my life. The memories are now gardenia-sweet. I miss her every day, which explains the melancholic feelings. But I can easily live with that sweet feeling.

I've done a lot of work on the grieving front in the last 50 days. Lots of reading. And thanks to Kathy #2, I discovered Shelly Kagan's lectures at Yale on the topic of death—24 hours of free lectures. The lectures were therapeutic and served to reinforce my world views. They resonated with what I had previously written in my "Surfer Spirit" e-mail to you. For a while, I thought that I was alone working on these issues.

The other big news is that I'm writing a book called *Grieving a Soulmate.* It's really about what happens to soulmates when "death do us part." It provides a secular way of dealing with death and grieving. It's mostly for the post-60's generation: My group of lost souls who tried to change the world and are now facing death. It's a big cohort— 76 million strong in the U.S. alone. Most of us are death virgins.

I've read most of the literature; I think that I can do better. If I couldn't make a small contribution, I wouldn't go through the hassle. If the book turns out not to be good, I'll just press the delete button—the world does not need another crappy book. I just think it could help people in my situation. The computer books we wrote contain 90% of the knowledge Jeri and I acquired in the industry. I hope this book will capture the knowledge I acquired in the last ten years. I plan to donate all proceeds from the book to charity (preferably, the hospice where Jeri died).

From a grieving perspective, writing this book while I'm still actively grieving is quite tricky, almost recursive. At this point, I don't know what the ending is going to be. I find some of the research on death to be painful at times. Upon closer examination, the source of this last pain was not Jeri's death, but rather the way the rest of us may end up dying in this age. My research on end-of-life in the age of chronic disease is absolutely terrifying. I can now understand Woody Allen's phobias better. In comparison, Jeri had a very soft landing and a wonderful death. As I told Mike, our friends who live in Oregon are much safer. (They have legalized physician-assisted dying.) The rest of us should lobby to become more like Oregon. I have read almost ten books on dying, and now I can't wait to go back to the grieving topic. It makes for much more pleasant reading and writing.

As always, I don't mean to depress you. A few days ago, I was sitting on the beach working on my book's outline. Ritchie, my beach boy friend, was unfortunate enough to ask me what the book was about. I told him about some of the issues I had encountered. You should have seen his face. It was the look of pure terror. I discovered in my readings that people, on the average, can only take 15 minutes of this talk before they give me the stink eye—the literature calls it, "turn hostile." So my 15 minutes are up. Again, thank you all for your patience.

Aloha, Robert

Find Out More

The easiest way to find out more is to follow the footnotes that are sprinkled throughout this book. In this appendix, I try to organize some of these resources into lists to make them more accessible to readers who like lists. If you're time restricted, then go to a specific category and start at the top of the list. If you have the time and are academically inclined, then by all means just keep reading until you hit to the bottom of a list. Note: One resource, *Widowed,* appears on more than one list.

Grief Self-Help: Books

- Joyce Brothers, *Widowed* (Ballantine Books, 1990).
- Alan D. Wolfet, *Understanding Your Grief* (Companion Press, 2003).
- Julie K. Cicero, *Waking Up Alone* (AuthorHouse, 2007).
- Genevieve Ginsburg, *Widow to Widow* (Fisher Books, 1995).
- Brook Noel and Pamela D. Blair, *I Wasn't Ready to Say Goodbye* (Sourcebooks, 2008).
- Janet B. Wright, *The Widow's Journey* (BookSurge, 2009).

Grief Narrative: Books

- C.S. Lewis, *A Grief Observed* (Harper, 1961).
- Joyce Brothers, *Widowed* (Ballantine Books, 1990).
- Joan Didion, *The Year of Magical Thinking* (Vintage Books, 2005).

Grief Theory: Books

- Elizabeth Kübler-Ross and David Kessler, *On Grief and Grieving* (Scribner, 2005).

- George A. Bonanno, *The Other Side of Sadness* (Basic Books, 2009).
- Robert Neimeyer, *Meaning Reconstruction & the Experience of Loss* (Sheridon, 2000).
- Linda Machin, *Working with Loss and Grief* (SAGE Publications, 2009).
- John Archer, *The Nature of Grief* (Routledge, 1999).
- Thomas Attig, *The Heart of Grief* (Oxford University Press, 2000).
- John Bowlby, *Attachment and Loss Trilogy, Vol. 3* (Basic Books, 1982).
- Jeremy Holmes, *John Bowlby and Attachment Theory* (Routledge Press, 1993).
- M. Stroebe et al. (editors), *Handbook of Bereavement Research and Practice* (American Psychological Association, 2008).
- Joyce Brothers, *Widowed* (Ballantine Books, 1990).
- William Worden, *Grief Counseling and Grief Therapy* (Routledge, 2003).
- M. Stroebe et al. (editors), *Handbook of Bereavement Research and Practice* (American Psychological Association, 2008).
- Peter Gay (editor), *The Freud Reader* (Norton, 1989).
- Julia Kristeva, *Black Sun* (Columbia University Press, 1989).
- Jonathan Lear, *Happiness, Death, and the Remainder of Life* (Harvard Press, 2001).

Grief Theory: Articles

- Meghan O'Rourke, "Good Grief," *The New Yorker* (Feb., 2010).
- Fran Schumer, "After a Death, The Pain That Doesn't Go Away," *New York Times*, September 28, 2009.
- Margaret Stroebe and Henk Schut, "The Dual Process Model of Coping With Bereavement," *Death Studies* (Vol. 23, 1999).

- G. Bonanno et al., "Prospective Patterns of Resilience and Maladjustment During Widowhood," *Psychology and Aging* (Vol. 19, 2009).

- M. Stroebe et al., "Attachment and Coping in Bereavement," *Review of General Psychology* (Vol. 9, 2005).

- M. Stroebe et al., "Broken Hearts or Broken Bonds," *American Psychologist* (Vol. 47, 1992).

- P.K Maciejewsky et al., "An Empirical Examination of the Stage Theory of Grief," *Journal of the American Medical Association* (Feb., 2007).

Grief and Grieving: Websites

- AARP Grief and Loss Program (http://www.aarp.org/family/lifeafterloss/).

- WidowNet Self-Help (www.widownet.org).

- GriefNet Internet Support Group (www.griefnet.org).

- Jeri's memorial website (www.JeriOrfali.com).

Death and Dying: Books

- Virginia Morris, *Talking About Death* (Algonquin Books, 2004).

- David Kessler, *The Needs of the Dying* (Harper, 2007).

- Marilyn Webb, *The Good Death* (Bantam Books, 1997).

- David Feldman and Andrew Lasher, *The End-of-Life Handbook* (New Harbinger, 2007).

- Sherwin Nuland, *How We Die* (Vintage Books, 1995).

- Ira Byock, *The Four Inner Things That Matter Most* (Free Press, 2004).

- Elizabeth Kübler-Ross, *On Death and Dying* (MacMillan, 1969).

- Elizabeth Kübler-Ross, *Death: The Final Stage of Growth* (Touchstone, 1986).

- Ernest Becker, *The Denial of Death* (Free Press, 1973).
- Susan Sontag, *Illness as Metaphor* (Picador Press, 1978).
- Paul Tillich, *The Courage To Be* (Yale University Press, 1952).
- Lewis Cohen, *No Good Deed: A Story of Medicine, Murder Accusations, and the Debate over How We Die* (Harper, 2010).

Death and Dying: Articles

- Anemona Hartocollis, "At the End, Offering Not a Cure but Comfort," *New York Times*, August 20, 2009.
- Dan Barry, "My Brain on Chemo Alive and Alert," *New York Times*, August 31, 2009.

Death and Dying: Websites

- Hospice Patients Alliance (www.hospicepatients.org).
- The National Hospice and Palliative Care Organization (www.careinfo.org and www.nhpco.org).
- Hospice Net (www.hospicenet.org).
- Hospice Foundation of America (www.hospicefoundation.org).
- Growth House End-of-Life Planning (www.growthhouse.org).
- Shelly Kagan's Lectures on Death at Yale University (www.academicearth.org/speakers/shelly-kagan-1).
- AARP Grief and Loss Program (http://www.aarp.org/family/caregiving/).
- Compassion & Choices (www.compassionandchoices.org).
- ERGO (www.finalexit.org).
- National Alliance for Caregiving (www.caregiving.org).

Acknowledgments

It takes a village to create a great book (and multiple e-books). Luckily, I was able to enlist a small support group of friends who read the manuscript and helped channel my thinking. It's hard to remain coherent when writing about death and grief. My support group kept me on track with their constant and helpful feedback. My professional editors, on the other hand, provided the less gentle feedback; they made sure the book was perfect.

I want to thank my friends who read the manuscript from cover to cover and commented on the chapters. They include Norah T., Brian H., Kathy #1, Maureen D., Kathy #2, Spinner, Mike M., Deborah #2, Deborah #3, Dan H., Anita T., Carey S., Alexandra A., Greg W., Marilyn K., Ryan S., Christa Freeze, and Dr. Keith Terada. I was very lucky to have your comments, suggestions, and recollections.

I thank my three professional editors for improving the manuscript and making it flawless. Thank you Nadine Newlight, Kimberly Fujioka, and Kevin Anderson. I thank the good people at Mill City Press for producing a superb book and then publishing it. I thank the folks at Publish Green for exquisitely handcrafting and customizing each e-book to take full advantage of the unique features of iPad, Kindle, iPhone, Sony, Nook, Palm, Nokia, and many more. I was lucky to work with all of you.

Finally, I want to thank Jeri, my soulmate and late coauthor, for being a constant source of inspiration and support. As I wrote and rewrote each chapter, I kept asking myself, "What would Jeri have said?" Consequently, we had some very stimulating inner discussions that covered every aspect of this book—including the content, interior layout, and cover design. As always, Jeri was a great source of critical advice; she kept me honest at all times. In a sense this makes her the coauthor of this book, in absentia. Our latest collaborative effort is a concrete demonstration of the power of *continuing bonds*.

CPSIA information can be obtained at www.ICGtesting.com
Printed in the USA

268258BV00003B/70/P